S0-DSP-083

Money, Banking, and Financial Markets in China

Money, Banking, and Financial Markets in China

Gang Yi

Westview Press
BOULDER • SAN FRANCISCO • OXFORD

In memory of my late parents

Published in 1994 in the United States of America by Westview Press, Inc., 5500 Central Avenue, Boulder, Colorado 80301-2877, and in the United Kingdom by Westview Press, 36 Lonsdale Road, Summertown, Oxford OX2 7EW

Library of Congress Cataloging-in-Publication Data
Yi, Gang.
Money, banking, and financial markets in China / Gang Yi.
p. cm.
Includes bibliographical references and index.
ISBN 0-8133-8441-9
1. Finance—China. 2. Monetary policy—China. 3. Money—China.
4. Banks and banking—China. I. Title.
HG187.C6Y4 1994
332'.0951—dc20 92-11411
CIP

Printed and bound in the United States of America

∞ The paper used in this publication meets the requirements of the American National Standard for Permanence of Paper for Printed Library Materials Z39.48-1984.

10 9 8 7 6 5 4 3 2 1

Contents

PART TWO
THE MONEY SUPPLY PROCESS

PART THREE
THE DEMAND FOR MONEY

Figures

Tables

Preface and Acknowledgments

Writing a book on money, banking, and financial markets in China is a difficult task, because the Chinese economy is in a rapid transition and its financial sector has been constantly changing since the late 1970s. The present book offers a comprehensive review of the reform process of the financial sector in China since the establishment of the central bank (1984-1993). The emphasis is on providing institutional and statistical information, rather than drawing conclusions. The transitory nature of the financial sector does not prevent us from recording what has happened during the reforms and providing an economic analysis based on theory and statistical evidence.

The book consists of five parts and sixteen chapters. Part One of this book reviews how the current banking system has emerged from the all-inclusive monobank system in the past. Part Two discusses the money supply mechanism and evaluates monetary policies. Part Three analyzes the monetization process and estimates the demand for money. Part Four examines the price reforms and causes of inflation. Part Five provides a summary of the recent development of financial markets in China. For the econometric results reported in this book, the original data are attached whenever possible, so that readers can verify the results.

This book includes a series of my research papers published in the recent past (Yi 1990a, 1990b, 1991, 1992a, 1992b, 1993). The following sources are gratefully acknowledged:

Chapter 5 and Chapter 6: reprinted with revision, by permission from *Journal of Asian Economics*, Vol. 3, No. 2, pp. 217-238. Copyright © 1992, JAI Press, Inc. Greenwich, Connecticut.

Chapter 8 and Chapter 9: reprinted with revision, by permission from *China Economic Review*, Spring, 1991, pp. 75-95. Copyright © 1991, JAI Press, Inc. Greenwich, Connecticut.

Chapter 10: reprinted with revision, by permission from *China Economic Review*, Vol. 1, No. 2, pp. 155-165, and *China Economic Review*, Vol. 3, No. 2, pp. 219-223. Copyright © 1990, 1992, JAI Press, Inc. Greenwich, Connecticut.

I am greatly indebted to those who kindly provided their invaluable comments and criticism on my research papers, on which this book is based:

Duoguang Bei (Ministry of Finance)
Gene H. Chang (University of Toledo)
Xiwen Chen (Development Research Center)
Gregory Chow (Princeton University)
Robert Dernberger (University of Michigan)
Ying Du (Ministry of Agriculture)
Gang Fan (Chinese Academy of Social Science)
Gao Shangquan (State Commission for Economic System Reform)
Guo Shuqing (State Commission for Economic System Reform)
Wen Hai (Fort Lewis College)
Peter Harrold (World Bank)
E. C. Hwa (World Bank)
Gary Jefferson (Brandeis University)
Jiang Sidong (State Commission for Economic System Reform)
Li Yining (Peking University)
Lizuo Jin (Oxford University)
Justin Y. Lin (Peking University)
Lou Jiwei (State Commission for Economic System Reform)
Yushi Mao (Chinese Academy of Social Science)
Stephen McGurk (Ford Foundation)
Barry Naughton (University of California, San Diego)
Dwight Perkins (Harvard University)
Yingyi Qian (Stanford University)
Duo Qin (Queen Mary College)
Bruce Reynolds (Cornell University)
Jeffrey Sachs (Harvard University)
Peter Schran (University of Illinois)
Inderjit Singh (World Bank)
Guoqiang Tian (Texas A & M University)
Yan Wang (World Bank)

Yijiang Wang (University of Minnesota)
Shangjin Wei (Harvard University)
James G. Wen (Baruch College, CUNY)
Jinglian Wu (Development Research Center)
Geng Xiao (Hong Kong University)
Xie Ping (The People's Bank of China)
Xu Meizheng (State Commission for Economic System Reform)
Xiaonian Xu (Amherst College)
Xiaokai Yang (Monash University)
T. S. Yu (Chung-Hua Institute for Economic Research)
Xiaochuan Zhou (Bank of China)
Fan Zhang (Wayne State University)
Wei Zhang (Harvard University)
Weiying Zhang (Oxford University)
Min Zhu (World Bank).

Special thanks to the anonymous referees of the *China Economic Review*, *Comparative Economic Studies*, ***Economics of Planning***, ***Journal of Asian Economics***, and ***Journal of Comparative Economics***. Any remaining errors in this book are solely my responsibility.

I wish to say a specially emphatic thank you to my mentor, Professor George Judge, who taught me economic analysis and econometric modeling, the basic tools used in the book.

I am particularly grateful to my colleagues Roko Aliprantis, Paul Carlin, Subir Chakra-barti, Partha Deb, Monte Juillerat, Robert Kirk, Peter Rangazas, Robert Sandy and Martin Spechler for their support and help. I wish to thank Dan McKiernan, Peggy Huston and Carol Morgan for their able research assistance and editorial help. I am also grateful to Alison Auch and Amos Zubrow of Westview Press for their encouragement and helpful suggestions. The research for this book is partially supported by the Committee on Scholarly Communication with P. R. China (CSCC).

Of course, my greatest debt is to my wife, Jingping, who has borne most of the cost of this project. All the figures in this book are made by her. My five-year-old son, Justin, has been extremely supportive. He is the first one who has committed to buy this book. The price he agrees to pay is one dollar.

Gang Yi

Acronyms

ABC	The Agricultural Bank of China
ACFB	Almanac of China's Finance and Banking
BIE	Bounded Influence Estimation
BOC	Bank of China
BOCOM	Bank of Communication
CCP	China's Communist Party
CDs	Certificates of Deposit
CELC	China East Leasing Company
CEO	Chief Executive Officer
CFSA	China Financial Security Association
CIA	The Central Intelligence Agency of the US
CIB	China Investment Bank
CITIC	China International Trust and Investment Corporation
CITICIB	CITIC Industrial Bank
CSRS	Commission on Security Regulation and Supervision
CVTIC	China Venturetech Investment Company
GDP	Gross Domestic Product
GLS	Generalized Least Squares
GNP	Gross National Product
HCBP	Handbook of Chinese Banking Practices
ICBC	The Industrial and Commercial Bank of China
IMF	International Monetary Fund
MPI	Market Price Index
MSC	Model Selection Criteria
MSE	Mean Squared Error
OLS	Ordinary Least Squares
OPI	Official Price Index
PBC	The People's Bank of China
PCBC	The People's Construction Bank of China
PICC	The People's Insurance Company of China
PPP	Purchasing Power Parities
PRC	The People's Republic of China
RCCs	Rural Credit Cooperatives
SAEC	The State Administration of Exchange Control
SHSE	Shanghai Security Exchange
STAQS	Security Trading Automated Quotation System
TVEs	Township and Village Enterprises

1

Introduction

China is now at a critical moment of economic transition from a centrally planned economy to a market economy. The Chinese experience is truly unique in the sense that it has used a gradualist approach to transition. The reforms in China are successful by almost any economic standard. The average Gross National Product (GNP) growth rate of China was 9.0 percent for the 14-year period from 1979 to 1992. Per capita national income increased on average by 5.5 percent annually for the same period, making this the most rapid growth period in Chinese history. Given that it has 22 percent of the world's population, China's achievement is very significant. Figures 1.1 and 1.2 illustrate the level of GNP and its growth rate in China during the reform period. Recently the International Monetary Fund and the World Bank have more astonishing estimations of Chinese GDP figures according to purchasing-power parities (see Appendix to Chapter 1).

After about 15 years of economic reform, the Chinese economy has changed significantly. First, the state-owned proportion of the economy has been shrinking continually. The economy has been changed from a predominantly state-owned, centrally-planned economy to a mixed ownership economy. In 1992, the output produced by non-state sector was already 54 percent of GNP.

Second, China is now an open economy. In 1992, total exports were 85 billion US dollars and total imports were 80.6 billion US dollars, an increase of 18.2 percent and 26.4 percent respectively over the previous year. The total value of China's foreign trade accounted for about one-third of its GNP (calculated by the official exchange rate), much higher than the equivalent figure for the United States (16.4 percent), and the trade superpower Japan (17.1 percent). In 1992, the total value of newly signed foreign investment contracts was 68.5 billion US dollars, an increase of 2.4 times over the year before. The amount of actually used foreign capital in 1992 was 18.8 billion US dollars. Figures 1.3 and 1.4 demonstrate the trade growth and foreign direct investment in China respectively.

Third, China is now a market-oriented economy. The prices of more than 90 percent of consumer goods are determined by the market. Most producer goods are allocated by markets. Almost every year since 1985, the government has decontrolled the prices of some producer goods. Now there are only a few producer goods prices that are still controlled by the government. Although China still has a long way to go in the prices of factor markets (capital, labor, and land), price reform in the commodity market has been successful and is close to completion.

Fourth, the perceptions and attitudes toward a market economy have changed, which is probably a deeper and more fundamental achievement of economic reform. Farmers know that a responsibility system focused on households is better for agricultural production than the commune system. Rural entrepreneurs have realized that on average industrial and service businesses are far more profitable than agricultural production. A lot of private businesses and self-employed people have experienced success. More importantly, local governments have enjoyed the decentralized reforms which have brought enormous economic benefit to their localities and personal success to the officials. Therefore, demand for further reform and a market economy comes now from the bottom, from ordinary people such as farmers, workers, private entrepreneurs, and local government officials. The emerging consensus among the Chinese people that the market mechanism is superior to the centrally-planned system is probably the greatest event in Chinese history. A market economy can make most participants better off, and the Chinese people are adapting well to such an economy. This was proved in Hong Kong, in Taiwan, and in Singapore; the Chinese people on the mainland are proving it now.

1.1 Further Reforms in the Future

Most experts agree that the next stage of reform in China should focus on (1) fiscal (tax system) reform, (2) enterprise (ownership) reform, (3) reform in the financial sector, and (4) social safety net.

Economic reform so far has eroded the tax base of the government. Before reform, the government controlled the entire economy. It chose to set the prices of agricultural products much below the equilibrium level, and to set the prices for industrial products arbitrarily high. Wages and salaries of workers and government employees were low because the prices of necessities were low. Consequently, the profits of the government-owned modern industrial and service sectors were very high and naturally the profits were retained by the government. There was no income tax, no sales tax. All profits were surrendered to the government, and all expenditures and investment were from the government; there was no need for value-added taxes. As long as the government could maintain the distorted price structure and directly control the modern sectors of the economy, its revenue was guaranteed. On average, the government collected about one-third of national income before reform. Now the reform has, to a large degree, corrected the distorted price structure and the government-owned proportion of the economy has been shrinking. As a result, government revenue, as a percentage of GNP, has declined during the reform period, from 35 percent in 1978 to about 19 percent in 1992. At the same time, the explicit and implicit commitments of government expenditures in terms of the percentage of GNP have not declined by the same proportion. Consequently, a huge government deficit has resulted every year since 1979. Therefore, it is urgent to establish a new, feasible tax system, without which it is impossible for the central government to function.

Enterprise reform is absolutely necessary and urgent, because one-third of government-owned enterprises are losing huge amounts of money every year. The other one-third have been breaking even on an accounting basis, but losing money implicitly. Only one-third of the state-owned enterprises are profitable. The nature of enterprise reform is ownership reform, in which property rights must be defined clearly. The loss-making state enterprises are the biggest burden to the government and the largest waste of scarce resources. It is inevitable that some inefficient state-owned enterprises will go bankrupt if the government stops the subsidies, which implies that some workers will be unemployed. Therefore, some kind of social safety net and job training programs should be established in the process of reforming the state-owned enterprises.

The financial sector is affected on the one hand by fiscal reform and government deficits, and on the other hand by the enterprise reform. When the government has deficits, after borrowing domestically and abroad, it has to monetize the deficit (printing money to finance it). The ultimate burden of the loss-making state enterprises would lie on the state-owned banking system. The state enterprises and the government-owned banking system are two pockets of the government; money may be taken from one to replenish the other, but the government is confronted with the same amount of losses. Without reforming the financial sector to make the specialized banks truly independent commercial banks, the soft budget problem of the state enterprises would never be solved. At the same time, the government has to rely on the banking system to monetize its deficits until its tax base is solid and tax revenue is adequate.

1.2 A Blueprint

The third plenum of the fourteenth China's Communist Party Central Committee was held in Beijing, November 11-14, 1993. More than 300 ranking leaders from the central and provincial party organizations participated in the meeting, which was widely regarded as China's most sweeping attempt in recent years to push the economic reform forward. The most important document produced by the meeting, "The Resolution on Several Issues of Establishing a Socialist Market Economy" (hereafter "the resolution"), was passed on November 14.

What's New in the Resolution?

The resolution consists of 50 points, which are organized into ten sections. It lays out a blueprint of economic reform for the near future. The important "breakthroughs" in the document are the following:

1. *Tax reform.* A comprehensive tax reform started at the beginning of 1994. The new tax law is closer to the standard tax system used in a market economy, which is characterized by separating the tax belonging to the central government from that belonging to local governments. The new tax-share scheme will replace the current tax method, a lump-sum, fixed amount of tax under the tax responsibility system which is negotiated between Beijing and local governments. Local government currently receives on average 70 percent of total tax collected. It is expected that under the new system local governments will pay more to the central government. As far as the concrete plan is concerned, the following points would be implemented at the beginning of 1994. First, the existing tax collection system will be reorganized into two separated sets of government bureaus for central and local tax collection respectively. Second, profit tax on Chinese enterprises will be reduced to 33 percent from 55 percent. A new value-added tax, to be levied on the value of a product at various stages of production and sales, will replace the consolidated industrial and commercial tax. Third, the law on individual income tax will be revised, in which the concept of "resident" will be defined by using the international concept. Individual income tax will be applicable to Chinese citizens, self-employed workers, and foreigners who earn income in China. The revised version of individual income tax law became effective January 1, 1994.

2. *Banking Reform.* The resolution emphasizes the role of the central bank (the People's Bank of China) in macroeconomic control. A committee on monetary policy will be established under the central bank. The first objective of the central bank is to maintain price stability. Several development and policy-oriented banks will be created to take over responsibility for policy loans from the existing specialized banks. This new arrangement attempts to make the specialized banks real independent commercial banks, which is a necessary condition to cut off the special relationship between the state-owned enterprises and the banking system. The development-oriented banks will support industrial, agricultural, and infrastructure projects that may not be commercially profitable but are crucial to the economic development of the country. The financial resources of the policy and development-oriented banks will mainly come from the central government's budget.

3. *Foreign Exchange Reform.* The two track foreign exchange system will be gradually replaced by the a free market rate. The official exchange rate will be abolished soon. Although there are still some regulations regarding foreign exchange, it is expected that the currency will be convertible or close to convertible in terms of merchandise trade in the near future. There are consistent indications in the document that China will reduce its tariff on imports and reform its international trade system in line with the requirements of the General Agreement on Tariffs and Trade. In fact, right after the plenum, the Chinese government announced another round of tariff reduction by 8.8 percent on average, starting in 1994.

4. *Fostering the Market.* The resolution devotes a whole section to the issues of developing and fostering a market system. It emphasizes the importance of financial and labor markets, real estate, technology transfer and information markets. This point is regarded as a breakthrough because for a long time, due to the ideological consideration (orthodox Marxist theory), the official party documents have been extremely sensitive to the discussion of labor and real estate markets. Although the resolution discusses the problems existed in the above markets, it has a positive tone that recognizes the necessary roles of these markets in general. As a matter of fact, this is the most favorable official party document regarding those markets.

5. *Social Safety Net.* The document outlines the principle for the social safety net in the future. It promotes a multi-track social security system. The urban employees' retirement saving program will be co-paid by the employer and employee. Unemployment insurance will be paid by employer as a proportion of the total wage. Specialized institutions will be established for social security management. The functions of administrative management and investment operation will be separated. At this point

no detailed information for the implementation of the social safety net is available.

The resolution is a comprehensive document which addresses most aspects of the economy. It repeats the previous policies on the following aspects:

State-Owned Enterprises. There is little news on ownership reform. There is no clear direction regarding the reform of the state-owned enterprises. The document devotes a whole section to the state-owned enterprises, in which it recapitulates the two previous documents: The Law of State-Owned Industrial Enterprises and The Guidelines on Reforming the Management Mechanism of State-Owned Enterprises.

However, there is an indication that China will push large state-owned enterprises to form large industrial groups as holding companies. The government grants those large groups the full rights to manage the state-owned assets and encourage institutional ownership of other companies' stocks. Before the plenum, the Xinhua News Agency reported that eight such large industrial groups had been established. The direction and implications of such large groups are far from clear.

Agriculture. There are many urgent problems in the agriculture sector. Rural per capita income has increased very slowly since 1989. Employment pressure is much higher now than before, because the township and village enterprises (TVEs) have absorbed very little surplus labor in the rural area for the period 1989-1993. However, the document does not offer new solutions to the agricultural problems.

As in many other documents, the resolution repeats the party's policies on education and sciences, establishing and improving the legal system, and the party's leadership in the socialist market economy.

Some Concerns

Most western observers applaud the new movements of the Chinese economic reform outlined by this document. It is a strong indication of the determination and will of the Chinese government to push economic reform forward in the direction of a market economy. Of course there are limitations and ideological constraints. But the direction is right. This generates many optimistic forecasts on the Chinese economy. However, it is worth pointing out the following concerns.

Local governments are resistant to the tax reform. After 15 years of the decentralized reform, local government in China has become a powerful institution in terms of both the political and economic power under its control. All reform plans implemented by the central government will be either discounted or amplified by local government in the direction in favor its locality's interest. The results of the implementation of the new tax system remain to be seen.

The ultimate solution to the problems of the banking system lies in the ownership and property rights reform. Establishing several development oriented banks does not solve the problem. It merely shifts the problem of bad loans of commercial banks to the financial burden of the newly established development banks, which would eventually become gigantic government deficits.

The most urgent problem in the Chinese economy is still potential runaway inflation. China is still in the stop-go cycle on macroeconomic control, which has swung between pursuing a rapid economic growth to fighting inflation. After a low inflation period 1990-1992, the official inflation rate reached 13 percent in 1993. Potential runaway inflation has eroded the confidence of many foreign and domestic investors and will most likely cause the next round of crackdowns on the economy.

1.3 The Focus of the Book

This book focuses on the financial sector. After more than a decade of reform, the money, banking, and financial sectors in China have changed profoundly. Because the situation in China is so dynamic, the aim of this book is to provide updated information on the financial sector in China, rather than to draw conclusions. To facilitate later discussion, let us first compare briefly the money and banking system under the centrally-planned economy with that of a market system.

1. In the centrally-planned economy before the reform, resources were allocated by the government through a mandatory plan, which was made in terms of physical distribution of the resources. Money was passive and accommodating. The money supply was endogenously determined by the physical allocation plan. In a market-oriented economy, the money supply is an active and largely exogenous variable which is typically controlled by the central bank.

2. The centrally-planned economy was characterized by an all-inclusive monobank system, whereas a market economy needs a banking system which consists of a central bank and commercial banks.

3. Currency in circulation and credit loans were strictly controlled in the planned economy; cash money and credit money were separated. In a market economy, the money supply process is based on the monetary base (high power money), and a multiplier mechanism.

4. Interest rates were controlled arbitrarily at a level far below the equilibrium level in the planned system. Furthermore, there was little flexibility to adjust interest rates; they were fixed and frozen for many years. A market economy needs flexible equilibrium interest rates to allocate one of the most important factors, capital.

5. The instruments of monetary control in the planned economy were administrative orders, whereas in a market system, adjustment and control are being made by economic levers, mainly through instruments like reserve ratios, open market operations, and interest rate policy.

6. Monetization in the planned economy was very limited, meaning that a large proportion of resources were allocated by mandatory plan through rationing devices. The involvement of money in economic transactions was restricted and money only played a subordinate role in resource allocation. The economic reform has been a process of monetization. As the proportion of resources allocated by the government gets smaller, more and more economic activities are conducted solely through monetary transactions in the market places. The economy has been much more monetized during the reform.

7. Under the centrally-planned economy, prices and wages were frozen for about 20 years in China (1958-1978). There was neither inflation nor inflationary expectations during this period. Since reform started in the late 1970s, inflation has been a concern for both the government and ordinary people in China. Inflationary expectations become an important factor to consider for macroeconomic stability.

8. Demand for money was a questionable concept in the centrally-planned economy, in which consumers had very few alternatives in allocating their wealth. China is becoming a market-oriented economy during the reform, in which more and more financial assets are available. It makes sense to discuss and estimate money demand in China now.

9. In the centrally-planned economy, there were no nonbank financial institutions. The all-inclusive monobank system had an absolute monopoly position in China. During the reform, more and more nonbank financial institutions emerged. They compete with the banks both in attracting deposits and in providing loans and making direct investment.

10. The centrally-planned economy was by and large a closed economy. Firms, consumers, and local governments did not have the right to deal in foreign exchange, which was tightly controlled by the central government. The reform is also a process of opening up the Chinese economy. With the increasing degree of openness of the economy, more and more individuals and firms and local governments have obtained access to foreign exchange

one way or the other, directly or indirectly, legally or semi-legally. Consequently, official exchange rates are closer to the equilibrium level now than before.

The present book addresses the issues listed above. Part One of the book contains two chapters. Chapter 2 introduces the banking system of China before reform. Chapter 3 provides a brief review of the reform process in the financial sector and gives an overview of the new banking system established during reform in China.

Part Two is about the money supply process, and consists of four chapters. Chapter 4 defines money. Chapter 5 discusses the money supply process after the establishment of the central bank. Chapter 6 introduces the control instruments of the central bank and evaluates the effectiveness of its monetary policies. Chapter 7 focuses on the discussion of interest rates in China.

Part Three focuses on the demand for money in China. Chapter 8 explains why the income velocity of money has decreased during the reform period. Chapter 9 provides a detailed discussion on the monetization process in China. Chapter 10 addresses the problems of inflationary expectations. Chapter 11 discusses alternative models of demand for money.

Part Four addresses the problems of inflation within three chapters. Chapter 12 discusses the relationship between price reform and inflation. Chapter 13 introduces several useful models to explain inflation in China from different angles. Chapter 14 examines the relationship between the monetary variable and economic activity.

The last part of the book provides updated information on the recent development of the financial markets in China. Chapter 15 discusses the current situation of the nonbank financial institutions and the implications for future monetary policy. Finally, Chapter 16 introduces the rapid development of stock and bond markets in China.

One of the features of this volume is that it provides a large amount of data on recent developments in the financial sector in China. The emphasis is on providing information rather than on reaching conclusions. Therefore, this book should be regarded as a starting place for research. For the preliminary econometric results reported in this book, the original data are provided whenever it is possible, so that readers can verify the results.

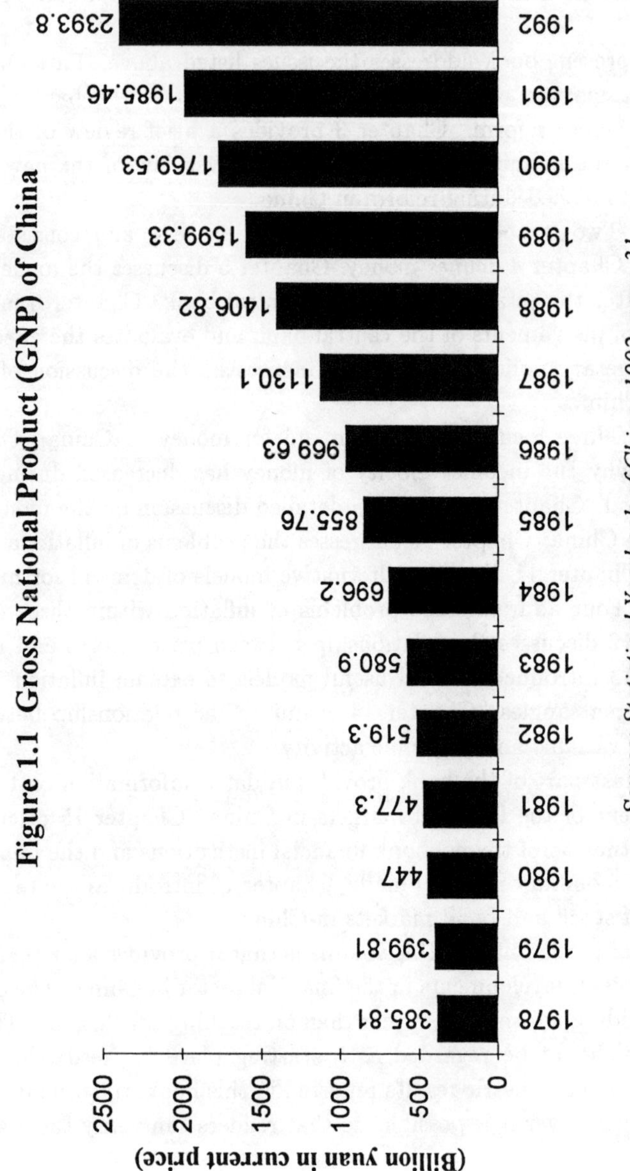

Figure 1.1 Gross National Product (GNP) of China

Source: Statistical Yearbook of China, 1992, page 31.

Figure 1.2 The Growth Rate of GNP in China

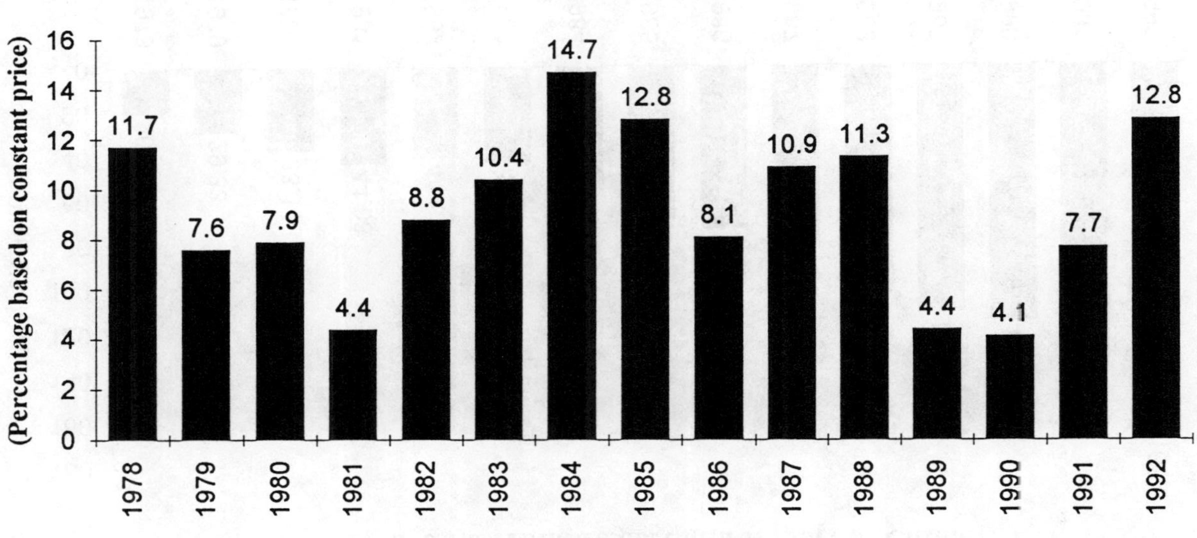

Source: Statistical Yearbook of China, 1992, page 31.

Figure 1.3 Total Export and Import of China

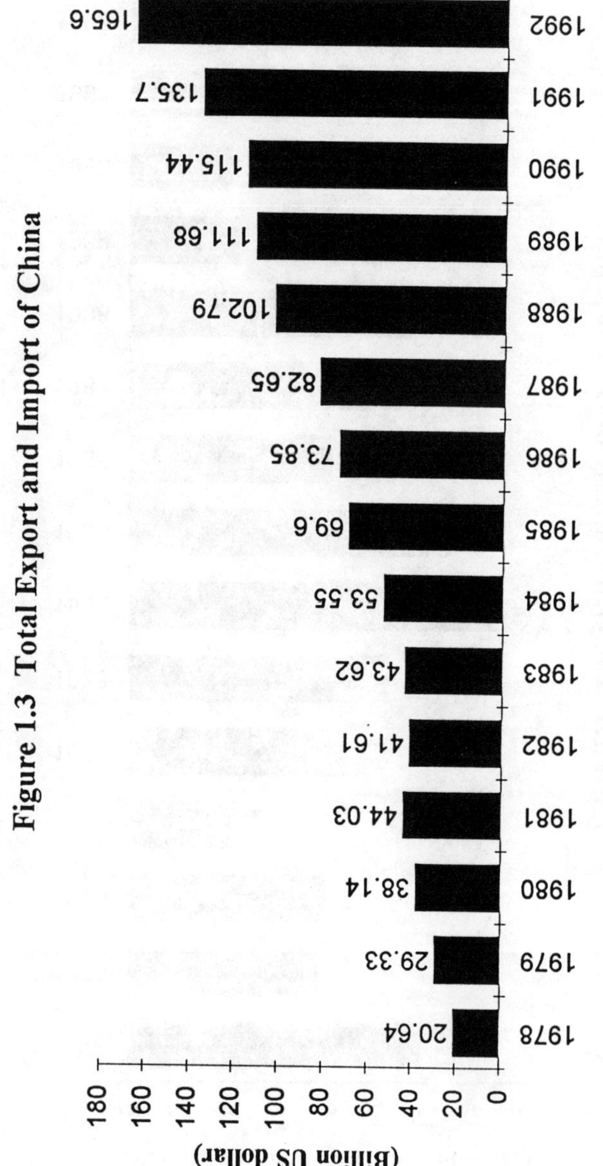

Source: Statistical Yearbook of China, 1992, page 627.

Figure 1.4 Foreign Investment (Contract) in China

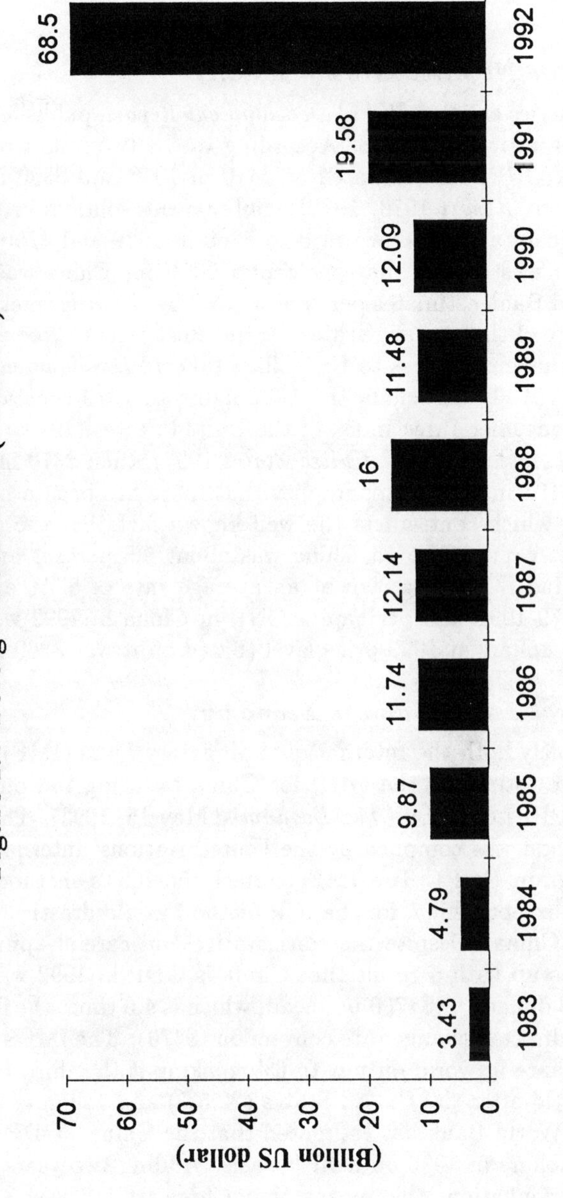

Source: Statistical Yearbook of China, 1992, page 641.

Appendix to Chapter 1

Chinese GNP Puzzles

Positive or Negative Growth Rate?

The series entitled *World Development Report*, published by the World Bank, was initiated in 1978. According to the two initial reports, China's per capita GNP was estimated at $410 in 1976 and $390 in 1977 (*World Development Report* 1978, 1979). Subsequent volumes of the reports revised per capita GNP downward to $260 in 1979 and $290 for 1980. The World Bank estimated that per capita GNP for China was $370 in 1992. The World Bank estimates per capita GNP by the *Atlas* method which uses the average of the exchange rates for the most recent three years to convert national currency figures to US dollars (*World Development Report*, 1991, pp. 273-275). If we deflate the 1992 figure to 1979 constant price by using the Consumer Price Index of the United States (1979=100, 1992=193; *Statistical Abstract of the United States* 1993), then $370 in 1992 is equivalent to $191 in 1979. This implies that there has been a negative growth in China, which contradicts the well known fact that the average growth rate of per capita GNP in China was about 5.5 percent annually for this period. Had it really grown at an average rate of 5.5% annually for the period 1979-1992, the per capita GNP in China in 1992 would have been $1063 US dollars at 1992 price level (based on it was $260 in 1979).

How Large Is the Chinese Economy?

Recently both the International Monetary Fund (IMF) and the World Bank have estimated the GDP for China by using the purchasing-power parities (PPP) criterion (*The Economist* May 15, 1993). The most popular PPP method was compiled by the United Nations' International Comparison Program (ICP). The IMF applied the ICP's method to almost all countries except China, for the ICP method would drastically overestimate GDP for China. Despite the conservative and careful approach, the IMF still comes up with a result that China 's GDP in 1992 was about $2,000 billion US dollars, or $1700 per head, which is 4.6 times the figure estimated from the direct exchange rate conversion ($370). The IMF's new figures lift China's share in world output to 6%, making it the third largest economy in the world after the United States (22.5%) and Japan (7.6%).

The World Bank has estimated that the China's GDP was $2,210 billion US dollars in 1990 on a PPP basis. Adding two years of 10% growth and dollar inflation, this means that China's GDP was $2,870 billion in 1992 (or $2,460 per head), which makes China the second largest economy in the world. Unbelievable results! Table 1.1 and Figure 1.5 provide a summary of the World Bank's estimation.

Table 1.1
GDP Per Head of Developing Countries
(All in US dollar)

1992	— **GDP per head in $** — Exchange rate	Purchasing power parity	**GDP, $bn** Purchasing power parity
China	370	2,460	2,870
India	275	1,255	1,105
Brazil	2,525	4,940	770
Mexico	3,700	6,590	590
Indonesia	650	2,770	510
South Korea	6,790	8,635	380
Thailand	1,780	5,580	320
Pakistan	400	2,075	240
Argentina	6,870	5,930	190
Nigeria	275	1,560	190
Egypt	655	3,350	180
Philippines	820	2,400	155
Malaysia	2,980	7,110	130

SOURCE: The World Bank, OECD, from *The Economist*, May 15, 1993 page 83.

Figure 1.5 The World GDP League

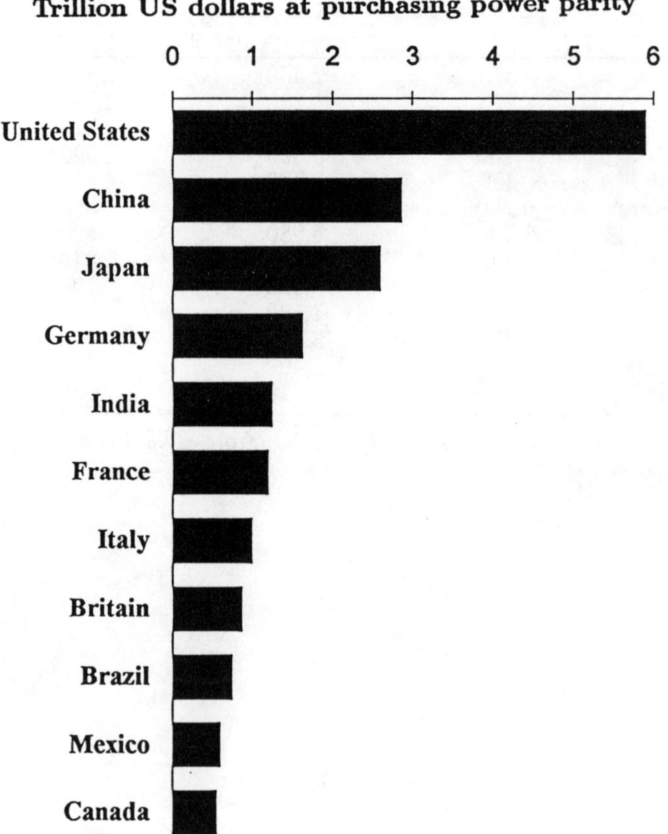

Comparable Russian data not available.

Source: World Bank, OECD, see The Economist, May 15, 1993.

PART ONE

Financial System in China: An Overview

2

The Money and Banking System Before the Reform

The banking system before the reform was characterized by an all-inclusive mono-bank system established in the 1950s. Under that system, the People's Bank served as both a central bank and a commercial bank, which controlled about 93 percent of the total financial assets of the country. The People's Bank of China acted as the "center of cash, credit and settlement," from which currency and credit were issued, into which cash held by urban residents and credit held by state enterprises and institutions were deposited, and through which the payments within the state sector were cleared (Liu 1980).

Although there were specialized banks under the People's Bank, such as the Agricultural Bank, Bank of China, and the People's Construction Bank, they were not independent. The People's Bank monopolized almost all banking activities. The specialized banks virtually served as departments of the Peoples' Bank, or departments of the Ministry of Finance. During the 30-year period from the time the People's Republic was established to the beginning of the reform (1949-1978), there were several institutional changes to the banking system in China. However, the nature of the all-inclusive mono-bank system had never changed before the reform.

The main task of the banking system was to provide working capital (circulating capital) to enterprises. The composition of national savings at that time was consistent with the above observation. The savings of the economy were mainly generated through the current account surplus of the state budget. In 1978, the savings provided by the government were 15.5 percent of GNP, whereas household financial saving was only 1 percent of GNP (De Wulf and Goldsbrough 1986). The total (cumulated) household bank deposits was only about 6 percent of GNP in 1978 (Qian 1988). Therefore, the government saving was much larger than household saving at that time. For most years during the period 1962-1978, the government had a small surplus after all the expenditures and budgetary investment allotments. The government had neither domestic nor foreign borrowings for the period 1958-1978.

The role of financial intermediation was very limited on resource allocation before the reform, because most investments were financed directly from the government budgetary allotments rather than through the banking system. The limited amount of banking business was monopolized by the all-inclusive mono-bank system led by the People's Bank of China. There were no financial markets, no alternative ways of financing, and no financial assets except bank deposits.

It is not very informative to review the institutional changes in the banking sector for the period 1949-1978, because they were out of date and some changes were done back and forth several times (Liu 1980). In this chapter, we just focus on one important aspect of the banking system before the reform: the two circuits of money flows, which were in place when the reform began, making them essential to understanding both the overall process of the reform and analyses presented later in this book.

2.1 The Two Circuits of Money Flows

Before the reform, the liquidity provided in China consisted of two circuits: a cash circuit and a bank transfer circuit. Generally speaking, most transactions involving non-state parties were conducted by cash; and most transactions within the state sector were facilitated by bank transfers. In other words, we can say that transactions in the consumer goods market were carried out primarily by cash, whereas most transactions in the producer goods markets were cleared by bank transfers since the former market involved mostly individual consumers and the latter mostly state enterprises. The Chinese monetary authority used the so-called "cash plan" to control the currency flow and "credit plan" to control the bank transfer flow.

The Currency Circuit

The amount of currency was measured by cash in circulation (usually at the end of the year). Roughly speaking, there were five channels to put currency into circulation as indicated in Figure 2.1. Among these five channels, wage payment and state procurement of agricultural products were the two large items, together accounting for about 80 percent of the total currency supplied.

Figure 2.1 also illustrates the five ways that currency was withdrawn from circulation, of which retail sales was the most important item, accounting for about 70 percent of the cash withdrawn from circulation (People's Bank of China, 1984).

The change of the currency in circulation was defined as the difference between the inflow and outflow of currency in a certain period of time and it was heavily influenced by two factors: people's income, and supply of consumer goods. The ability of the People's Bank of China to control the change of currency in circulation was limited. It had little control over people's income and supply of consumer goods. It was the government, not the bank, who set up the wage and procurement plan, and production targets. The banking system had to supply enough money to accommodate the government's economic growth targets.

There was a strict control on currency in circulation in China that began in the early 1950s. The currency flow was basically restricted in the area of the individual consumer's income and expenditures, while bank transfer money was for firms' transactions. Generally speaking, state-owned firms were required to conduct their transactions by using their bank transfer money. They could not freely withdraw currency from their bank accounts. This rule was also applicable to the specialized banks. They had to submit most cash received to the People's Bank, keeping only a small proportion for liquidity purposes. Therefore, to a large degree, the natural convertibility relationship between currency and bank transfer money was strictly regulated. The rationale of this kind of arrangement was to make the amount of cash transactions among firms as small as possible in order to supervise firms easily. This kind of arrangement was not fundamentally changed until several years after the establishment of the central bank system. By the end of 1986, the amount of cash in circulation was 120 billion yuan in China, of which the state enterprises had just 20 billion (Huang, Xu 1988).

The Bank Transfer Money Circuit

A number of authors have used the currency in circulation as the measure of the money supply. This was obviously a rough approximation, since the bank transfer money provided another circuit of liquidity and most transactions in the producer goods markets among state-owned enterprises were conducted by the bank transfer money.

Figure 2.2 offers a demonstration of the bank transfer money flow. There were three sources of the bank transfer money. The first one was government allotment from the central and/or local government's budgetary plan. Government allotments were originally designed primarily for fixed capital investments. The theoretical justification for using government allotments was that firms were owned by the socialist public. Government allotments came from the social savings and the government made the investment decisions on behalf of the public to the publicly owned enterprises. Once a firm received an investment allotment, it immediately became a bank deposit of that firm. Firms paid neither the principle nor any interest back to the government on the fund allotted. It was a one-way transfer from the government to firms. All centrally-planned economies had been perplexed by the low efficiency and waste caused by this kind of fund allotments.

The second source of the bank transfer money was bank loans from the credit plan. Bank loans were originally designated to be working capital (or circulating funds) for industrial production and commerce. Because the demand for working capital was influenced by season, market condition, and other random variables, it was more efficient to use bank loans as the major source of working capital. The proportion of working capital financed by bank loans changed from time to time and also varied across sectors. On average more than 50 percent of the working capital of industrial production and about 80 percent of the working capital of commerce had been financed by bank loans, which were usually in short to medium terms and, of course, charge interest. A typical firm had to pay principle plus interest back to the lending bank when it was due. Similarly, once a loan was lent to a state enterprise, it became the deposit of the firm.

The third source of the bank transfer money was firms' retained earnings deposited in banks, which was not large before the reform and has become more and more important recently.

2.2 The Characteristics of the Money and Banking System Before the Reform

The characteristics of the money supply process under the mono-bank system can be summarized as follows: First, the State Council was the authority of issuance of currency and determining the total amount of loans. The banking system was not independent; it was just a government agency. The responsibility of the banking system was to carry out government monetary policy and to police all state enterprises and institutions according to the financial discipline of the government.

Second, the basic apparatus of money flow in China consisted of two circuits: a bank transfer balance flow circulating among enterprises and institutions within the state sector, and a cash flow serving primarily households and the non-state owned enterprises. The monetary authority used a "cash plan" to control the currency flow and a "credit plan" to command the transfer balance flow. As a result, money was disintegrated into two blocks and there were regulatory barriers in between. In a typical market economy, a large proportion of transactions among firms are also settled by bank transfers and do not cause a currency flow. The difference, however, is that in market economics, firms do so by choice whereas in China, they did so by coercion.

Third, the separation of currency from the bank transfer money made the money creation process in China unique in the following two ways. On the one hand, due to the denial of free convertibility between the bank transfer money and cash, the uniformity property of money was seriously constrained. Modern money creation theory based on the monetary base, reserved ratio, and multipliers does not apply to the banking system in China before the reform, because there was no central bank and no required reserves. On the other hand, it was inevitable that the two circuits were interactive and influenced each other in a way such that deposits created loans. In other words, the multiplier effect partially worked even in the mono-bank system. However, compared to the mandatory cash and credit plans, the multiplier effect was a second-order factor.

Fourth, money supply targeting was subordinated to the implementation of the output targets in the central plan (physical plan). Since most fixed capital investment projects were financed by budget allotments, the primary objective of the credit plan was to provide working capital to industries and commerce. Bank loans to enterprises were based on a "real bills" doctrine, which stated that there would not be an over issue of credit as long as bank credit was restricted to financing the production and sale of real goods. The cash plan was designed to facilitate transactions for consumer goods. An empirical rule, the so-called 1:8 rule, was the yardstick for deciding the amount of currency in circulation for a long time, which stated that for every 1 yuan cash in circulation, there should be 8 yuan worth of consumer goods available on markets in a given year. In other words, the velocity of cash was equal to 8. Consequently, money supply was passive and accommodating, and it was basically endogenous in the sense that it was determined by the physical production plan and the amount of consumer goods available.

Fifth, it was always controversial which measure should be used for money. If macro control was the primary concern, then the focus should have been on the measure that influenced the demand the most. For this purpose, currency in circulation was a simple and appropriate measure of money under the mono-bank system, because the net changes of currency in circulation were equal to the difference between total deposits and loans. Control over currency was tantamount to control of the deposit and loan plan. Furthermore, the aggregate demand for consumer goods was a function of currency in circulation. The control of currency implied restraining aggregate demand and maintaining price stability. It was not surprising that the Chinese monetary authority and scholars in the academic circle often used currency in circulation as the measure of money before reform (Chow 1987).

Figure 2.1 Currency Flow Before the Reform

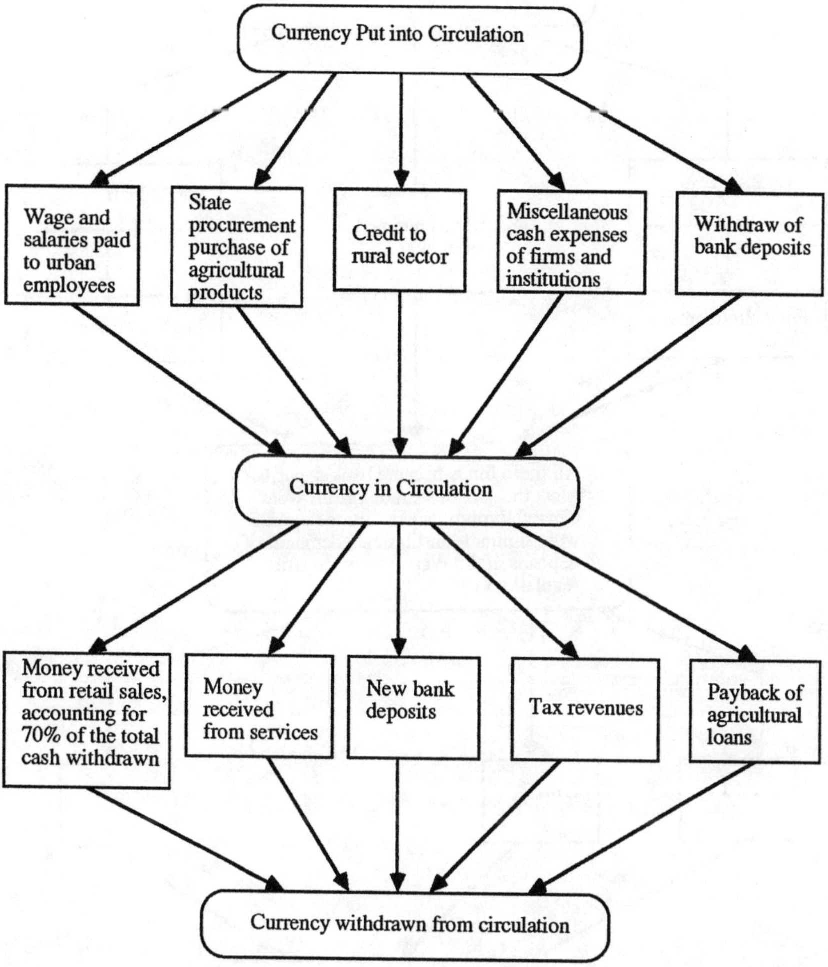

Figure 2.2 Bank Transfer Money Flow

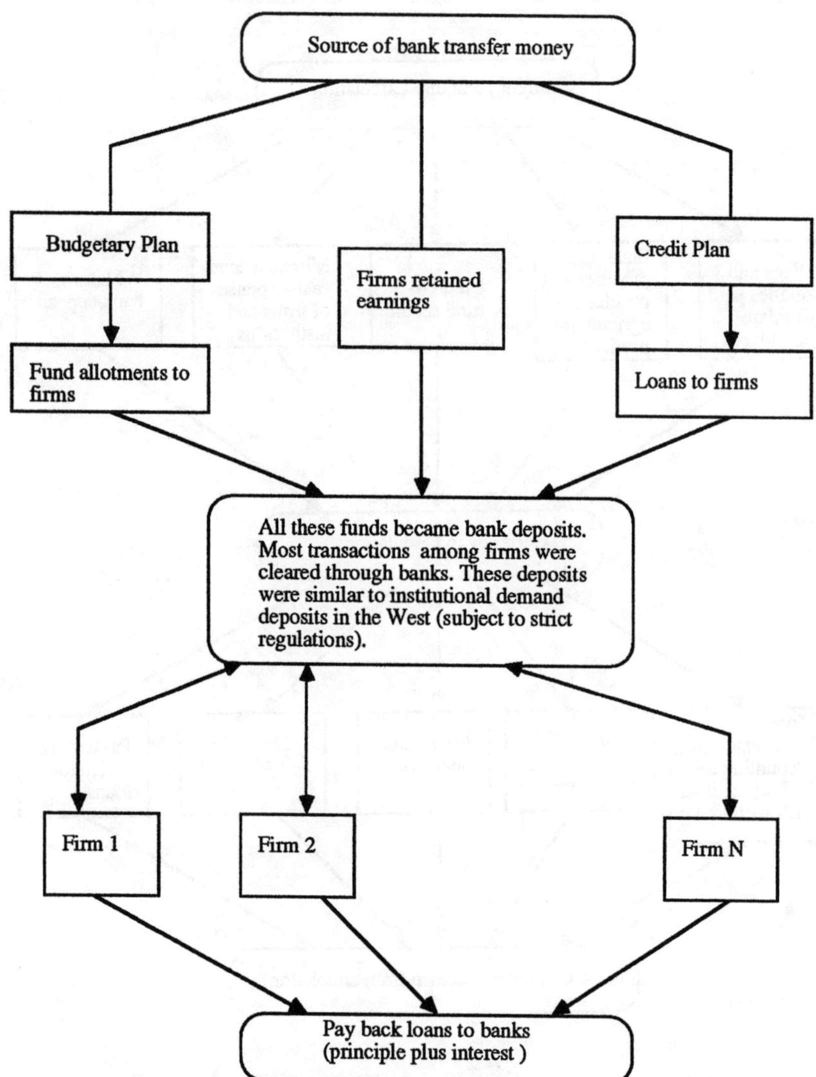

3

Reforming the Banking System

The objective of the economic reform, according to official documents, was to establish a socialist market-oriented economy based primarily on public ownership (Zhao 1987). Reform in the banking sector was necessary to achieve this goal. The design of the new banking system aimed at promoting the economic leverage function of the banking system by giving more freedom of operation and profit motives to specialized and other commercial banks, making them independent economic entities while macro monetary policy was controlled by the central bank. The restructuring of the banking system can be summarized as follows.

3.1 The Structure of the New Banking System

In 1978, the People's Bank of China (PBC) was formally separated from the Ministry of Finance and was granted a ministerial rank. In January 1984, the PBC became the central bank, and its commercial banking business was taken over by the newly established Industrial and Commercial Bank of China (ICBC) as well as other specialized banks. The purpose of this move was to separate the administrative functions of the banking system from its commercial functions.

By the end of 1991, PBC had its headquarters in Beijing, 44 first level branches in all provinces and large cities, more than 400 second tier branches at the regional level (between province and county), and about 2000 branches at the county level. PBC employed more than 166 thousand people at the end of 1991.

As the central bank, PBC is a government administrative organization directly led by the State Council. Its main responsibilities are to make macro monetary policies; control the money supply, interest rates, and exchange rates; serve as the treasury of the central government; regulate financial markets; and formulate the overall credit and loan plan.

PBC is also the official representative for China in international monetary organizations, such as the International Monetary Fund (since 1980) and Asian Development Bank (since 1985). In addition, the State Administration of Exchange Control (SAEC) is affiliated with the PBC. SAEC is a government agency that controls and regulates foreign exchanges.

Under the central bank, the banking system consists of specialized banks and commercial banks. There are four government-owned specialized banks in China: the Industrial and Commercial Bank of China (ICBC) for urban areas, the Agricultural Bank of China (ABC) for rural areas, the People's Construction Bank of China (PCBC) for long-term investments on a large scale, and the Bank of China (BOC) for foreign exchange. Rural credit cooperatives (RCCs) are collectively owned rural financial institutions and they are affiliated with (or led by) the ABC. Closely associated with the PCBC is the China Investment Bank (CIB), the main function of which is to channel loans from international sources (mainly from the World Bank). Besides the four specialized banks, there are several more comprehensive commercial banks have been established during the reform period. Among them, the Bank of Communications (BOCOM), and CITIC Industrial Bank (CITICIB) have a national network of branches; others are regional banks, such as Shenzhen Merchants Bank, Fujian Industrial Bank, Guangdong Development Bank, Shanghai Pudong Development Bank, etc.

During the reform, the existing specialized banks have been restructured and new commercial banks and financial institutions have been established. The primary responsibility of the specialized banks is to conduct commercial banking activities in their specialized areas. At the same time, they have the responsibility to carry out economic policies by providing policy loans as directed by the government. The following is a brief summary of the major banks and financial institutions in China.

The Industrial and Commercial Bank of China (ICBC) was founded on January 1, 1984, the same time the central bank was established. The primary mission of the Industrial and Commercial Bank was to take over the commercial banking operations of the People's Bank in order to make the latter a true central bank. The Industrial and Commercial Bank attracts all sources of deposits and provides commercial banking services to urban residents, enterprises, and institutions. It is the major source of working capital loans to state and collective firms. It also serves as a clearing house for transactions among firms and institutions, by virtue of which it supervises the economic activities of firms.

The Agricultural Bank of China (ABC), founded in 1955, provides its financial services primarily to rural residents and institutions. It is the main channel through which government loans for various purposes, including procurement purchases, are provided to the countryside. It is also the leading force and supervisory body of the rural credit co-ops.

The People's Construction Bank of China (PCBC), established in 1954, specializes in managing budget allotments and loans to large scale, fixed capital formation and innovation projects. The Construction Bank functions as a bank as well as an organ of the Ministry of Finance. Starting in 1985, all basic construction budgetary allotments have been allocated in terms of loans. Hence, the Construction Bank has become more like a real bank rather than an organ of the Ministry of Finance.

The Bank of China (BOC) specializes in the management of foreign exchange and international payments. It serves as the clearing house for trades and other international transactions and provides loans to international trade-related businesses as a State-appointed import-export bank. The Bank of China implements exchange control, conducts international loans, and handles foreign securities. However, since the beginning of the reform, the monopoly position of the Bank of China in international financial business has been challenged by the newly established financial institutions discussed below.

The China Investment Bank (CIB), established in December, 1981, specializes in raising foreign long- and medium-term credit and loans for use in China (mostly for small- to medium-sized projects). It has worked closely with the World Bank, the Asian Development Bank, and other international monetary institutions and serves as an intermediary to dispense loans under the lending institutions' guidance.

The Bank of Communication (BOCOM), resurrected in July, 1986, has two characteristics that other Chinese banks do not possess. First, it is an institution owned by shareholders, the largest of which is the central government. Second, its area of operation is not as restricted as that of other specialized banks. It is actually a conglomerate that deals with a wide range of financial activities.

Formed in 1979, the China International Trust and Investment Corporation (CITIC) is the largest firm in the area of international finance in China. Its task is to attract foreign capital and advanced technologies to China. It is authorized to issue bonds, underwrite stocks in foreign countries, provide consulting services to foreign investors, and sponsor joint venture projects world-wide.

The Rural Credit Co-ops (RCCs) are collectively owned. They are independent credit unions in rural areas. They function as basically the grassroots units of the Agricultural Bank. Their scales are generally small;

they make autonomous decisions regarding their operations. They are solely responsible for profits and losses.

The People's Insurance Company of China (PICC) is by far the largest insurance company in China. It was founded in 1949 and has branches in every province. It resumed its domestic insurance business in 1979. Its services include property damage (household and enterprises), transportation, auto, life, and agriculture insurance.

The central bank, the specialized banks, and financial institutions constitute the banking system of China, based on which the money supply mechanism operates. Figure 3.1 illustrates the framework of the financial system in China. The non-bank financial institutions and capital markets will be discussed in detail in Chapters 15 and 16 of this book. Table 3.1 summarizes some general information on the banking system in China, which includes the number of branches, total employees, total assets, and net earning information for all the major banks and financial institutions in 1991. For a more detailed description of the specialized banks and the reform process in the banking sector in China during the reform period, see *China: Financial Sector Policies and Institutional Development*, World Bank (1990), De Wulf and Goldsbrough (1986), and Qian (1993).

During the reform, tremendous efforts have been made to replace budgetary allotments by bank loans. The proportion of investments financed by budgetary allotments has declined rapidly. The use of bank loans has expanded to fixed capital investments to make the cost of capital more explicit in order to improve efficiency. More and more fixed capital investments, including large key projects, have been financed by bank loans instead of budgetary allotments. The role of the banking system becomes very important. On one hand, savings from households have grown rapidly and have become the largest source of saving for the economy. The banking system is now the main financial intermediary to channel the savings of the economy to investments. On the other hand, the banking system not only provides most of the working capital for the economy (as it did in the past), but also provides most of the investment (fixed capital) through loans. Bank loans have become very crucial in smoothing the day-to-day operation of the economy and control of the macro credit conditions of the country.

3.2 The Relationship Between the Central Bank and Specialized Banks

Since the four specialized banks dominate the bulk of the banking business and all of them are owned by the government, it is interesting to look at the relationship between the specialized banks and the central bank. One of the goals of the banking reform is to give more management freedom and control to the specialized banks and enable them to be independent, profit-driven enterprises. The central bank, as a government agency, is responsible for formulating monetary policy and controlling macroeconomic conditions. According to official documents (the People's Bank of China, 1984), the relationship between the central bank and specialized banks can be described as:

1. *Under the guidance of one plan.* The amount of money available to specialized banks for credit and loan purposes is part of the country's comprehensive credit plan and subject to the approval of the central bank. The credit plan has been implemented increasingly by economic levers (such as interest rates, reserve ratio, etc.). The traditional imperative administrative order has been gradually reduced.

2. *Dividing the financial capital.* The old mandatory hierarchical quota management method of credit has been changed to a more flexible credit and loan policy, under which the specialized banks use the funds they control (the deposits that they obtain, their own capital, plus the amount of money they are allowed to borrow from the central bank according to the credit plan) to make loans. They are supposed to make their own lending decisions and to be responsible for the consequences (profits or losses).

3. *Foreign exchange control.* The central bank controls loans and investments of hard currencies. Banks dealing with foreign exchange must submit their hard currency credit and loan plan to the central bank for approval.

4. *Required reserve.* The specialized banks submit a certain proportion of their deposits to the central bank as the required reserve. In 1985, the required reserve ratio was 10 percent. Recently, it has been about 13 percent. The central bank may change the reserve rate as an instrument of monetary policy.

5. *Competition among banks.* Competition among specialized banks is still very limited. They are pretty much specialized (or monopolized) on their own turf, although mutual borrowing among banks is allowed (usually within the same region).

From the above five points, we see that the new policy emphasizes two aspects. The first is to give specialized banks more incentive to make profits. The second is that the central bank controls the money supply and the overall credit condition. Because of the establishment of the central bank and the reserve system, bank deposits are now connected with loans. Theoretically speaking, this implies that a modern money creation theory based on the monetary base and multiplier is applicable to China. On the other hand, since it is difficult to phase out the old system and the new system needs to adjust, one could not expect the central bank and the reserve system to be functioning effectively in a short period of time. It would be surprising to see that the central bank system, which was founded by a series of government decrees, works well while a large proportion of the economy is still centrally-planned. In Chapter 5, we will examine the new money supply process in China by looking at the monetary base and the multiplier mechanism.

The most important consequence of the decentralized economic reform is that the market share of the economy has been increased. Before the reform, aggregate demand was controlled by a double lock: the credit plan plus the physical plan. To start a project, a state firm had to first get the physical plan allotment and then either apply a loan or a grant to finance the project, which was entitled under the physical plan. As the producer goods market grows, firms can buy producer goods as long as they have money. By the end of 1992, about 80 percent of the producer goods and more than 90 percent of consumer goods were allocated by the market. Consequently, the double lock became a single lock. The physical plan is no longer relevant for a lot of resources. There are all sorts of loopholes and tricks that firms can use to get around the cash and credit regulations and somehow obtain what they need from markets. After all, it is part of their autonomous managing power to which they are entitled from the reform. For example, firms can sell their products in the market for cash, which can be used to buy whatever they need. Two firms can buy and sell to each other and clear their transaction by paying the balance, which may well be within the regulation's limit for the free movement of the bank transfer money. In this sense, the growth of the producer goods markets increased the proportion of transactions that are conducted in cash and also to a certain degree made the liquidity of the bank transfer money higher than before. Therefore, during the reform, the boundary of the two money circuits discussed in the previous chapter has been blurred.

3.3 Foreign Banks in China

Before 1949, Shanghai was the financial center of the Far East. There were more than 200 foreign bank branches in Shanghai alone. Compared to Shanghai, Hong Kong was relatively primitive in terms of the development in financial markets at that time. Most of those foreign banks had been driven out of China after the People's Republic was established. In 1978, when the economic reform started, there were only four foreign banks in Shanghai: Hong Kong Shanghai Banking Corp.Ltd.(UK), Standard Chartered Bank PLC (UK), The Bank of East Asia (Hong Kong), and Overseas-Chinese Banking Corporation (Singapore). Most of their businesses were related to trade finance. In 1984, the People's Bank of China authorized the above four banks in Shanghai to expand their business to a certain degree.

On September 8, 1990, the People's Bank of China promulgated *Regulations On Foreign and Joint Venture Financial Institutions in Shanghai*, which was the first systematic regulation regarding foreign financial institutions. The regulation described both the requirements and procedures for establishing a branch of foreign financial institutions in Shanghai and outlined the scope of their businesses. Since then, many foreign banks and financial institutions have established their branches and representative offices in Shanghai, Beijing, and other cities. Most bank branches, however, have been established in Shanghai, Shenzhen, Zhuhai, and Shantou. For example, by the end of 1991, the following banks had opened their branches in Shanghai in additional to the four banks mentioned above: Sanwa Bank (Japan), Industrial Bank of Japan, Citibank, N. A. (US), Bank of America (US), Banque Indosuez (France) , Credit Lyonnais (France), Bank of Tokyo (Japan), and Dai-Ichi Kangyo Bank (Japan).

By the end of 1993, there were hundreds of branches and representative offices of foreign financial institutions in China. Japan was by far the largest presence in terms of the number of branches and offices in China, types of services, and the volume of transactions. The Appendix of this chapter provides selected branches and representative offices of foreign financial institutions in China and their addresses and phone numbers.

Although there have been strict restrictions for what types of business foreign banks can do in China, it is clear that the restrictions are gradually easing and regulations and laws are moving toward the direction of the international standard. The following businesses are fairly common for foreign banks and financial institutions: Trade financing, all kinds of deposits and loans in hard currencies, demand deposits and checking services in foreign exchange and bank transfers, consulting, insurance services, underwriting ,and corporate finance. Most clients of foreign financial institutions in China are foreign firms, joint-venture firms, foreign individuals, and some domestic firms that are engaging in export and import businesses. By the end of 1993, foreign banks were not allowed to do business in domestic currency, although there have been some indications that the government will release this restriction soon.

3.4 The Problems of the Banking System

The banking system in China has changed during the reform from a mono-bank system to a more or less market oriented banking system with a central bank and a variety of specialized and commercial banks plus non-bank financial institutions. The Chinese financial sector may appear like a market oriented system. However, if we look underneath, we will find the banking system is still far away from a real market system. The following are some problems worth mentioning.

The Central Bank

The central bank does not behave like an independent central bank. Generally speaking, the primary objective of a central bank is to control money supply and maintain the price stability. In order to achieve this goal, a central bank should be relatively independent of the government and have the power to make monetary policies. The organization structure of PBC coincides exactly with the government hierarchy at every level. The central government controls the headquarters of PBC. Its first level branches are led by its headquarters and the corresponding provincial governments. The same thing is true all the way to the county level. It is extremely difficult for PBC to act independently under this arrangement.

Historically, PBC was an all-inclusive mono-bank. When PBC became the central bank, its commercial banking activities were transferred to the four specialized banks. However, this separation has not been completed. The objective function of PBC is a mixed one: on the one hand it acts as a central bank, on the other, it continues to engage in some profitable activities and is responsible for some special policy loans, such as loans to gold production, technology development, and loans to poor and minority regions.

The financial relationship between PBC and the central government is not clearly defined. PBC has to provide unlimited loans to the central government unconditionally. There is neither a formal legal procedure to go through for the central government to borrow money from the central bank nor a definite date to pay it back. There is little check and balance from the legislative body—the People's Congress—either.

The Specialized Banks

All four specialized banks are government owned. Their branches are led by the headquarters as well as the governments of their localities. The specialized banks have to take on many tasks assigned by the government.

For instance, all specialized banks have to provide policy-oriented (subsidized) loans to some key projects of the government and social welfare programs. The percentage of these policy loans in their total loan portfolio are: 20 percent for ICBC; 30 percent for ABC; 15 percent for BOC; and 45 percent for PCBC (Hui 1994). Presumably the rest are commercial loans. The fact that the specialized banks have the dual responsibilities of commercial banking business and policy loans has created tremendous moral hazard problems. The specialized banks could always use policy loans as an excuse for their low efficiency and mistakes in commercial lending decisions. Furthermore, they have often diverted the funds for policy loans for more profitable commercial business and used their power of policy loans as leverage for rent seeking.

At the same time, all the specialized banks have suffered from government intervention. They often have to lend to the government for its deficits and to pay government deposits at a premium interest rate. The government often has imperative "recommendations" for the specialized banks and asks them to provide loans under certain conditions to "high priority projects." Of course the priority was decided by the government. This kind of government intervention has definitely had a negative impact on the bottom lines of the specialized banks.

By definition, all specialized banks have their own turf. The government has allowed competition among specialized banks to a certain degree. For example, ABC now has many branches in urban areas; ICBC has engaged in foreign exchange. However, it takes a long time to establish a competitive environment. The specialized banks have operated on their own turf for many years and are well entrenched. Lack of competition is a major obstacle on the road to an efficient banking system.

Other Problems

Establishing a competitive and efficient banking system is a complicated process. The following are some related issues. First, more and more foreign banks have established branches or representative offices in China. However, they have not entered the domestic currency banking business. Financial liberalization and gradually releasing the restrictions on foreign banks are definite trends. Allowing foreign banks to compete in China to a certain degree would exert pressures on domestic banks, which is good for speeding up reforms in the financial sector. Second, the problems of the banking sector are connected with the state-owned enterprises. Many problems of the banking system will not be solved until property rights are clearly defined for the large scale state-owned enterprises, which in turn depend on the establishment of a proper social safety net. Third, one of the most important aspects of the reforms in the banking sector is the establishment of a legal environment. By the end of 1993, China did not have a "Bank Law" yet. It is expected the "Bank Acts of China" will be approved by the People's Congress soon. From the experiences of the past, it is not so difficult to promulgate such a law. The real problem is the enforcement and transaction costs of the enforcement.

Table 3.1
Survey Information on Financial Institutions in China in 1991

Name of Bank	Branches[a]	Employees (person)	Total assets (million *yuan*)	Profit (million *yuan*)
The central bank				
The People's Bank	2,531	166,309	901,080	—[b]
The specialized banks				
The Industrial and Commercial Bank	30,834	504,554	1117,469	15,941
The Agricultural Bank	55,614	483,763	686,848	1,605
The Bank of China	6,362	87,626	1107,739	8,333
The Construction Bank	27,586	238,789	669,742	1,880
The Communication Bank	418	18,182	106,069	2,050
The Investment Bank of China	—	—	17,434	116
Other financial institutions				
The People's Insurance Corporation of China	3,383	93,394	35,158	2,238
The International Trust and Investment Corp.	29,565	—	45,263	369
The Rural Credit Co-ops[c]	103,834	539,226[d]	368,966	796

SOURCE: *Statistical Yearbook of China*, 1992, p. 655. *Almanac of China's Finance and Banking*, 1992, pp. 517-547, p. 583.

NOTE:

a. The sizes of branches vary tremendously. A provincial branch is a very large branch whereas a local deposit office could be a small branch of only three employees. Nevertheless, both of them are counted as one "branch" here.

b. No information.

c. The data for the Rural Credit Co-ops are 1990 data.

d. Not including part time employees.

Figure 3.1 Financial Institutions in China

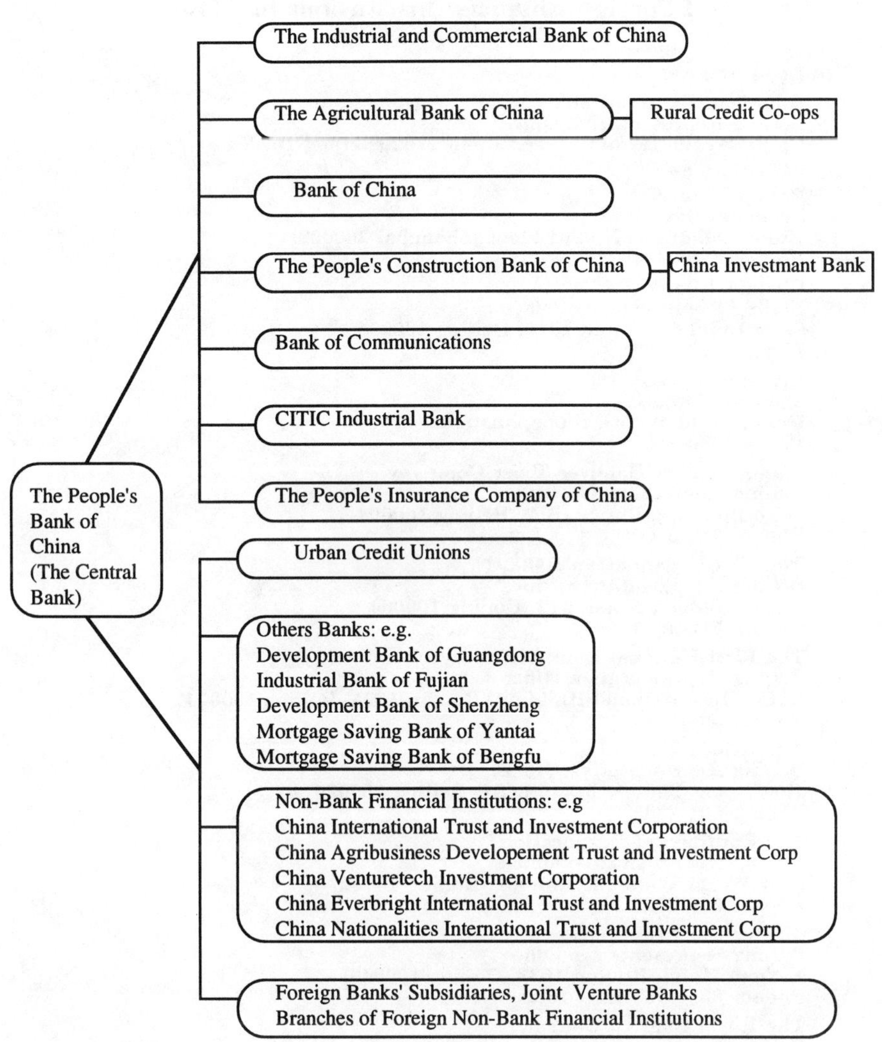

Appendix to Chapter 3
Selected Branches and Representative Offices of Foreign Financial Institutions in China

North America

American Express Bank
Beijing Representative Office
China World Trade Center, Room 2702, Beijing 100004
Phone: 505-2838

Bank of America
Shanghai Branch
Union Building, Ground Floor, Shanghai 200002
Phone: 320-2491

Chemical Bank
Beijing Representative Office
Saite Building, Room 1812, Beijing 100004
Phone: 512-3722

Citibank, N.A.
Shanghai Branch
Union Building, 5th Floor, Shanghai 200002
Phone: 320-8661

Manufacturers Hanover Trust Company
Beijing Representative Office
Saite Building, Room 1812, Beijing 100004
Phone: 512-3700

The Chase Manhattan Bank, N. A. C
Beijing Representative Office
Saite Building, Room 512, Beijing 100004
Phone: 512-3693

The First National Bank of Chicago
Beijing Representative Office
CITIC International Building, Rooom 1604, Beijing 100004
Phone: 500-3281

American International Group, Inc.
Beijing Representative Office
JingGuang Center, Room 3407, Beijing 100020
Phone: 501-2889

The Continental Corporation
Beijing Representative Office
New World Tower, Room 901, Beijing 100027
Phone: 500-7799

Master Card International Inc.
Beijing Representative Office
XiYuan Hotel, Rooom 1633, Beijing 100046
Phone: 831-3388 Ext. 1633

The Royal Bank of Canada
Beijing Representative Office
China World Trade Center, Room 618, Beijing 100004
Phone: 505-0358

Canadian Imperial Bank of Commerce
Beijing Representative Office
International Club, Beijing 100004
Phone: 532-3164

Bank of Montreal
Beijing Representative Office
Saite Building, Room 707, Beijing 100004
Phone: 512-2288

Europe

**Societe Generale de Banque (Belgium)
Beijing Representative Office
ZiJin Hotel No. 3, Beijing 100046
Phone: 55-5725, 54-6189**

**HongKong and Shanghai Banking Corp. Ltd. (UK)
Beijing Representative Office
JianGuo Hotel, Room 145, Beijing 100020
Phone: 500-1074, 500-2233 Ext. 145**

**HongKong and Shanghai Banking Corp. Ltd. (UK)
Shanghai Branch
YuanMingYuan Avenue, No. 185, Shanghai 200002
Phone: 329-1775, 329-1659**

**Standard Chartered Bank PLC (UK)
Beijing Representative Office
HongKong Macao Center, 14th Floor, Beijing 100027
Phone: 501-1578**

**Standard Chartered Bank PLC (UK)
Shanghai Branch
Shanghai Center, 7th Floor, Shanghai 200002
Phone: 279-8823**

**Crosby Securities Lts. (UK)
Beijing Representative Office
HongKong Macao Center, Beijing 100027
Phone: 501-2288**

**Unibank Denmark (Denmark)
Beijing Representative Office
LiangMa Office Building, Room 1110, Beijing 100026
Phone: 501-1904**

**Union Bank of Finland (Finland)
Beijing Representative Office
LiangMa Office Building, Room 1110, Beijing 100026
Phone: 501-6688**

**Banque National de Paris (France)
Shenzhen Branch
XinDu Hotel, Room 301, Shenzhen 518000
Phone: 23-8031, 22-0379**

**Banque Indosuez (France)
Shanghai Branch
Lainyi Tower, Room 502, Shanghai 200002
Phone: 329-2228**

**Credit Lyonnais (France)
Shanghai Branch
Shanghai Center, 8th Floor, Shanghai 200040
Phone: 329-2228**

**Bayerishe Vereins Bank (Germany)
Beijing Representative Office
LiangMa Office Building, Room 1010, Beijing 100026
Phone: 501-2105, 501-2106**

**ABN AMRO Bank (Netherland)
Beijing Representative Office
JingGuang Center, Room 3306, Beijing 100020
Phone: 501-2055, 501-5110**

**Swiss Bank Corporation (Switzerland)
Beijing Representative Office
China World Trade Center, Room 3624, Beijing 100004
Phone: 505-2213**

**UnioBank of Switzerland (Switzerland)
Beijing Representative Office
China World Trade Center, Room 1231, Beijing 100004
Phone: 505-2283**

Asia and Pacific Region

National Australia Bank Limited (Australia)
Beijing Representative Office
International Building, Room 1943, Beijing 100004
Phone: 500-2255 Ext. 1943

Westpac Banking Corporation (Australia)
Beijing Representative Office
Saite Building, Room 506, Beijing 100004
Phone: 512-2288 Ext. 506

Heng Sheng Bank (Hong Kong)
Shanghai Representative Office
Ruijin Building, Room 1301, Shanghai 200020
Phone: 471-8781

Nan Yang Commercial Bank (Hong Kong)
Shenzhen Branch
JianShe Avenue No. 31, NanYang Building, Shenzhen 518000
Phone: 22-8153, 22-8155

Johnson & Higgins (H.K.) ltd. (Hong Kong)
Beijing Representative Office
JingGuang Building, Room 2708, Beijing 100020
Phone: 501-3388 Ext. 2708

The Bank of East Asia (Hong Kong)
Shanghai Branch
SiChuan Zhong Lu Line No. 229, Shanghai 200002
Phone: 321-6863

Sanwa Bank (Japan)
Shanghai Branch
Ruijing Hotel, Room 1510, Shanghai 200020
Phone: 433-6400

Mitsubishi Bank (Japan)
Beijing Representative Office
CITIC International Building, Room 1901, Beijing 100004
Phone: 500-3345

Fuji Bank (Japan)
Beijing Representative Office
CITIC International Building, Room 1901, Beijing 100004
Phone: 512-3047

Industrial Bank of Japan (Japan)
Shanghai Branch
International Trade Center, Room 1601, Shanghai 200335
Phone: 275-1111

Bnak of Tokyo (Japan)
Shanghai Branch
Ruijing Hotel, Room 1207, Shanghai 200020
Phone: 433-4036

Sanyo Securities Co. ltd. (Japan)
Beijing Representative Office
Fortune Building, Room 1002, Beijing 100004
Phone: 501-3110

United Overseas Bank Ltd. (Singapore)
XiaMen Branch
XinHua Road No. 10-14, Overseas Chinese Building, XiaMen 361003
Phone: 22-0100

Overseas-Chinese Banking Corporation (Singapore)
Shanghai Branch
JiuJiang Road No. 120, Shanghai
Phone: 323-3888

SOURCE: The foreign bank branches and representative offices in this appendix are selected from a list of more than 300 compiled by the People's Bank of China in 1992. For the complete list, see *Almanac of China's Finance and Banking*, **1992, Beijing, pp. 713-741.**

PART TWO

The Money Supply Process

4

What Is Money?

Before economic reform, it was very difficult to obtain data from China. Most economic data were classified documents. Even Chinese scholars, university professors, and research fellows in academic institutions did not have access to economic data of China. At that time, Chinese economists relied on the data from abroad to study the Chinese economy (e.g. from the World Bank, International Monetary Fund, and the Central Intelligence Agency (CIA) of the United States). The author of this book has vivid memories of studying the Chinese economy at Peking University in 1978, based on the data estimated by the CIA.

The Chinese government started publishing economic data systematically at the beginning of the 1980s. As far as the financial sector is concerned, many sources are now available, among them the *Almanac of China's Finance and Banking*, the *Statistical Yearbook of China*, and the *Almanac of China's Economy* are probably the most important. It is also worth mentioning that, in recent years, discrepancies among the data published by various sources both inside China and abroad are becoming smaller and smaller. When one looks at the recent report on the Chinese economy from the CIA of the United States, the World Bank, and International Monetary Fund, all report figures very similar to those in official documents published in China. The data collected by different sources are pretty much the same, which indicates that the data collection process in China is closer to the international standard. The data from China is getting more and more reliable.

4.1 The Definition of Money

We start with the definition of money. The official name of the Chinese money is *Renminbi*, or the People's Money, the unit of which is *yuan*. The official exchange rate in early 1994 was 1 US dollar to 8.72 *yuan*.(*People's Daily*, February 1,1994).

For a long time, economists and government officials in China used the currency in circulation as the primary measure of money. As far as controlling aggregate demand is concerned, using currency in circulation as the measure of money is no longer appropriate today. We shall use broader measures of money, M1 and M2, in this book for the following reasons.

First, bank transfer money consists of deposits of enterprises and institutions. These deposits are very similar to the demand deposits of institutions in the West. Although their movement is restricted within the intra- and inter-bank transfer system and they are not freely convertible to cash, they can be used to clear transactions among firms. They are demand deposits in the sense that they can be used directly as the means of purchase. The total amount of deposits of enterprises and institutions reflects the degree of tightness of monetary policy and has a significant effect on aggregate demand for the country. Therefore, when we consider a proper conception of money, the bank transfer money is certainly an important ingredient.

Second, it should be emphasized at this point that there is no clear-cut border between the two circuits (cash vs. bank transfer) regardless of how rigorous the regulations might be. In reality, the two circuits are closely related. An easing of credit policy increases loans to firms, which would eventually increase the currency in circulation, even if all of the loans went to purchase capital goods. It is estimated (Yi 1988) that 40 percent of investment in capital goods (most of which would be through the bank transfer circuit) would be converted to demand for consumer goods, simply because, among other things, to produce capital goods workers must be hired. The wage bill is paid in cash, which would undoubtedly increase the currency in circulation, and consequently the demand for consumer goods. During the decentralizing reforms, the boundary between the two money circuits has been blurred further. Firms can use the management power gained from the reforms to manipulate or circumvent, legally or semi-legally, the restrictions between the two money circuits.

Third, how about the deposits held by households? There are very few individual checking accounts in China. In 1989, it was reported that banks in China started checking account services for some qualified individuals, mostly private businessmen or celebrities. The amount of individual checking deposits was still relatively small by the end of 1992. Household deposits consist mainly of two parts: passbook saving deposits, and time deposits. An individual is free to convert his savings deposit into cash at any time with little transaction cost (ordinary people in China tend to ignore the cost of time). Time deposits can be converted into cash subject to some interest penalties. By the end of 1991, the total amount of household bank deposits in China was 911.03 billion yuan, of which 156.84 billion were passbook deposits, the remaining (754.19 billion) were time deposits (*Statistical Yearbook of China*, 1992, p. 281). Passbook saving and time deposits have potentially important effects on aggregate demand, although they are considered to be less liquid and households have to convert them into cash before making a purchase.

Now let us define money supplies in order of decreasing liquidity. First, currency in circulation is defined as M0. We define the sum of M0 and demand deposits of firms and institutions as M1. Since the household passbook savings and time deposits are less liquid in the sense that one can not write checks on them, we define M1 plus passbook savings and the time deposits (held by households and institutions) as M2.

4.2 Different Measures of Money

It is easy to measure currency in circulation. Before reform, most economists in China and the monetary authority of China regarded currency in circulation as money. There was not very much research literature on money at that time in China. For the little existing, the focus was on currency in circulation. In terms of money management and macro control, the emphasis of the monetary authority was also on cash. The net difference between the newly increased total deposits and total credit loans of the banking system was the net cash issuance. If the monetary authority constrained the quantity of currency in circulation, it actually controlled both the cash circuit and the credit money circuit. As far as measurement is concerned, there was no debate on cash in circulation. It is easily measured. The People's Bank has cash-in-circulation data from 1952, when the communist government unified the fiat money in China. The currency data are quite accurate.

For the measurement of M1 and M2, it is a little complicated. Perhaps there are three measures of M1 and M2 in China that are widely used. The first one is the monetary survey published in the recent *Almanac of China's Finance and Banking* (ACFB) by the Finance and Banking Association, which is actually compiled at the Finance and Banking Institute of the People's Bank. The second measure is from the same source, but derived from the balance sheet of the banking system. The third measure is by the International Monetary Fund in their money survey published in the *Yearbook of International Financial Statistics.* Tables 4.1 to 4.3 summarize the above three measures. Let us look at these three tables in detail.

The ACFB Money Survey

The money survey published by the People's Bank in the *Almanac of China's Finance and Banking* is compiled from the balance sheet of the banking system. The monetary survey has adopted modern definitions of money and standard statistical measurement methods of the International Monetary Fund (IMF). Therefore the statistics in the new money survey are very similar to those in the survey of the IMF, although there are still some differences. Table 4.1 provides survey data.

In Table 4.1, data are summarized from the balance sheets of the banking system owned by the government and the rural credit co-ops. This kind of comprehensive data is available only for 1985 on. The monetary survey consists of two parts, assets and liabilities. First, let us look at the assets part. **Assets** are equal to the sum of foreign assets (net) and domestic credit (net). **Loans** are total loans provided by the banking system and rural credit co-ops. **Claims on Government (net)** refers to the difference of central government borrowings from the banking system and total deposits of the central government in the banking system. In all the years represented in Table 4.1, government borrowings are greater than the total government deposits. The other important relationship in the assets part is that domestic credit (net) is equal to (Loans - Other assets (net) + Claims on government (net)).

Second, on the liability side, M0 is defined as cash in circulation. Money (M1) is equal to the sum of M0 and the demand deposits of institutions. Quasi-money is equal to the sum of time deposits of institutions and total household savings (which is the total savings of urban and rural households). Broader money (M2) is defined as the sum of money (M1) and quasi-money.

Obviously, the new monetary survey by ACFB is very well done. The definition is clear. The data collection process is systematic and carefully implemented. The standard is the international standard. This is perhaps the most simple, clear and reliable data available. The disadvantage of this data is that it is available only from 1985 and on. Notice that this data does not include deposits and loans of the nonbank financial institutions, mainly investment and trust companies. In 1990, the total amount of loans made by the investment and trust companies was 89.06 billion yuan, about 5.8 percent of M2. Loans made by investment and trust companies increased more rapidly in the 1991-1993 period.

The Data from the Balance Sheet of the Banking System

The change in the money and banking sector in China since economic reform is so profound that it is probably justifiable to argue that the data before reform and after reform are not comparable. Any direct comparison or econometric work that pools that data together without some sort of careful adjustment would be subject to the Lucas Critique. It is obvious that the monetary regime has been changed enough to make direct comparison difficult.

Nevertheless, sometimes readers still want to have data series that run from the beginning of the People's Republic to the present, despite the differences of the periods before and after the reform. The only series that is available is the fund source and usage information of the state banking system, which covers the period of 1952 to 1992. Table 4.2 summarizes information derived from this source on M0, M1, and M2.

The currency in circulation in Table 4.2 is straightforward. M1 is the sum of currency in circulation and demand deposits of firms and institutions. In other words, in the balance sheet of the state-owned banking system published by the monetary authority, M1 is equal to M0 plus the total amount of deposits, then minus the total amount of household savings, then minus the central government deposits in the central bank. M2 is equal to M1 plus the total amount of household savings.

There are several points worth mentioning here. First, the data in Table 4.2 are from the state banking system, which does not include the rural credit co-ops. If we added the liquidity provided by the rural co-ops, the M2 number would be larger. Second, the statistical measurements are different for data in Table 4.1 and Table 4.2. Therefore, they are not quite comparable. For example, for the recent monetary survey data in Table 4.1, M2 is equal to M1 plus total household savings plus the time deposits of enterprises and institutions. However, the time deposits of enterprises and institutions were not significant before the reform and the data were not available. Items such as self-raised funds for construction did not exist before reform. Therefore, the M2 in Table 4.2 is just the sum of M1 and total household savings. The advantage of the data in Table 4.2 is that it is the most comprehensive monetary survey data and it covers the entire period 1952-1992. Using this data without any adjustment might be subject to the Lucas Critique. Nevertheless, the data are provided for convenience of readers.

The Monetary Survey of International Monetary Fund

The monetary survey data of the International Monetary Fund is provided in Table 4.3. First, Money (M1) in Table 4.3 is defined as currency in circulation plus deposits of other domestic transactors plus demand deposits in the banking system plus demand deposits in rural credit co-ops. Second, quasi-money is defined the same as in Table 4.2, which is equal to the sum of the time deposits of institutions plus urban and rural household savings. Third, M2 is equal to M1 plus quasi-money. Fourth, the reserve money in Table 4.3 is equal to currency in circulation plus bank reserves plus deposits of other domestic transactors. By comparing Table 4.1 and 4.3, we see that the measurements of money (M1) and broad money (M2) between the ACFB monetary survey and the IMF monetary survey are different. Lastly, the IMF monetary survey started in 1977. The data before 1977 are not available.

In the literature, some authors use M0 as money (Chow 1987), which was the predominant opinion of both the monetary authority and the scholars in China before the reform. A lot of authors rely on the data provided by the International Monetary Fund and World Bank. Also many authors used quarterly data along the lines of Table 4.2; this data is drawn from a monetary survey of the state-owned banking system (Feltenstein and Ha 1991; Yi 1993). It is probably not very fruitful to debate which measure is right. Perhaps on some occasions, one data series is better than the other for a particular purpose. However, it is important to identify the source of the data used. Bear in mind the advantages and disadvantages of different measures, and be cautious when interpreting the econometric results from different data sets.

Table 4.1
ACFB Money Survey in China
(All in billion yuan)

Year	1985	1986	1987	1988	1989	1990	1991
Asset	520.7	674.8	839.0	1017.5	1201.9	1538.6	1948.2
Foreign asset (net)	20.83	3.89	26.13	30.25	37.14	92.67	137.36
Domestic credit (net)	499.88	670.88	812.82	987.29	1164.73	1445.90	1810.84
Loans	627.19	811.65	976.63	1142.50	1346.95	1654.13	1981.03
Claims on Govt (net)	9.33	5.86	20.80	30.56	24.66	42.06	84.59
Other assets (net)	117.98	146.63	184.61	185.77	206.38	250.29	-255.69
Liability	520.7	674.8	839.0	1017.5	1201.9	1538.6	1948.2
Broad Money (M2)	519.89	672.09	833.09	1009.98	1194.96	1529.37	1934.99
Money (M1)	334.09	423.22	494.86	598.59	638.22	760.89	935.83
Cash in circulation (M0)	98.78	121.84	145.45	213.40	234.40	264.44	317.78
Demand deposits of institutions	235.31	301.38	349.41	385.19	403.82	496.45	618.05
Quasi-money	185.80	248.87	338.23	411.39	556.74	768.48	848.33
Time deposits of institutions	23.54	25.11	30.90	31.24	42.05	65.06	88.46
Households savings	162.26	223.76	307.33	380.15	514.69	703.42	910.70
Bond	0.82	2.68	5.86	7.56	6.91	9.20	13.21

NOTE:

1. ACFB = *Almanac of China's Finance and Banking* 1992, Beijing, p. 451.

2. Money survey includes both the banking system and rural credit cooperatives.

3. (Demand deposits of institutions) = (enterprise demand deposits + institutional deposits + rural deposits + other deposits).

4. (Time deposits of institutions) = (enterprise and institutional time deposits) + self-raised funds for construction)

SOURCE: *Almanac of China's Finance and Banking*, 1992, page 451.

Table 4.2
Money, National Income, and Household Savings
(All in billion yuan)

Year	M0	M1	M2	National income	Household savings
1952	2.75	9.27	10.13	58.9	0.86
1953	3.94	10.14	11.37	70.9	1.23
1954	4.12	11.65	13.24	74.8	1.59
1955	4.03	12.60	14.59	78.8	1.99
1956	5.73	14.83	17.50	88.2	2.67
1957	5.28	16.25	19.77	90.8	3.52
1958	6.78	25.80	31.32	111.8	5.52
1959	7.51	32.34	39.17	122.2	6.83
1960	9.59	34.28	40.91	122.0	6.63
1961	12.57	38.44	43.98	99.6	5.54
1962	10.65	39.51	43.62	92.4	4.11
1963	8.99	39.09	43.66	100.0	4.57
1964	8.00	37.92	43.47	116.6	5.55
1965	9.08	43.24	49.76	138.7	6.52
1966	10.85	49.40	56.63	158.6	7.23
1967	12.19	55.58	62.97	148.7	7.39
1968	13.41	58.86	66.69	141.5	7.83
1969	13.71	58.33	65.92	161.7	7.59
1970	12.36	57.16	65.11	192.6	7.95
1971	13.62	62.46	71.49	207.7	9.03
1972	15.12	64.97	75.49	213.6	10.52
1973	16.61	74.91	87.03	231.8	12.12
1974	17.66	80.03	93.68	234.8	13.65
1975	18.26	86.79	101.75	250.3	14.96
1976	20.40	92.55	108.46	242.7	15.91
1977	19.54	92.57	110.73	264.4	18.16
1978	21.20	94.85	115.91	301.0	21.06
1979	26.77	117.71	145.81	335.0	28.10
1980	34.62	144.34	184.29	368.8	39.95
1981	39.63	171.08	223.45	394.1	52.37
1982	43.91	191.44	258.98	425.8	67.54
1983	52.98	218.25	307.50	473.6	89.25
1984	79.21	293.16	414.63	565.2	121.47
1985	98.78	326.17	488.43	704.4	162.26

Table 4.2 continues on the next page

Table 4.2 continues from the previous page

Year	M0	M1	M2	National income	Household savings
1986	121.84	402.40	626.16	789.9	223.76
1987	145.45	459.12	766.45	936.1	307.33
1988	213.40	548.74	928.89	1177.0	380.15
1989	234.40	577.31	1092.0	1312.5	514.69
1990	264.44	687.46	1390.9	1438.4	703.42
1991	317.78	844.58	1755.6	1611.7	911.03
1992	432.18	1131.7	2299.9	1989.5	1154.5

NOTE:
M0 is defined as currency in circulation by the end of the year;
M1 is equal to M0 plus demand deposits of firms, institutions;
M2 equals M1 plus passbook saving and time deposits of households;
National income is measured in current price;
Household saving is the total urban and rural residential savings.

Notice that the data provided in Table 4.2 are from the state-owned banking system alone, it does not include the data of the rural credit co-ops. Therefore, the definitions used in Table 4.1, 4.2 and 4.3 are different. Consequently they are not directly comparable.

SOURCE: *Almanac of China's Finance and Banking*, 1992, Beijing, China; *Statistical Yearbook of China*, 1992, Beijing, China. *Statistical Abstract of China*, 1993, Beijing, China.

Table 4.3
IMF Money Survey of China
(All in billion yuan)

Year	Money(M1)	Money plus quasi-money(M2)	Reserve money (base)
1977	58.01	85.84	–
1978	58.04	88.97	–
1979	92.15	132.78	–
1980	114.88	167.11	–
1981	134.52	197.77	–
1982	148.84	226.57	–
1983	174.89	271.28	–
1984	244.94	359.85	–
1985	301.73	487.49	228.41
1986	385.90	634.86	281.86
1987	457.40	795.74	318.17
1988	548.74	960.21	398.36
1989	583.42	1139.31	491.12
1990	700.95	1468.19	638.73
1991	898.78	1859.89	793.14
1992	1171.43	2432.73	922.80

NOTE:

1. Money (M1) = (Currency in circulation + Deposits of other domestic transactor + Demand deposit in the banking system + Demand deposit in rural credit co-ops).

2. Quasi-money is defined as the sum of time deposit of institutions plus the total urban and rural households' saving.

3. M2 is defined as money plus quasi-money.

4. Reserve money = currency in circulation + Banks' reserve + Deposits of other domestic transactor.

SOURCE: *International Financial Statistics Yearbook*, 1993, International Monetary Fund (IMF), Washington, D.C.

5

The Money Supply Process

There are many articles in the recent literature that discuss different aspects of the financial sector in China. For example, Feltenstein and Farhadian (1987) construct a model of inflation by using a general equilibrium (or disequilibrium) framework. Chow (1987) estimates the demand for money in China. Perkins (1988) discusses the relationship between price reform and inflation. Feltenstein and Ha (1989) estimate the repressed inflation and liquidity overhang. Yi (1991b) discusses the monetization process. The task of this chapter is to investigate the money supply process.

During economic reform, the banking system in China has changed from an all-inclusive mono-banking system to a more or less market-oriented central bank system. The money supply mechanism in this semi-reformed environment is unique in the sense that it has attributes of both a centrally planned economy and a market economy. Study of the money supply mechanism is the primary focus of this chapter, which is organized as follows. Section 5.1 defines the monetary base and examines its components. Section 5.2 discusses the factors that influence the monetary base. The next section analyzes the multiplier effect of the money creation process. The fourth section addresses the factors that influence the multiplier and its predictability. The final section summarizes the relationship between the money supply and the monetary base, the multiplier.

5.1 The Monetary Base and Its Components

The monetary base (also called high-powered money) can be expressed as

$$B = C + R \tag{5.1}$$

where B is the monetary base, C equals currency in circulation, and R is equal to the total reserves in the banking system.

In the balance sheet of the central bank, the monetary base is part of its liabilities to the public and to commercial banks. From the point of view of the public and of commercial banks, the monetary base is an asset, and if held by depository institutions, can be used to satisfy the central bank's legal requirement for reserves. The monetary base puts the ultimate constraint on monetary growth through the multiple expansion mechanism. Now we analyze the monetary base in more detail by using a hypothetical balance sheet of the central bank in Table 5.1.

Let's first look at the liabilities side of Table 5.1. The monetary base consists of L_1 (currency in circulation), L_2 (required reserves), and L_3 (excess reserves). The issuance of currency is controlled by the central bank subject to approval of the State Council. It is one of the most important monetary policy targets. L_2 is the legally required reserve that specialized banks must remit to the central bank. Since 1985 the required reserve ratio has been about 10 percent. The central bank has the power to change this ratio as a tool for conducting monetary policies. For example, to tighten the money supply, the People's Bank mandated that all specialized banks must submit a 6 percent prepaid reserve for their payable in the near future in 1989 (Xia and Sun 1990). In addition to required reserves, deposits of financial institutions in the central bank are also part of the monetary base, since they can be regarded as excess reserves. The central bank pays interest (for instance, 4.32 percent annual rate in 1985) to deposits of specialized banks.

Table 5.1
A Hypothetical Balance Sheet of the Central Bank

Assets	Liabilities and Equity
A_1 Loans to specialized banks	L_1 Currency in circulation
A_2 Loans to other financial institutions	L_2 Required reserves
A_3 Gold and silver	L_3 Deposits of financial institutions
A_4 Foreign exchange	L_4 Postal deposits
A_5 Government's borrowings	L_5 Deposits of organizations
A_6 Funds to be remitted	L_6 Deferred availability cash items
A_7 Cash items in process of collection	L_7 Self owned capital
A_8 Other assets	L_8 Other liabilities

L_4, postal deposits, and L_5, deposits of government agencies and organizations, are sources of funds that belong to the central bank. The remaining sources of funds of the central bank (L_6, L_7, and L_8) are self-explanatory.

The asset side of the balance sheet of the central bank is straight forward. The largest item is A_1, loans to specialized banks (accounting for 78 percent of the total assets in 1986 (Bei 1989)). From the hypothetical balance sheet in Table 5.1 we have

$$\sum_{i=1}^{8} A_i = \sum_{i=1}^{8} L_i \tag{5.2}$$

Then the monetary base can be expressed as

$$B = L_1 + L_2 + L_3 = \sum_{i=1}^{8} A_i - \sum_{i=4}^{8} L_i \tag{5.3}$$

5.2 Factors that Affect the Monetary Base (B)

The monetary base is the amount of assets available to be used as reserves for depository institutions. It also represents the liabilities of the central bank. Since the composition of the monetary base is part of the liabilities of the central bank, we can investigate change of the monetary base by examining the central bank's assets and liabilities. It is clear from equation (5.3) that the monetary base is equal to the sum of the central bank's assets minus its liabilities that are not in B. As a matter of fact, every item in the balance sheet of the central bank may affect the monetary base.

Let us look at the asset side first. When the central bank acquires an asset, the monetary base is increased, because the payment will either increase the amount of currency in circulation or increase the reserves of depository institutions. The term "asset" is here used in its broad (or accounting) sense. It includes government securities, loans to depository institutions, commercial paper, foreign currency or gold, etc. All of the above transactions result in a payment from the central bank to the public, which increases the monetary base.

On the liability side, any rise in L_1, L_2, or L_3 will directly increase B. Any increase of those liabilities that are not in the monetary base will cause a decrease in B, assuming that total liability is fixed. For example, in Table 5.1, L_4, postal deposits, and L_5, deposits of government's agencies and institutions, are liabilities that are not in the monetary base. Postal deposits are deposits absorbed by the post office network all over the county. In 1985, the central bank authorized the postal network to start a deposit business. However, postal offices can only attract deposits from the public; they are not allowed to make loans and all deposit proceeds must be remitted to the central bank. The central bank pays the postmaster a fee for the service.

As a result, the postal deposit is a leakage in the money creation process. The public has the choice of putting their money into specialized banks or into the post offices. If a consumer chooses to put 100 yuan into a post office, then this 100 yuan leaks out from the money creation process. An extreme scenario would be if all consumers decided to put their money into post offices; then the specialized banks receive no money and consequently, there would be no multiple money creation process at all. It is easy to see that an increase in postal deposits leads to a decrease in B.

A similar argument applies to the deposits of government agencies and institutions. A government deposit in the central bank is a liability to the central bank that is not in the monetary base. The smaller are government deposits, the greater is the monetary base for a given amount of assets. According to the regulations of the State Council, all deposits of government agencies (above the county level) belong to the central bank. However, the general practice has been that a significant proportion of those deposits went to specialized banks or other depository institutions for the purposes of escaping regulations and for other profit motives. There are many ways for depository institutions to treat these as some kind of regular accounts, subsequently using these funds to make loans. This practice definitely influences the money supply. The higher the proportion of deposits illegally used by depository institutions, the larger the monetary base.

The other two factors that affect the monetary base are government deficit-financing and the float. Generally speaking, government expenditure won't change the monetary base as long as it is financed either by tax collection or by issuing new debt. When the public pays taxes or buys government bonds, the monetary base decreases temporarily. However, as the government spends the proceeds, the funds are put into circulation. This will restore the monetary base to its original level. If we assume that the money comes and goes in the same period, the net effect on the monetary base is zero for the period. However, the above description is an exception rather than a rule for China in the 1980s. The Chinese government financed its deficits by printing money every year in the period 1980-1993 except 1985.[1] The average amount financed by printing money in the 1980s was 5.74 billion yuan per year. As a result, the monetary base increased and the money supply expanded by a multiple factor.

The central bank float is the amount of credit given to depository institutions by the central bank as a result of the check-clearing process. The float is equal to the cash items in the process of collection minus the deferred availability cash items. The float has been effectively an interest-free, short-term loan to depository institutions. Hence, the greater the float, the greater the monetary base. During the 1980s, the check-clearing mechanism was reformed three: times (1981, 1985, 1987) in China. The main objectives of these reforms were (1) to separate funds of the central bank from funds of specialized banks; (2) to enable the specialized banks to be independent economic entities that are responsible for their profits and losses; (3) to speed up the process of clearing funds and to improve economic efficiency. The next step of reform would be to establish a clearing center in the central bank by using computer networks and satellite communication. The new technology can shorten the process of check-clearing, but will not be able to eliminate the float. The float will continue to be a factor that influences the monetary base.

In summary, every item on the central bank's balance sheet will have an effect on the amount of currency outstanding or on the reserves of the specialized banks and will alter the monetary base subsequently. If $\sum_{i=1}^{8} A_i$ is fixed, an increase in $\sum_{i=4}^{8} L_i$ will lead to a decrease in the monetary base. On the other hand, If $\sum_{i=4}^{8} L_i$ is fixed, any increase in the asset side will expand the monetary base. The composition of the monetary base is equally as important as its size. One yuan of currency in circulation is equal to one yuan of money supply. It is the deposits in the banking system that create money through a multiple expansion mechanism. We discuss the multiplier in the next section.

Having analyzed the components of the monetary base, let us look at the real balance sheet of the central bank, which is given in Table 5.2 at the end of the chapter. We will leave readers the task to apply the theoretical framework provided above to the real data in Table 5.2.

5.3 The Multiplier

The establishment of the central bank and the reserve system provide the foundation for the multiple money creation process. In this section, we focus on the multiplier of the broad money, M2, which is defined as

$$M2 = C + D + T \tag{5.4}$$

where C equals the currency in circulation, D is the total amount of transaction deposits, and T is equal to the total amount of time deposits.[2] The multiplier for M2 can be written as

$$K = M2/B \tag{5.5}$$

where B is the monetary base, which can be expressed as

$$B = C + R = C + (r_1 D + r_2 D + r_3 T) \tag{5.6}$$

where $R =$ total reserves held by the depository institutions; $r_1 =$ the required reserve ratio for transaction accounts; $r_2 =$ the excess reserve ratio expressed as a proportion of transaction accounts; and $r_3 =$ the required reserve ratio for time deposit.

Now we substitute equations (5.4) and (5.6) into equation (5.5) and get

$$K = M2/B = \frac{C + D + T}{C + r_1 D + r_2 D + r_3 T} \tag{5.7}$$

Dividing both the numerator and the denominator of equation (5.7) by D, we have

$$K = \frac{1 + c + t}{c + r_1 + r_2 + r_3 t} \tag{5.8}$$

where $c = C/D$, $t = T/D$ are the ratio of currency to transaction deposits and the ratio of time deposits to transaction deposits respectively. It is obvious that K is jointly determined by the central bank (r_1, r_3), depository institutions (r_2), and the public (c, t).

5.4 Predictability of the Multiplier

If the multiplier is constant, then the central bank can control the money supply exactly by manipulating the monetary base. However, the multiplier is usually not a constant; the following factors alter the multiplier.

The central bank controls r_1, r_3, the legal reserve requirement for transaction and time deposits. The negative relation between r_1, r_3 and the multiplier is obvious. Generally speaking, the central bank can ease or tighten the money supply by changing the required reserve ratio.

The public's behavior determines c, the ratio of currency to transaction deposits, and t, the ratio of time deposits to transaction deposits. These two ratios depend on the interest rate differential between transaction deposits and time deposits, and inflationary expectations. For instance, during the first half of 1988, the inflation rate was high, the real interest rate was negative, and people's inflationary expectations were high. Consequently, consumers responded by withdrawing their bank deposits, by panic buying, and by hoarding behavior. The bank deposits decreased 2.6 billion yuan in August, 1988. The government quickly raised the nominal interest rate and introduced the so-called "guarantee value program for time deposits," which linked the return of deposits to the inflation rate. As a result, household deposits, especially time deposits, soared in 1989. By the end of 1989, total deposits reached 514.69 billion yuan (*Statistical Yearbook of China*, 1990). Consequently, the two ratios c and t changed significantly.

The excess reserves ratio is determined by the specialized banks, the objective of which is profit maximization subject to a series of regulations and to considerations of liquidity and safety. The following elements influence the opportunity costs of holding the excess reserve: the return on the excess reserve, which is determined by the central bank; the discount rate and the degree of difficulty to get a discount loan application approved; and the interest rates on loans that specialized banks lend out to their customers.

Nuojin Xu (1989) estimates the multiplier for the money creation process by using monthly data for the period of June, 1985 through December, 1988. His main findings are: (1) For the period studied, the monthly average of the multiplier is 2.31 with a maximum value of 2.66 and a minimum value of 1.97. The standard deviation is 0.45. (2) There is an upward trend for the estimated multipliers during the period 1985-1988. (3) The multiplier moves upward for the first six months of a calendar year, and moves downward for the second half of a year. The turning point is usually in July or August.

The change of the multiplier within a year is mainly determined by the pattern of the currency injected into circulation. The first half of the year is usually the period when currency flows back to the banking system. If we assume that the monetary base is fixed, then the decrease of currency in circulation implies an increase in reserves. The second half of the year is the period during which currency is injected into the economy (e.g., through the procurement of agricultural products, etc.). Other things being equal, the increase of the share of the currency in the monetary base would lower the multiplier. This can easily be seen by taking the partial derivative of the multiplier with respect to c, the ratio of currency to the transaction deposits.

$$\frac{\partial K}{\partial c} = \frac{-(1+t)+(r_1+r_2+r_3t)}{(c+r_1+r_2+r_3t)^2} \tag{5.9}$$

The derivative is negative as long as

$$-(t+1)+(r_1+r_2+r_3t)<0 \tag{5.10}$$

The above condition is easily met for the following reasons. The average value of t, the ratio of time deposits over the transaction deposits, was between 1.0 and 2.0 during the 1980s. The legal required reserve ratio for the transaction deposits has varied. It equaled 7 percent in 1985, 11 percent in 1986, 8 percent in 1987, and 10 percent in 1988 (N. Xu 1989). The excess reserve ratio had a downward tendency from 11 percent to 5 percent for the period 1985-1988 (J. Xu 1989). The required reserve ratio for time deposits has been much lower than that for transaction deposits.

To sum up, the multiplier is a variable rather than a constant. It is jointly determined by the interaction of the central bank, specialized banks and the public. Although it is predictable to a certain degree, there is a lot of uncertainty and endogeneity involved in determining the multiplier, which is outside of the control of the central bank. Furthermore, a small error in estimating the multiplier could lead to a large error in money supply prediction. Therefore, the central bank is better off focusing on the monetary base only, if the objective is to control macro credit conditions.

5.5 The Money Supply, the Monetary Base, and the Multiplier

The growth rate of the money supply is equal to the sum of the growth rate of the monetary base and the growth rate of the multiplier. Taking the natural log of equation (5.5), then differentiating with respect to time, we get

$$\dot{M}2=\dot{B}+\dot{K} \tag{5.11}$$

where the dot notations denote the growth rate of the corresponding variable. The growth rate of the monetary base and the multiplier can move up and down together, or one goes up and the other goes down. If the multiplier is constant, then any increase in B will cause the money supply to go up by $K\Delta B$. If the monetary base is fixed, a change in the multiplier will cause the money supply to change by the amount ΔKB, where Δ denotes the change of the variable.

As far as the relationships among the money supply, the monetary base, and the multiplier are concerned, the following points can be observed from Table 5.2. First, the product of the monetary base and the multiplier is a reasonable predictor of M2; the difference can be explained as a result of a credit ceiling and other mandatory regulations and random events. Second, the growth rate of M2 can be decomposed into two parts: the growth rate of the monetary base and of the multiplier. The changes of the monetary base and the multiplier could be in different directions. For example, in 1989, the growth rate of the monetary base was much larger than that of the period 1986-1988. However, the growth rate of M2 in 1989 was smaller than the average of the 1986-1988 period due to the slow (or negative) growth in the multiplier. Third, the main engine of the growth of the money supply was the increase of the monetary base. In the period 1986-1989, about 75 percent of the growth of M2 came from the increase of the monetary base, the remaining 25 percent came from the growth rate of the multiplier.

It is worth mentioning that, generally speaking, any change in the components of the monetary base will cause a change in the multiplier unless the changes are canceled out by each other. The opposite is also true. If the amount of B is unchanged, any change in the multiplier will cause the structure of B to change unless the changes are canceled out by each other.

Xia and Sun (1990) provide an example which substantiates this point. In March, 1986, the monetary base decreased 1.76 percent (currency in circulation dropped 6.15 billion) from the previous month. However, the proportions of the three components of the monetary base, cash, required reserve, and excess reserve changed from 53.44, 22.19, and 24.37 in February to 50.91, 24.06, and 25.02 in March, respectively. Consequently, the money supply rose by 1.37 billion and total loans expanded by 7.7 billion. On the other hand, when the central bank increased the monetary base, the money supply did not necessarily increase. In October, 1988, the monetary base was 8.11 billion higher than the previous month, and the central bank's loans to specialized banks went up by 8.3 billion. At that time, the public was running on banks and panic buying. Most of the increase in the monetary base was converted to cash. The proportions of cash, required reserve, and excess reserve in the monetary base changed from 57.69, 25.76, and 16.56 at the beginning of the year to 64.5, 26.04, and 9.48 in October, respectively. As a result, there was a contractionary effect. The money supply shrank by 2.37 billion in October and the amount of total loans decreased by 10.16 billion. Table 5.3 provides the quarterly data for money supply, monetary base and the estimated multiplier for the period 1985 to 1989.

Notes

1. In the official data, domestic and foreign borrowings are part of government revenue. The government deficit item listed in the *Statistical Yearbook of China* is basically the deficit financed by printing money (or overdrawing from the central bank). The total deficit should be equal to the listed government deficit plus total borrowings.

2. Actually, the exact term for T should be "the total amount of non-transaction deposits" that are included in M2. Because time deposits consist of the bulk of it, we use the notation T, and call it "time deposit" in our discussion for simplicity.

Table 5.2
The Consolidated Balance Sheet of
The People's Bank of China, 1987-1991
(in Billion yuan)

	1987	1988	1989	1990	1991
Assets					
Loans to banks	275.65	336.44	420.95	509.07	591.88
Loans to nonbank financial institutions	1.74	2.36	3.65	5.70	7.37
Other loans	22.68	30.56	34.53	40.67	44.91
Gold	1.20	1.20	1.20	1.201.20	
Foreign exchange	13.21	15.84	26.46	59.95	122.81
Assets in int'l financial institutions	17.88	18.71	19.16	25.90	26.20
Government's borrowing	51.50	57.65	68.46	80.11	106.78
Total assets	383.86	462.76	574.41	722.60	901.08
Liabilities and capital					
Government budgetary deposits	30.70	27.09	43.80	38.04	48.58
Public Institutions' deposits	44.92	39.27	48.40	61.48	75.28
Other deposits	4.47	7.61	10.95	18.99	32.55
Required reserves	67.02	84.14	104.17	139.06	180.98
Excess reserves	52.75	50.88	81.21	141.46	203.15
Currency in circulation	153.20	223.76	247.20	278.82	333.63
Liabilities to int'l financial institutions	14.19	14.86	13.87	18.57	18.47
Self-owned capital	22.90	25.21	25.21	29.15	34.53
Other liabilities	-6.29	-10.06	-0.40	-2.97	-26.09
Total Liabilities and capital	383.86	462.76	574.41	722.60	901.08

SOURCE: *Almanac of China's Finance and Banking*, Beijing, China, 1992, p. 517.

Table 5.3
The Money Supply, the Monetary Base, and the Multiplier
(Quarterly Data in Billion yuan Except the Multiplier)

Quarter	M0	M2	Monetary Base	Multiplier
1985.4	98.78	489.3	228.4	2.05
1986.1	89.88	480.7	216.2	2.08
1986.2	88.85	511.0	231.1	2.10
1986.3	97.86	544.1	242.8	2.15
1986.4	121.84	628.9	281.9	2.12
1987.1	114.26	633.7	256.6	2.22
1987.2	113.54	659.8	262.3	2.36
1987.3	126.99	709.6	272.4	2.46
1987.4	145.45	772.0	318.2	2.43
1988.1	144.25	779.4	305.7	2.46
1988.2	154.31	837.6	322.1	2.62
1988.3	185.03	881.7	346.9	2.65
1988.4	213.40	928.9	398.4	2.47
1989.1	209.91	928.6	395.1	2.34
1989.2	208.11	961.3	399.9	2.41
1989.3	208.24	1000.9	417.6	2.42
1989.4	234.40	1092.0	491.1	2.24

NOTE:
M0 = currency in circulation;
M2 = M0 plus transaction demand deposits and time deposits defined in Table 4.2.

SOURCE: M0 and M2 are from various issues of *China's Finance*, and *Almanac of China's Finance and Banking*; the monetary base is from various issues of *International Financial Statistics* published by IMF; the multipliers are from Nuojin Xu (1989) execept the multipliers of 1989, which are estimated by the author.

6

Monetary Policies

Based on the discussions of the previous chapters, we now analyze the apparatus of credit control and evaluate the monetary policies since the establishment of the central bank.

6.1 The Apparatus of Macro Credit Control

The apparatus of macro credit control consists of the following three parts: formulation of an overall plan, allocation of funds, and the instruments for adjustment and control.

The overall comprehensive credit plan is formulated by the central bank under the direction of the State Council and the Planning Bureau. The process of making a credit plan can be summarized as: "From the top to the bottom, and then from the bottom to the top" (The People's Bank of China, 1984) The process of formulation of the credit plan starts with the central bank. A money supply target is calculated by the central bank according to the needs of economic growth, price level increase, and other factors like velocities of money and the monetization process. The plan includes the quota for new loans and the targets for deposits for specialized banks. Then the central bank informs specialized banks of its tentative plan and asks them for inputs. The headquarters of specialized banks allocate the quotas and required deposit targets to their provincial and regional branches. Then regional specialized banks make their own plans.

The remainder of the process goes from the bottom to the top. The provincial branches of the central bank summarize the deposit and credit plans of all local specialized banks' branches and formulate a provincial plan for deposits, loans, and cash issuance. All provincial branches of the central bank submit their plans to their headquarters. Then the central bank revises its original plan and makes final the overall credit plan. Once the plan is approved, it becomes the yardstick according to which monetary policy is conducted. This process can be interpreted as a Bayesian estimation process. The central bank has a prior estimation, then it asks the specialized banks to collect information from their branches. The central bank then revises its tentative plan by combining its prior estimation with the collected information and formulates its posterior estimation, which is the final credit plan.

Funds allocation refers to the distribution of funds quota. It includes the allocation of funds between the central bank and the specialized banks, and the allocation between the central bank and its branches.

Instruments for adjustment and control are: (1) The central bank's loans to specialized and commercial banks which include regular loans and temporary loans. From the balance sheet of the central bank (Table 5.2), we can see that the claims on banks have been always the largest item on the asset side (from 2/3 to 3/4 of the total assets). (2) The reserve ratio, which is about 13%. (3) Interest rates and the discount rate. The central bank decides the rate of its loans to banks (discount rate) and regulates almost all lending and deposit rates. Generally speaking, banks are allowed to float their deposit and loan rates in a range of 10-35% of the rate set by PBC. Chapter 7 will discuss interest rates in detail. (4) Required special deposits of banks. This can be regarded as an extra-reserve requirement (about 5-7% in addition to the 13% reserve ratio), which provides a way for the central bank to freeze part of the deposits of the specialized banks. (5) A deposit-lending ratio requirement plus an overall quota on the total amount of loans that the specialized banks can make. The first three instruments are commonly used by central banks all over the world. They are economic levers of monetary control. The last two instruments are used by the monetary authorities of centrally-planned economies. They have the attributes of administrative orders rather than economic levers. As the monetary authority of China, the People's Bank often uses special deposits, the reserve ratio, and loans to specialized banks as a means to control the money supply. Interest rates (including the discount rate) have not been frequently used until recently. The quota on loans is always a last resort for control, by which it orders the specialized bank to restrain their loans within the quota limit regardless. The formulation of the plan, allocation of funds, and the five instruments for adjustment and control constitute the monetary control apparatus with Chinese characteristics.

6.2 Is Currency in Circulation A Good Target?

Generally speaking, the central bank can control the monetary base to a large degree. The composition of the monetary base and the demand for currency are determined by the interaction of the central bank, the commercial banks, and the public. For a long time PBC used currency in circulation as the principal target of controlling the money supply. Although in recent years, there have been some emphases on controlling the monetary base, it seems that the central bank still has focused on the cash target too much. Using currency as the main target for monetary policy has been detrimental to financial stability and economic development.

First, currency control has damaged the reputation of the banking system. In order to maintain the currency layout within the mandatory quota, many specialized banks deliberately postponed cash payments, by means such as decreasing their working hour, computer system maintenance, meetings, etc. Consequently, the average time of a payment through the bank system increased.

Second, currency control has stimulated more demand for cash. Firms and individuals know that the efficiency of banks is low and they have a strong preference for cash transaction among themselves rather than through banks. This certainly reduces the speed at which currency flows back to the banking system. Rational firms and individuals demand more currency for transaction purposes.

Third, currency control has increased the transaction cost of money flow. Among the three main forms of money flow – cash, check and electronic transfer – the transaction cost for cash is usually the highest to an economy. Note that a rational firm will pick up the method of payment to minimize its transaction cost. Apparently, if many firms prefer cash transactions, it indicates that the transaction cost of cash payment is smaller than payment through banks. Regulations distorted the order of the transaction cost and forced many firms to use cash transactions instead of bank transfers. This is obviously a waste for the society.

Fourth, there are other negative implications for currency control. It increased the influence of administrative control in financial activities. For example, many farmers sold their agricultural products to the government and could not get their money in cash; instead they got IOU's from the government. The banking system essentially told the farmers: "We are running out of cash, here is an IOU, we will pay you when cash is available." Farmers were openly angered by this kind of treatment. This definitely had a negative effect on incentive to sell their products to the government in the future (Tian 1990). The above discussion suggests that using currency in circulation as the principal control target was not effective and had many detrimental effects.

6.3 Monetary Policies for the Period 1984-1988

The objective of the establishment of the central bank was to separate the administrative functions of the banking system from its economic functions and strengthen macro control through monetary policy. During the economic reform in the 1980s, the banking system was restructured; the economy was changed profoundly by the responsibility system reforms in the agricultural sector and a rapid growth of the township and village enterprises and of the private sector. The monetary authority was inexperienced in this new economic environment.

Monetary policy for the second half of the 1980s was characterized by great swings between pumping too much money into the economy and overtightening the money supply. In 1984 (the first year that the People's Bank became the central bank), the central bank pumped too much liquidity into the economy. The net issuance of currency in 1984 was 26.2 billion yuan, which was greater than the total currency issuance for the period 1949-1979. As a result, the economy was overheated. The central bank had to tighten the money supply in 1985. At the beginning of 1986, the industrial output declined to the bottom of the trough. Under the political pressures from both the central and local governments, the central bank started to ease again. Inflationary pressure forced the central bank to tighten the money supply in 1987, which was quite effective. By the end of 1987, the money supply increased 19%, which was below the average growth rate of money during the 1980s (*Economic Daily*, Nov. 3, 1989).

At the beginning of 1988, the central bank decided to tighten the money supply and planned to issue 20 billion yuan cash for the year. However the central bank gave up its tightening policy soon because the government decided to prevent the decline of industrial output. By the end of June, the loans that the central bank provided to specialized banks went up only 3.2%, and the total amount of loans outstanding dropped 3.5% compared to the same period of 1987. However, by the end of July the net issuance of currency was already near 20 billion yuan, compared to a 4.35 billion net receiving of cash by the banking system for the same period in 1987. The components of the monetary base changed; the proportion of currency in circulation increased, and the proportion of excess reserve declined to 8.81%, the minimum level since the central bank was established. (The proportion of excess reserves in the monetary base was 25.7% and 19.6% for 1986 and 1987, respectively). The proportion of the required reserve in the monetary base climbed to 27.3%, the highest level since 1985. By the end of the year, the net issuance of currency was 68 billion, 3.4

times of what was originally planned! The official inflation rate for 1988 was 18.5%, the highest in the history of the People's Republic (Xia and Sun 1990).

The central bank did not utilize the reserve requirement to control the money supply successfully. Since 1984, there has been a trend toward the proportion of excess reserves in the monetary base decreasing. For that reason, the growth rate of loan creation by the specialized banks has been greater than the increase of loans that the central bank provided to the banking system. For example, in June 1988, loans provided by the central bank to the banking system increased 12.8% compared to March, 1987, but total loans of the banking system went up 28.6% for the same period (Xu, J. 1989).

Another aspect worth mentioning is that the loans that the central bank provides to specialized banks are based on credit; that is to say that usually there is no collateral or mortgage at all. The basis for credit is that every bank is owned by the government, and it is impossible for one of them to go bankrupt. Furthermore, most loans that specialized banks make are loans to state-owned enterprises. There is usually no collateral or mortgage either. If a significant number of enterprises default on obligations to a specialized bank, then the specialized bank has to default on obligations to the central bank.

As a result, a lot of loans were bad and have been written off from both the lender's and the borrower's books. It is estimated that about 15% of loans were delinquent on average in the second half of the 1980s (Zhu 1989). At the end of 1989, the total amount of loans of the state banking system was 1240.9 billion yuan. The above estimation suggests that about 180 billion yuan loans were delinquent. In this sense, we say that the budget constraints of both the state-owned enterprises and specialized banks are soft.

6.4 Monetary Policies for the Period 1988-1991

Monetary control since the fourth quarter of 1988 has been very effective. The monetary authority has achieved the following three targets.

First, during the fourth quarter of 1988, the banking system successfully eased inflationary expectations and promptly stopped the running on banks by introducing the so-called "value guarantee deposit programs," which was an indexing scheme that linked the return of deposits to the inflation rate. Table 6.1 provides the return information for a value guarantee program on a three-year time deposit. The second column of the table is the interest rate of the deposit; the third column is the inflation compensation in addition to the interest rate, which has been announced quarterly; the last column is the total nominal return of the deposit, which is the sum of the previous two columns. Consumers responded quickly to these kinds of programs. The time deposit increased rapidly in 1989 and 1990. By the end of 1989, the total deposit reached 514.69 billion yuan, which was 134.54 billion yuan higher than the year before. If we look at the composition of the increase of the deposits, the entire increment went to time deposits. That is, by the end of 1989, the passbook saving deposits balance was the same (96.48 billion yuan) as the end of 1988; the time deposits increased 134.54 billion yuan (47.4 percent) compared to the end of 1988 (*Statistical Yearbook of China*, 1990). This trend continued in the early 1990s. At the end of 1991, the total residential deposits was 911 billion yuan, which was 46% of the GNP of that year (1985.5 billion).

Table 6.1
Returns of Three-Year Time Deposits
(All in percentage)

Quarter	Interest rate (annual)	Inflation compensation	Total return (nominal)
1988.4	9.71	7.28	17.00
1989.1	13.14	12.71	25.85
1989.2	13.14	12.59	25.73
1989.3	13,14	13.64	26.78
1989.4	13.14	8.36	21.50

SOURCE: *Almanac of China's Finance and Banking*, 1990, Beijing, China, p. 187.

Second, in addition to the value guarantee program, the monetary authority successfully reduced inflationary pressure by imposing a ceiling of the total loans and a credit quota system. The cost of such measures was an economic recession. The growth rate of the industrial output declined drastically and reached zero growth in September, 1989. The growth rate of the industrial output in 1990 was 6 percent, the slowest one-year growth since reform started in 1979. Total retail sales decreased 2.4 percent and the official inflation rate was only 2.1 percent in 1990. As a result, thousands and thousands of township and village enterprises went bankrupt and numerous rural workers who worked in the urban areas lost their jobs. Notice that the tightening program in 1988-90 had an asymmetric result. It hurt the non-state sector more than the state enterprises. The inefficient non-state firms went bankrupt whereas inefficient state enterprises made heavier losses. Consequently, the economic structure was adjusted and optimized in the non-state sector during the tightening period, but not for the state sector.

Third, the central bank started to ease constraints on the money supply during the first half of 1990 by providing massive amounts of loans to the state-owned enterprises. Credit control over the non-state sectors has been also eased. It seems to have jump-started the economy quite effectively. The growth rate of industrial output was 13.7 percent for the first eight months in 1991 on average.

However, while most outside observers recognized the successes of monetary policy in the late 1980s, not enough attention was being paid to the potentially insolvent position of the banks in China. Since the adjustment period started in 1989, the Chinese economy has been perplexed by the low efficiency of the state-owned large and medium size enterprises. By the end of 1991, the loss-making state enterprises have accumulated a chain of inter-enterprise debt amounting to about 200 billion yuan. To maintain political stability and help state-owned firms (the backbone of the socialist economy), the government has injected 35 billion yuan into the state sector (Xiao 1991). In other words, the government ordered the banking system to provide new loans as "seed money" to those enterprises in financial trouble. As a result, loan rollovers have disguised the delinquency problem temporarily. Most loans have been converted to stocks of unsold products. Consequently, government policy is most likely to exacerbate the existing inter-enterprise debt problem because it would increase the size and the probability of future delinquencies. Furthermore, during the period of 1989-1990, there were negative spreads between lending and deposit rates because the interest rates paid to depositors were increased drastically to curb inflation, while the lending rates were fairly rigid, because a large proportion of state enterprises would have gone bankrupt had the lending rates been increased to cover costs. The bad loans plus the increase of cost of funds have contributed to a fast de-capitalization of the banking system in China. For the period 1985-1991, the capital to asset ratio of the specialized banks decreased from 9.6% to 6.0%. This problem was alleviated somewhat after the second half of 1991 by a combined efforts of lowering deposit rates and increasing lending rates. But the underlying problem is still there, unsolved. The potential danger of insolvent banks is still very real and worth further investigation.

6.5 The Austerity Program of 1993

After three years of low inflation in 1990-1992, the economy started to heat up after Mr. Deng Xiaoping's trip to southern China in 1992. In the first half of 1993, the inflation pressure was high and the financial sector was in disorder. Thousands of new nonbank financial institutions were formed. A huge amount of funds was in the real estate market along the coastal areas. Banks, financial institutions and local governments have circumvented the rules and regulations of the central bank on raising funds and financing their projects. The central government found more and more institutions were outside of the control of the cash and credit plans. The government and central bank were on the verge of lost control.

After a long time of hesitation and debate, the central government finally reached the consensus to implement an austerity program in the summer of 1993. Vice Premier Zhu Rongji was in charge of the program. The then Governor of PBC, Mr. Li Guixian, was replaced and Mr. Zhu himself became the Governor of PBC. Mr. Zhu implemented the austerity program, which including: Strengthening the financial disciplines; separating the state-owned banks from their affiliated trust and investment firms; all specialized banks must call back all outside-credit-plan loans immediately; restricting the inter-regional lending; sending out working groups to provinces to check the implementation; etc.

The main consequences of the austerity program are as follows. First, the credit condition was really tight in general. Although the central bank repeated that the austerity program was not a comprehensive tightening, it aimed only at problems of the financial sector, especially at real estate market and nonbank financial institutions. But the central bank did not have the instruments, which had the flexibility to achieve its objectives without hurting the overall credit condition. Many local governments, especially those provinces along the coast complained that the austerity program hurt their economy more than necessary.

Second, the velocity of money decreased significantly. The tightening program has cracked down the inter-regional loans by requiring that all inter-regional (across provincial boarder) loans must be approved and supervised by the central bank. Notice that the macro credit condition in China depend on both the money supply and the velocity of money. The austerity program has tightened the macro credit condition much more than it appeared in the change of the growth rate of money supply, because the program have restricted the money flows among regions and consequently decreased the velocity of money drastically.

Third, as argued before, the austerity program has hurt the non-state sector more than the state-owned enterprises. Within the state sector, it probably hurt the efficient firms more than loss making firms. This observation was from the author's trip to Hainan and Zhejiang province during the summer of 1993. It has been found that when the banks asked enterprises to pay back the outside-plan loans as requested in the austerity program, most relatively efficient firms were able to pay back their loans, because firms wanted to keep a good relationship with banks for future credit. Generally speaking, efficient firms have a good cash flow position and were able to return the money to banks by postponing their new projects. The state-owned loss making firms had no money whatsoever, regardless of the austerity program.

Fourth, the difference between official and market interest rates increased. The author did an informal survey in several coastal provinces (Guangxi, Hainan, Shandong, Zhejiang) in the summer of 1993 (when the austerity program started). The official lending rates for main specialized banks were in a range of 10-16% whereas the market rates (black or gray) were in the range of 20-35%. Lastly, during the austerity program, the inter-enterprise debts problem emerged again.

Five months after the implementation of the austerity measures, Mr. Deng Xiaoping, the paramount leader, repeatedly emphasized that rapid development is the number one priority, and asked Chinese leaders to seize the rare opportunity for rapid economic growth and to solve the problems in the process of growth. The austerity program has achieved some of its objectives, but it was virtually aborted in the fourth quarter of 1993, when the central bank started to ease money supply. In early November, one of the Vice Presidents of the central bank announced that the financial situation in China had already been stabilized. The monetary policies in China have not been freed from the stop-go cycle.

6.6 Summary

The economic reform in the 1980's caused profound changes in the structure of the banking system in the following ways. (a) The establishment of the central bank laid the foundation of the money creation process through the monetary base and a multiplier effect. (b) Consequently, the money supply and credit conditions are controlled, at least partially, by economic instruments such as the monetary base, required reserve ratios, and interest rates. (c) The old money supply system is far from being phased out. As a matter of fact, it is the mixture of a central bank system and an administrative command driven centrally-planned system that constitutes the money supply mechanism with "Chinese characteristics."

The monetary policy of the central bank since 1984 has had some successes and some failures. Roughly speaking, it has not been very effective when the central bank tried to use economic levers to adjust the economy. When it lost the control, the central bank resumed the old credit control method mainly through administrative orders and it seems that they were quite effective. These phenomena demonstrate the central government's ability to control the macroeconomic conditions of the economy. At the same time, they indicate how fragile the market mechanism is after all these reforms. The money supply mechanism in China, by and large, is still controlled by the central government through administrative order rather than economic lever.

The central banking system in China is still in a very primitive stage, not because the central bank is not independent of the government, but because the central bank and specialized banks are not really separated. Even in a most advanced market economy, the central bank and the government are, generally speaking, connected to a certain degree. However, the difference is that commercial banks in a market economy are privately owned and have hard budget constraints. The savings and loan debacle in the United States provides an excellent example of what could happen if the government takes ultimate responsibility for the banking system even in a mature and developed market economy. The Chinese government's responsibility to its banking system is many times greater than that of its counterpart in the United States. Absence of real privately owned commercial banks is the fundamental reason why the instruments (economic levers) of a central bank did not work very well in China, whereas the administrative orders worked quite effectively.

7

Interest Rates

In the previous chapter, we discussed the instruments of monetary policy and the effectiveness of the control of the central bank. One of the most important tools in conducting monetary policy is the interest rate. The interest rate policy of the monetary authority in China has varied during the different periods since the founding of the People's Republic of China. Roughly speaking, the history since 1949 can be divided into three periods: 1950-1957; 1958-1978; 1979-1993. Of course, there are sub-periods in each period.

The Chinese monetary authority has had very different policies on interest rates in these three periods. The first period (1950-1957) is the transition period, in which the centrally-planned system was established by eliminating virtually all the privately-owned sectors of the economy. The government used interest rates as policy tools to foster the state-owned sectors and to squeeze the private sectors. During the second period (1958-1978), interest rates were basically frozen and did not play any active role at all in monetary policy. The third period (1979-present) is the reform period. The interest rate has been resurrected as a policy instrument to tune the economy. In this chapter, we briefly review the interest policy of the first two periods and then discuss the changes of interest rates during the reform period in detail.

7.1 Interest Rate Policies Before the Reform

China has never had an independent banking system. The fact that the banking system was controlled by the government can be traced back to the Nationalist government before 1949. In 1947, deposits in government-controlled banks accounted for 91.7 percent of total deposits (Liu 1980, page 32) and the government-controlled banks provided 93.3 percent of total loans.

When the communist government came to power in the mainland, it confiscated all the banking assets left by the Nationalist government and controlled the financial sector. However, the government did not immediately eliminate the privately-owned banks. In June, 1950, the loans provided by the communist government-owned banks accounted for 58.6 percent of the total loans; remaining loans were supplied by private banks. The privately-owned banks were squeezed out quickly during the two-year period 1950-1952. By the end of 1952, loans provided by government banks already accounted for 92.8 percent of total loans (Liu 1980, page 37).

Eliminating Privately-Owned Banks

The privately-owned banks were eliminated primarily by two methods. The first method was through outright confiscation. There were several political movements during the period 1950-1952: the land reform; the movement of suppressing counter-revolutionaries; and the so-called "against the three" (against corruption, waste and bureaucracy), and "against the five" movements (against bribery, tax loopholes, stealing government-owned materials and properties, cheating contracts by using cheap materials, and stealing classified economic information). Part of the privately-owned banking businesses were confiscated during the "against the three" and "against the five" movements, because the owners were accused of committing some economic crimes.

The other way to eliminate the privately-owned businesses was through the so-called " public and private joint venture" movement. A majority of the privately-owned banking businesses were squeezed out by the forced public and private "joint venture," which was a kind of forced buy-out program implemented by the government. The socialist transformation (government buy-out of the privately-owned enterprises) had two phases. The first phase was from 1950-1956, in which private entrepreneurs were forced to participate in the "public and private joint venture" program arranged by the government. The government dominated the joint ventures by appointing management, owning majority shares of the stocks, and regulating the production plans of these joint venture enterprises. The profits of the joint venture enterprises were divided into four parts: income tax, retained earnings, worker benefits, and bonus fund and dividend. Income taxes were surrendered to the government. Retained earnings were used for reinvestment and renovation. Dividends were distributed according to the split of public and private shares. The dividends of public shares again went to the government. The dividends of private shares went to the shareholders, who were previously owners of the enterprises. The privately-owned stocks were generally nonsalable and nontransferable. During this period, most private entrepreneurs still participated in, at least partially, the management of the joint venture enterprises.

The second phase of the socialist transformation started in 1956; the purpose of this phase was to further limit the role of capitalists in the joint venture enterprises. Starting in 1956, dividends for the private shareholder were replaced by a fixed dividend, which was paid by the government to the previous capitalists every month. The fixed dividend was about 5 percent (annual rate) of the estimated value of the assets previously owned by the capitalists (the value was vastly underestimated). The fixed dividend would be paid regardless of the operation (profit or loss) of the enterprises. The fixed dividend scheme was originally designed for seven years. Actually it was paid for ten years until September, 1966. After the fixed dividend program started, the government completely owned the joint-venture enterprises. Most previous capitalists were eliminated from important management positions except a few "model capitalists." In 1957, the government declared that the transition from a mixed economy to a socialist, centrally-planned system was complete.

Interest Rate Policies (1950-1978)

Interest policy for the period 1950-1957 was characterized by a transition from a backward market economy to a centrally-planned economy. The banking sector was one of the sectors that completed the socialist transformation first. By the end of 1956, the government controlled virtually all the banking businesses, and privately-owned banks practically disappeared in China. During the period of 1950-1957, the economy was transformed from a backward and underdeveloped market economy to a mixed economy and finally to a centrally-planned system. As far as interest policy was concerned, the monetary authority had gradually increased its control over interest rates. Interest rates had been, by and large, determined by the financial market, which reflected the scarcity of capital at the beginning of the period (in 1950). At the end of the period (1957), interest rates were firmly controlled by the monetary authority and were set at artificially low levels, which were no longer the price of capital. These changes can be clearly seen from Tables 7.1, 7.2 and 7.3.

Table 7.1 summarizes the changes of bank deposit interest rates for the period 1949 to 1980; Tables 7.2 and 7.3 contain information on interest rates of loans to industrial firms and to the commerce sector for the period 1949-1980, respectively. From these three tables, we can see the following points.

First, for the period 1950-1952, interest rates were close to market rates. During this period, the economy was a mixed one and resources were allocated to a large degree by a market mechanism. The government dominated the banking sector during these three years, but privately-owned banks still existed. Interest rates were controlled by the government and changed frequently to stabilize financial markets. Interest rates were high because inflation was high. The new government used high interest rates to tightened the money supply, and successfully stopped the hyperinflation. Starting April, 1950, the price level measured by the new currency (Renminbi, the people's money) was stabilized and the total of bank deposits in September, 1950 was 16 times of that in December 1949 (Zhou Enlai, *People's Daily*, October 1, 1950).

Second, the government used the interest rate as a weapon to squeeze the private sector out. The socialist transformation movement was basically a political campaign. Capitalists were eliminated primarily by political force rather than by economic competition. Here, we just focus on the discrimination against the private sector in terms of interest rates charged by the government-owned banking system. From Tables 7.2 and 7.3, we see that the interest rates of loans to the private sector were on average 30 percent higher than rates on those to the state-owned enterprises. Large scale private enterprises were practically wiped out by the end of 1958. The amount of bank loans to the private sector was negligible thereafter. Interest rates of bank loans since 1958 can be regarded as the rates that banks charged to the state-owned or collectively-owned enterprises.

Third, the period 1958-1978 was a dark age for interest rates, which were basically frozen for 20 years. Interest was a natural enemy of the communist ideology generated from the theory of surplus value of Karl Marx, according to which interest is part of the surplus value. Therefore interest was seen as exploitation by capitalists. Several times in the history of the People's Republic of China, Marxist economists argued that interest should be eliminated. Some of them even wanted to get rid of money in order to speed up the transition to a communist society (Liu 1980). Since interest was regarded as an evil, the interest rate was tightly controlled at a fixed level that was far below the equilibrium level for more than 20 years. We will discuss the consequences of the artificially low interest level in Section 7.3.

7.2 Interest Rate Policies for the Reform Period: Theory

During the economic reforms, the perception of interest has gradually changed. The government and the central bank have started to acknowledge that interest rate policy is one of the important components of monetary policy. The central bank now uses the interest rate as an instrument to tune macroeconomic conditions by influencing aggregate supply and demand. However, it is mistaken to think that the Chinese monetary authority is completely market-oriented. Its perception and philosophy on interest policy are still quite different from those of a market economy. While the Chinese monetary authority has started to recognize the importance of in terest rates, there are still many features of a centrally-planned economy in its policy-making criteria. This can clearly be seen from the recent publication of the central bank, *Handbook of Chinese Banking Practices* (hereafter HCBP), published in 1991, which summarizes the procedures and principles that the central bank follows to make interest rate policies. Let us look at these procedures and principles in detail.

Interests Rates Are Determined by The Central Bank

There are three concrete aspects when we say that the central bank determines the interest rates. (1) It determines its lending rates to specialized banks and other financial institutions (the discount rate) and the rates on the deposits of the specialized banks. (2) It regulates the interest charged by the specialized banks and other financial institutions. (3) It provides guidance on rates charged to each other among financial institutions (similar to the federal funds rate). Let's discuss these three aspects in order.

First, after the establishment of the central bank in 1984, the management of credit and loans has changed profoundly. The fund of the central bank is separated from that of the specialized banks. The fund allocation mechanism has been changed from a rationing allocation system to a credit and loan relationship between the central bank and specialized banks. The interest rate that the central bank charges specialized banks to borrow money (counterpart of the discount rate in the West) plays a key role in this new relationship. The central bank considers the following two factors to determine the discount rate. (1) Generally speaking, the base rate that the central bank charges the specialized banks should be higher than the rate paid by the central bank on the deposits of the specialized banks. It also should be higher than the cost to the specialized banks of attracting deposits from the public. (2) The rates on deposits of the specialized banks (reserves and excess reserves) paid by the central bank should be higher than the average rate paid by the specialized banks to their depositors in order to somewhat guarantee the profitability of the specialized banks.

Second, the central bank regulates the rates of specialized banks, both the lending rates and deposit rates. After the reform of the banking system, specialized banks became more or less independent financial enterprises that are responsible for their profits and losses. At the same time, most of the fixed capital and working capital of firms are provided by the banking system in the form of loans. Therefore, interest rates on loans have a significant impact on the costs of firms. The central bank considers both the profitability of firms and of the specialized banks in regulating the rates. About 60 percent of the profits of specialized banks are surrendered to the government. Therefore, interest regulation influences the revenue of the central government to a large degree.

Third, the central bank also provides guidelines for the rates charged to each other among financial institutions (similar to the federal funds rate). Furthermore, private lending and borrowing among consumers are subject to regulation by the central bank, the basic objective of which is to protect normal lending and borrowing and punishing usurious loans. Now the maximum interest rate charged by private lending should not exceed 3 times that of the same length loan by the government-owned banks.

The General Principles of Interest Rate Policies

1. *The principle of differential treatments.* Differential interest treatments are based on the following criteria. First is difference in length. There are mainly two kinds of loans in China, loans for working capital and loans for fixed capital. Roughly speaking, working capital loans are those which are short, whereas loans for fixed capital are long. Consequently, interest rates on short-term loans are lower than those of long-term loans. The same thing is true for deposits. Interest rates on time deposits are higher than the passbook saving deposits. This is the Chinese yield curve; the only difference from the familiar yield curve is that it is determined by the central bank.

Second is the difference among industries. Interest rates are used as tools of industrial policy in China to help the infrastructure industries, such as energy, transportation, and communication. Usually the internal return rates of these infrastructure industries are relatively low, but their marginal social benefits are high. It is absolutely necessary to support these bottleneck industries in order to achieve sustainable long-run economic growth. The interest rates on loans to 13 infrastructure industries have been 10-30 percent lower than regular loan interest rates in the late 1980s. Loans for procurement purchases of grain, edible oil, cotton, and to export goods are also at lower rates than the regular rates for working capital. This can be regarded as part of the Chinese industrial policy implemented by the central bank.

Third, Rates for the special economic zones (SEZs). In order to speed up the construction of the SEZs and economic development areas (EDAs), the People's Bank of China provided loans to SEZs and EDAs with lower interest rates in the 1980s; for loans under 5 years, the annual rate was only 2.88 percent, for 5 to 10 year loans, the annual rate was 4.32 percent (HCBP, page 46).

Fourth are differences among regions. The differential treatment is for egalitarian considerations. The banking system provides loans to some regions of the country at special low rates. Regions that qualify for these special loans are minority and poor areas, the remote border regions, and those regions that were the bases for the communist party before 1949. The interest rates charged to welfare programs are also low.

2. *The principle of the autonomous adjustability.* Autonomous adjustability refers to the power that the provincial and large municipal branches of the specialized banks of China are authorized to adjust interest rates (within certain limits) in their localities. The rural co-ops also have power to determine their interest rates subject to guidance by the Agriculture Bank.

To be specific, for loans of working capital and fixed capital, bank branches have the power to charge a rate that is 60 percent higher than the regular rate determined by the central bank. To be more than 60 percent higher, it must subject to the approval of the local branch of the central bank. On the deposit side, the interest paid to time deposits with large denominations may be 5 percent higher than the regular time deposit rates for the same period. The interest on financial bonds may also be 2-3 percentage points higher than the regular time deposit of the same duration.

3. *The principle of calculating interest period by period.* Interest on deposits and loans in China is calculated period by period. For loans, no matter how high the interest rate is when the contract is signed, all interest rates will be adjusted when the central bank declares new rates. The banking system has to implement the new rates immediately and interest will be calculated separately for different periods. On the deposit side, the depositors are protected in a way such that when the interest rate is adjusted downward, time deposits will continue to pay the original high rates until their maturity date; when the interest rates are adjusted upward, depositors will received higher rates.

4. *The principle of profitability of the banking system.* The central bank also considers the profitability of the banking system when it decides the rates. The difference between the interest received by banks for their loans and interest paid by banks on deposits is the bulk of the total revenue. The (after tax) profits of the banking system can be calculated by subtracting the total costs of the bank's operation and taxes. Most profits of the banking system are surrendered as government revenue. Therefore, maintaining the profitability of the banking system is equivalent to guaranteeing a certain amount of government revenue.

Considerations in Regulating Interest Rates

The central bank considers the following factors in regulating the interest rates.

1. *Economic growth.* Interest policy is one of the most important tools of macro control, with which the central bank tunes the economy. Generally speaking, the central bank has three objectives. First, to promote economic growth. Second, to maintain economic stability, and primarily the stability of the price level. Third, to adjust the economic structure by providing low interest loans to so-called "bottleneck" industries, such as energy, transportation, etc.

2. *The average profit.* This policy consideration originates from Karl Marx's theory of average profit, which states that the rates of profit are different among industries because the capital/labor ratios are different, but that competition tends to equalize the profitability of different industries through free entry and exit. (Karl Marx, *Capital*, translated by Ernest Untermann and edited by F. Engels. Volume No.3. Charles Kerr & Company).

The central bank should determine interest rates based on the "average profit rate," which encourages the more efficient firms and drives the high cost firms out of business. However, in practice, it is difficult for the banking system to charge an interest rate uniformly to all firms. More often the bank system subsidizes inefficient firms by providing emergency loans and writing off bad loans due to the "public ownership" structure.

3. *The price level.* Price stability is one of the primary concerns of the central bank. When the rate of inflation is high and the real interest rate is negative, then the public tends to withdraw their money from the banking systems. The central bank should intervene by increasing the interest rate and tightening the money supply. The economic policy of 1988 and 1989 was a typical example of using interest rate as a weapon to fight inflation.

4. *Supply of and demand for funds.* The interest rate is the price of capital and therefore it should be determined by the supply and demand of funds in the capital markets. During the economic reform in the 1980s, consumer savings became the largest source of the supply of funds, whereas firm investment and the government deficit constituted the bulk of the demand for funds. The process of releasing artificial control over interest rates leads to the formation of a capital market and (quasi) market rates gradually appeared. If the reform continues, the supply of and demand for funds should be the dominant factor in determining interest rates. The fact that the central bank has to consider the supply of and demand for funds when it determines the rates (commercial banks' lending rates) indicates that there is no market rate in China yet.

5. *The interest rates of world capital.* Renminbi is not a convertible currency. Consequently, the interest rates of the world capital market have little influence on the domestic rates. However, as the Chinese economy became an open one in the 1980s, total imports and exports came to account for about 30 percent of China's GNP. The interest rate in the world capital market becomes an important factor to consider when the central bank determines domestic rates.

6. *The interest rate should be calculated in terms of a 360-day year.* Although it is already the computer age in the developed counties, a significant proportion of the branches of banks in China still use the abacus to do most of their calculating. When the central bank determines the annual interest rate, one of the requirements is that the annual rate should be calculated in terms of a 360-day year. Currently, the interest rate is calculated in China based on the assumption that a year is equal to 12 months, and a month is equal to 30 days. For instance, if the annual rate is 9.36 percent, then the monthly rate is .78 percent, and the daily rate is .026 percent.

7.3 Interest Rate Policies for the Reform Periods: Practice

As the central bank, the People's Bank is responsible for managing interest rates. There are two major aspects to routine interest rate management: adjusting interest rate levels and supervising and policing the specialized banks and other financial institutions.

Interest Rate Adjustment

The People's Bank of China uses interest rates as a tool to tune macroeconomic conditions. After more than a decade of economic reforms, the Chinese economy (both consumers and firms) has responded to credit conditions by adjusting their demand and supply behaviors. Consequently, the public's marginal propensity to save, the costs of firms, the banking system's profits, and the government's revenue depend on interest rates in an intelligible way. In practice, the central bank uses the following formulae to calculate the impacts of interest rates. Some of the formulae listed below are extremely trivial, the reason for listing them is that the central bank uses them in practice (see HCBP, page 49).

1. *The effect on interest income of the public.* The effect on interest income of the general public is calculated by:

(The change of interest income) =
(the change of interest rate) × *(total deposit before the interest change + the average increment of the deposit after the interest change).*

For a hypothetical example, in 1988, the average interest rate on deposits increased 1.50 percentage points; at the beginning of 1988 total deposits were 600 billion; the average increment of deposit during 1988 was 50 billion. Then the increase of interest income in 1988 is:

The change of interest income = 1.5 *percent* × (600+50) = 9.75 *billion yuan.*

2. *The effect on the costs borne by firms.* The primary concern of the central bank is the interest payment as a percentage of total costs borne by firms. Generally speaking, a firm has two accounts, deposits and a borrowing account. Since bank loans are the primary sources of the working capital of firms, the change of interest rates has a significant effect on total costs for firms. Interest payment as a percentage of total cost is calculated by

$$\left(\frac{Net\ \ interest\ \ payment}{Total\ \ cost}\right) \times 100.$$

The central bank has some internal benchmark as the appropriate average percentage of interest payment relative to total cost. Before the central bank changes interest rates, it calculates what would be the ratio of interest payments to total cost for the industrial sector, the commercial sector, etc., then decides whether the change is justifiable based on whether firms can tolerate it.

3. *Effect on the banking system and government revenue.* Here we use a hypothetical example to illustrate how the central bank calculates the effect of an interest adjustment on the banking system and government revenue. Suppose that on average the interest rate on deposits increases by 1 percentage point and so does the interest rate on loans in 1991. Suppose that before the interest rate adjustment (at the beginning of 1991) total

deposits were 500 billion, and deposits increased by 50 billion yuan during 1991. The total amount of loans at the beginning of 1991 was 700 billion and there was a 100 billion loan increase during 1991. Then the effect of the one percentage point change on the banking system and government revenue can be calculated as follows:

(a) The increase in interest income for the banking system is $(700 + 100) \times 1\ percent = 8$ billion. (b) The increase in interest payments is $(500 + 50) \times 1\ percent = 5.5$ billion. (c) The interest income of the banking system is subject to local business tax, which is, generally speaking, 5 percent. The change (increment) of total business tax is $(8 \times 5\ percent) = 0.4$ billion. Then the net interest income of the banking system is $(8 - 0.4) = 7.6$ billion. (d) According to current regulations, about 62 percent of net bank earnings are surrendered to the central government; the banking system keeps the remaining 38 percent. Then the net earning is $(7.6 - 5.5) = 2.1$ billion, out of which the central government gets 1.302 billion and the banking system retains 0.798 billion (38 percent).

The above calculation is oversimplified in the sense that it uses the "average interest rate." In practice, interest is calculated period-by-period when there is a rate adjustment. According to the regulations of the central bank, when interest rates are adjusted upward, all interest on deposits is calculated separately before and after the change; when interest rates are adjusted downward, previous deposits receive higher rates. Interest rates on loans are calculated separately before and after the change regardless of the direction of the change.

Supervision and Management of Interest Rates Policies

Interest policies in China are determined by the central government through the central bank, which is also in charge of supervision and management of interest policy. According to HCBP (page 49), the People's Bank makes monetary policy and regulates interest rates through its headquarters in Beijing and its local branches. The headquarters of the People's Bank has the following powers and responsibilities. First, it promulgates interest policy and regulations and supervises its branches and other financial institutions in carrying out interest policy. Second, it works as a coordinator to decide interest rates and serves as an arbitrator when there is a dispute. Third, it explains government policy and all regulations regarding monetary policy. Fourth, it determines benchmark rates and floating limits for deposits, loans, financial securities, and private lending. Lastly, it punishes those who violate government regulations.

The branches of the People's Bank play an important role in interest rate policy. First, the branches are responsible for checking how financial institutions in their localities carry out government policy on a regular basis and report to their headquarters. Second, following the general edicts of the People's Bank, the branches make the interest rate management regulations for their localities. Third, they serve as arbitrators for interest disputes, coordinate among financial institutions, and punish those who violate the regulations.

To sum up, the People's Bank has the sole authority of making interest policy. Other financial institutions must obey the regulations and have the power to float their interest rates only within the limits specified by the central bank.

To those who violate the interest regulations the punishments are the following: (1) For those who paid an interest rate higher or lower (than the regulated and the approved floating range) on deposits and financial securities, the fine is the amount of money that equals the interest overpaid or underpaid. Those who paid less interest must pay the difference to their holders of security deposits. From those who paid higher interest rates, the attracted deposits must be immediately transferred to the People's Bank until their maturity. (2) For those who charge higher or lower interest rates on loans, the fine is equal to the overcharged or undercharged interest. (3) To repeat violators, the People's Bank can give a warning, or temporarily or permanently suspend their business licence.

7.4 Other Interest Rate Data Provided

Table 7.4 illustrates the interest rates of the central bank in 1989, from which we see that the central bank actually used the rate as a economic lever to influence the specialized banks and other financial institutions. As we discussed in Chapter 6, using the interest rate as a policy tool started in the second half of the 1980s. At the same time the centrally-planned aspects of the banking system are still far from phased out.

Table 7.5 shows the deposit interest rates of the specialized banks, which followed fairly well the guidelines of the central bank. Table 7.6 provides interest rates charged by the Industrial and Commercial Bank of China (ICBC) in 1989, which have a clear pattern of industrial policy. For instance, in the item of fixed capital loans, there are three categories. Category one receives the best treatment and has a 30 percent discount on the rates. Category two and three have an interest rate discount of 20 percent and 10 percent respectively. Table 7.7 provides interest rate information on time deposits for the period 1980-1988.

From the information provided in this chapter, we see that the Chinese monetary authority has tried to use the interest rate as a policy instrument to tune economic conditions. Generally speaking, interest rates have been adjusted more and more by economic leverage during the reform period. The central bank has gradually released its administrative control over interest rates (in the centrally planned manner). Despite these improvements, interest rates, the most important price in the economy, are still far from the market equilibrium level in China. As a matter of fact, compared to price reforms in the consumer and producer goods markets, the speed of establishing a capital market with an equilibrium interest rate is lagging behind. Until the end of 1993, the central bank still behaved more like a government agency rather than an independent central bank in a decentralized market economy. The policy criteria and control instruments regarding interest rates discussed in this chapter have the dual characteristics of a centrally-planned economy and a market economy. Further reforms in the financial sector are necessary to establish an efficient capital market.

Table 7.1
Interest Rate Changes of Bank Deposits for 1949-1980
(Annual Rate %)

Date of change (month/day/year)	Passbook saving	Time deposits (3, 6 month, and one year)		
		3 month	6 month	One year
8/10/1949	60.0	120.0	168.0	252.0
4/10/1950	43.2	64.8	86.4	156.0
5/1/1950	21.6	54.0	64.8	86.4
5/15/1950	12.0	23.4	28.8	-
10/20/1950	12.6	27.6	31.2	34.8
3/26/1951	12.6	27.6	33.0	45.6
7/21/1951	10.8	22.8	28.2	36.0
12/1/1951	9.0	18.6	22.8	31.1
5/21/1952	5.4	10.8	12.6	14.4
9/15/1952	5.4	10.8	12.6	14.4
1/1/1953	5.4	9.6	10.8	14.4
9/1/1954	5.4	9.72	10.8	14.4
10/1/1958	2.88	5.04	6.12	7.92
1/1/1959	2.16		3.6	4.8
7/1/1959	2.16	2.88	3.6	4.8
8/5/1959	2.16	2.88	4.68	6.12
6/1/1965	2.16		3.24	3.96
10/1/1971	2.16			3.24
4/1/1979	2.16		3.60	3.96
4/1/1980	2.16		4.32	5.40

SOURCE: *Almanac of China's Finance and Banking*, 1990, Beijing, China; *Statistical Yearbook of China*, 1990, Beijing, China.

Table 7.2
Interest Rate Changes of Loans to Industrial Firms
(1949-1980 Annual Rates %)

Date of change (month/year)	State owned	Jointly owned	Collective	Self-employed	Private
5/1949	-	-	-	-	108-180
6/1950	-	-	-	-	36
2/1951	16.2-18.0[a]	-	-	-	46.8-50.4
7/1951	16.2-18.0[a]	-	-	-	30.0-86.4
6/1952	-	-	9.72	-	12.6-19.8
8/1953	5.58	5.76-16.8	5.04	10.8-16.2	12.6-19.8
1954	5.58	5.76-16.8	5.04	10.8-16.2	12.6-19.8
10/1955	5.58	8.28	5.76	10.8	11.88
1956	5.58	8.28	5.76	8.64	11.88
1957	5.58	8.28	5.76	8.64	11.88
1/1958	5.58	8.64	7.20	8.64	8.64
1/1959		7.20		7.20	
7/1959		7.20		7.20	
6/1960	7.20[b]				
5/1961	7.20				
1/1962	7.20				
4/1963	7.20				
10/1971	5.04				
1979	5.04				
1980	5.04				

NOTE:
a. Mortgage or collateral loans.
b. After 1960, the jointly-owned and privately-owned industrial firms were basically out of existence, therefore the rate since then can be regarded as the only one for both state and collectively owned industrial firms.

SOURCE: *Almanac of China's Finance and Banking*, 1990, Beijing, China; *Statistical Yearbook of China*, 1990, Beijing, China.

Table 7.3
Interest Rate Changes of Loans to Firms in Commerce 1949-1980
(Annual Rates %)

Date of change (month/year)	State	Joint	Private
5/1949	90.0-180.0	-	108.0-252.0
6/1950	25.2	-	46.8
2/1951	18.0	-	46.8
7/1951	18.0	-	30.0-86.4[a]
6/1952	12.0-14.4	-	16.2-23.4
8/1953	8.28	5.76-16.8	16.2-23.4
1954	8.28	5.76-16.8	16.2-23.4
10/1955	7.2	9.72	16.2
1956	7.2	9.72	16.2
1957	7.2	9.72	16.2
1/1958	7.2	8.64	8.64
1/1959	-	7.2	
1964	-	7.2	
6/1965	-	7.2	
11/1971	-	5.04	
1972	-	5.04	
1979	-	5.04	
7/1980	-	5.04	

NOTE:

a. Mortgage or collateral loans

Since 1959, state and collective firms dominated in commerce, the bank loans to private commercial firms were negligible. Therefore the rates after 1958 can be regarded as the uniform rate that bank charged both the state and collective owned firms in commerce.

SOURCE: *Almanac of China's Finance and Banking*, 1990, Beijing, China; *Statistical Yearbook of China*, 1990, Beijing, China.

Table 7.4
Interest Rates of the People's Bank of China in 1989
(Annual Rates %)

Item	Interest Rate	Effective Date
DEPOSITS		2/1/1989
I. Deposits of Financial Institutions[a]		
1. Legal reserves[b]	7.20	
2. Reserve for expected payment	8.64	
II. Deposit of Insurance Companies		
1. Passbook saving	2.88	9/1/1988
2. Reserve for property insurance	8.64	2/1/1989
3. Reserve for expected payment	8.64	2/1/1989
III. Special Deposits		
1. Under 6 months	float[c]	
2. 6 months	9.72	
3. 1 year	12.60	
LOANS[d]		
I. Loans to Financial Institutions		
1. Yearly loan	10.44	2/1/1989
2. Quarterly loan	9.72	2/1/1989
3. Daily loan	9.0	2/1/1989
4. Overdue loan	18.00	9/1/1988
II. Loans to Special Projects		
1. Economic development for BMRP areas[e]	7.02	2/1/1989
2. Regional development		
less than or equal to 1 year	11.34	
1 year to 3 year	12.78	
3 year to 5 year	14.40	
5 year to 10 year	19.26	

Table 7.4 continues

Table 7.4 continues from the previous page

Item	Interest Rate	Effective Date
3. Loans to		
Fourteen coastal cities and Special Economic Zones		2/1/1989
Loans to fixed capital investment		
less than or equal to 1 year	11.34	
1 year to 3 year	12.78	
3 year to 5 year	14.40	
5 year to 10 year	19.26	
4. Loans to gold and silver production		2/1/1989
1 year	8.46	
3 year	9.18	
5 year	9.90	
5. Loans to poor county-owned industries	7.02	2/1/1989
6. Loans to infrastructure of postal and telecommunication	11.34	2/1/1989
7. Low-interest loans to poor regions	3.6	2/1/1989
III. Loans within the People's Bank	8.892	2/1/1989

NOTE:

a. Financial institutions refer to specialized banks and other financial firms except the insurance company.

b. The People's Bank charges 0.03% daily rate on the overdue reserves; it charges 0.05% daily rate on those who delibertely delay the payment of the reserves.

c. Float with a maximun of 9.72%.

d. The branches of the People's Bank have the right to charge a rate that is 5-10% higher than the corresponding rate listed below.

e. BMRP stands for revolutionary bases, minority, remote and poor areas.

SOURCE: *Almanac of China's Finance and Banking*, 1990, Beijing, China, page 169.

Table 7.5
Deposit Interest Rates of Specialized Banks in 1989[a]
(Annual Rates %)

Item	Interest Rate	Effective Date
I. Urban and Rural Residents' Deposits		
1. Passbook saving	2.88	4/1/1980
2. Time deposits[b]		
1) TD type I[c]		
3 months	7.56	6/1/1989
6 months	9.00	2/1/1989
1 year	11.34	2/1/1989
2 year	12.24	2/1/1989
3 year	13.14	2/1/1989
5 year	14.94	2/1/1989
8 year	17.64	2/1/1989
2) TD type II and III[d]		
1 year	9.54	
3 year	11.34	
5 year	13.14	
II. Overseas Chinese Renminbi Deposits		2/1/1989
1 year	13.14	
3 year	14.94	
5 year	16.74	
III. Enterprises, Institutions and Private Firms Deposits[e]		
1. Passbook savings	2.88	9/1/1988
Seven day advanced notice of withdrawal	4.50	2/1/1989
2. Time deposits		
3 month	7.55	6/1/1989
6 month	9.00	2/1/1989
1 year	11.34	2/1/1989
2 year	12.24	2/1/1989
3 year	13.14	2/1/1989
5 year	14.94	2/1/1989
8 year	17.64	2/1/1989

Table 7.5 continues

Table 7.5 continues from the previous page

Item	Interest Rate	Effective Date
IV. Deposits of Insurance Company		
1. Passbook savings	2.88	9/1/1988
2. Reserves of property insurance	8.64	2/1/1989
3. Reserves of immature liabilities	8.64	2/1/1989
V. Large denomination transferable time deposit certificate		5/22/1989
1 month	7.02	
3 month	8.316	
6 month	9.9	
9 month	11.196	
12 month	12.60	

NOTE:

a. For deposits under 1 year, besides those regulated by the People's Bank, the specialized banks are allowed to provide their own deposit programs and decide the interest rates of those programs subject to the approval of the branch of the People's Bank in their locality. Other financial institutions can follow the programs of specialized banks. The rural credit co-ops can float their deposit interest rates upward by 70%. The below-county-level branches of specialized banks and other financial institutions (not including postal deposits) can float their deposit interest rate upward by 10-30%.

b. For those time deposits which have a term of 3 year or longer, the so-called "guaranteed value program" started on September 10, 1988.

c. TD Type I = Time deposit that requires a fixed amount deposited at the beginning of the term, and a customer gets the total amount plus interest at the end of the term with little flexibility.

d. TD type II and III refer to different variations of time deposits. TD Type II = A customer can frequently deposit his money into the account and gets the entire amount plus interest back at the end of the term. TD Type III = A customer gets the interest payment regularly, and gets his principal back at the end of the term.

e. When using a deposit as the collateral to get a loan, the deposit interest rate can be 1.5 to 2.1 percentage point higher than the rates listed here.

SOURCE: *Almanac of China's Finance and Banking*, 1990, Beijing, China, page 171.

Table 7.6
Interest Rates on Loans of the Industrial and Commercial Bank of China in 1989[a] (Annual Rates %)

Item	Interest Rate	Effective Date
I. Working Capital Loans (Circulating fund loans)		
A. Regular working capital loans	11.34	2/1/1989
B. Loans to private industrial and commercial firms	11.34-14.742 (may float up by 30%)	6/20/1989
C. Loans with favorable rates		2/1/1989
1. Loans to grain cotton and edible oil	10.08	
2. Minority trade and firms produce minority products	8.46	
3. Social welfare firms[b]	9.54	
4. Ship industry	10.62	
5. Shanghai MD-82 Aircraft	9.756	
6. College student loans	3.0	
II. Fixed Capital Loans		
A. Regular fixed capital loans		2/1/1989
less than or equal to 1 year	11.34	
1 year to 3 year	12.78	
3 year to 5 year	14.40	
5 year to 10 year	19.26	
above 10 year	compound interst at 11.34%	
B. Loans with favorable rates		2/1/1989
Category One Loans to agriculture, coal, petroleum, energy saving, salt industries and prisoners' factory	downward float by 30%	
1 year to 3 year	9.00	
3 year to 5 year	10.08	
5 year to 10 year	13.68	
Category Two Loans to electricity, transportation, railroad, postal service and communication airline, construction material, forest, etc.	downward float by 20%	
1 year to 3 year	10.26	
3 year to 5 year	11.52	
5 year to 10 year	15.42	

Table 7.6 continues

Table 7.6 continues from the previous page

Item	Interest Rate	Effective Date
Category Three Loans to iron and steel, nonferrous metal and chemical industry	downward float by 10%	
1 year to 3 year	11.52	
3 year to 5 year	12.96	
5 year to 10 year	17.46	
C. Fourteen coastal cities and Special economic zones (2 billion yuan)		12/21/1986
Less than or equal to 5 year	2.88	
Above 5 year	4.32	
D. Research and development loans (400 million yuan)[c]		2/1/1989
Less than or equal to 1 year	8.46	
1 year to 3 year	9.90	
E. Loans to purchase train, ship and aircraft	11.34	2/1/1989
F. Highway transportation and new vehicle purchase	11.34	
G. Loans for gold production[d] and equipments		
term $\leq$ 1 year	8.46	
1 year to 3 year	9.18	
3 year to 5 year	9.90	
III. Interest Penalty on Loans		
A. Overdue loans	additional 30% Interest	
B. Excessive inventory	additional 50% Interest	
C. Using loans for different purposes as specified	additional 100% Interest	

Table 7.6 continues

Table 7.6 continues from the previous page

NOTE:

a. For regular working capital and fixed capital loans, the branches of the Industrial and Commercial Bank of China (ICBC) may charge an interest rate that is 30% higher than the rates listed in this table. They can also charge different rates for different industries and the types of the projects based on risk assessment. For loans which have terms shorter than 1 year, the branches have the power to determine their own rates, which should be reported to the local branch of the People's Bank for record. Other financial institutions can follow the case of ICBC. The rural co-ops can float their rates on loans upward by 100%.

b. "Social welfare firms" refers to factories that hire primarily handicapped people.

c. For these loans, the People's Bank subsidizes ICBC at an annual rate of 2.88%.

d. For these loans, the People's Bank pays ICBC the difference between the low rates ICBC charged and 12.78% for different terms respectively. For instance, if ICBC charges 9.18%, then the People's Bank pays ICBC by the amount of 3.60% times the principle.

SOURCE: All calculations are based on the data from *Almanac of China's Finance and Banking*, 1990, Beijing, China, page 173-174. *Statistical Yearbook of China*, 1989, Beijing, China. *Almanac of China's Prices*, 1988, Beijing, China.

Table 7.7
Adjustment of Interest Rates on Time Deposits, 1980-1988
(Annual Rates %)

Date of change	Passbook saving	1 year	TD type I 3 year	5 year	TD type II 1 year	3 year	5 year	TD Type III 1 year	3 year	5 year
4/1/1980	2.16	5.40	6.12	6.84	4.32	5.40	6.12	3.96	5.40	6.12
7/1/1980	2.88	5.40	6.12	6.84	4.32	5.40	6.12	4.32	5.40	6.12
4/1/1982	2.88	5.76	6.84	7.92	4.68	6.12	7.20	4.32	5.76	6.48
4/1/1985	2.88	6.84	7.92	8.28	5.40	6.84	7.56	5.40	6.84	7.56
8/1/1985	2.88	7.20	8.28	9.36	6.12	7.20	7.92	6.12	7.20	7.92
8/1/1986	2.88	7.20	8.28	9.36	6.12	7.20	7.92	6.12	7.20	7.92
8/14/1987	2.88	7.20	8.28	9.36	6.12	7.20	7.92	6.12	7.20	7.92
9/1/1988	2.88	8.64	9.72	10.80	7.20	8.64	9.72	7.20	8.64	9.72

NOTE:

TD Type I = Time deposit that requires a fixed amount deposited at the beginning of the term, and a customer gets the total amount plus interest at the end of the term with little flexibility.

TD Type II = A customer can frequently deposit his money into the account and gets the entire amount plus interest back at the end of the term.

TD Type III = A customer gets the interest payment regularly, and gets his principal back at the end of the term.

SOURCE: *Almanac of China's Finance and Banking*, 1990, Beijing, China, page 168.

PART THREE

The Demand for Money

8

The Velocity of Money

During the first fourteen years of the Chinese economic reform (1979-1992), the real gross national product (GNP, deflated by the official price index) increased 231 percent. In 1992, the currency in circulation and the broad money were, respectively, about twenty times of that in 1978, whereas the official price index increased only 125 percent, and the free market price index went up 141 percent for the same period. According to the quantity theory of money, which assumes that the velocity of money is stable, the money supply growth rate above and beyond the GNP growth rate should be fully reflected by the increase in price level. However, in China, the inflation rates, measured by both official price index and free market price index, are much smaller than the difference between the money growth rate and the real GNP growth rate. In other words, the velocity of money was not constant in China. It was decreasing rapidly during the reform decade. The volume of money in circulation (relative to real GNP) has been getting larger and larger. This chapter defines the income velocity of money, discusses alternative theories that explain the excess money with the focus on the monetization hypothesis.

8.1 The Income Velocity of Money

Let us start with the exchange equation:

$$MV = Py \tag{8.1}$$

where M is nominal money supply, P is general price level measured by the official price index, y is real income measured by GNP, V is income velocity and is calculated by

$$V = Py/M \tag{8.2}$$

Taking the natural log of equation (8.1) and then differentiating, we get

$$\dot{V} + \dot{M} = \dot{P} + \dot{y} \tag{8.3}$$

where all the dot notations in equation (8.3) represent the growth rate.

During the reform period, the growth rate of money supply has been consistently greater than the sum of the growth rate of GNP and the inflation rate regardless of which measurement of money (M0, M1, M2) is used. To explain this phenomenon, let us define excess money as the growth rate of money minus the sum of the real GNP growth and the official inflation rate.

$$\text{EM} = \dot{M} - (\dot{y} + \dot{P})$$

where EM denotes the excess money, $\dot{M}$ is the growth rate of money, $\dot{y}$ represents the growth rate of real GNP and $\dot{P}$ is the official inflation rate.

For simplicity, we will concentrate our discussion on the excess money in the narrow sense (currency in circulation) in this chapter. Generalization to broader measurements of money can be done easily. Table 8.1 and 8.2 provide information on the growth rate of money, real GNP, and the inflation rate, the excess money defined as above and income velocity of money. The following three points can be observed from the two tables. First, the money supply increased rapidly during the period 1978-1992. The currency in circulation, M0 in 1992 was about 20 times of that in 1978. Second, the money supply increased more rapidly than the growth rate of real GNP plus the rate of inflation. From Table 8.2, we see that EM0 was all positive in this period except in 1989. This clearly indicates that there was excessive money supplies. Third, the income velocities of currency in circulation and M2 have decreased at a rapid rate for this period.[1]

From the point of view of the quantity theory of money, this was quite natural since the velocity is calculated by nominal GNP divided by nominal money. When the velocity V is constant, $\dot{M} = (\dot{P} + \dot{y})$. If $\dot{M} > (\dot{P} + \dot{y})$, then the only way for the equality (8.3) to have held is that $\dot{V}$ was negative, which means the velocity decreased.

The increase of money supply has been consistently greater than the sum of the GNP growth rate and inflation rate. Where did the money go? That is the basic question that this chapter tries to answer. There are several theories that explain the excess money supplies in the economy. The financial deepening theory proposed by McKinnon and Shaw (see Fry 1988, McKinnon 1993) is well known. Here we focus on three less well known hypotheses: the downward biased price index hypothesis, the forced saving hypothesis (Feltenstein and Ha 1991), and the monetization hypothesis (Yi 1991), with the emphasis on the last one.

8.2 The Downward Biased Price Index Hypothesis

The downward biased price index hypothesis asserts that the existence of the excess money is because the official price index of China is biased downward. Consequently, this hypothesis claims that if we use the "true" inflation rate, there would be no excessive money in the economy, because excessive money is calculated by using the growth rate of nominal money minus the sum of the growth rate of real GNP and the official inflation rate. This claim is obviously a serious challenge to the excess money data in Table 8.2. It is generally acknowledged that the official price index is biased downward. The question is downward by how much? How about the market price index? To answer these questions, let us look at how the official price index and market price index are constructed.

The official price index is calculated on a broad basis of commodities. For example, the official general retail price level in 1988 was calculated by random samples from more than 14,000 grassroots markets of 420 counties or cities all over the country. The samples contained almost every important retail commodity that one could think of and the final general retail index was computed by four rounds of weighted average at county, regional, provincial, and national level. However, there is no doubt that the official price index underestimated inflation, simply because it was calculated from the official prices, a great proportion of which were prices under a rationing system that did not reflect the true price level. For example, suppose color TVs were rationed and the official price was 1500 yuan each. This means that in order to purchase a color TV, one had to pay 1500 yuan plus a rationing coupon. If in the black market, the price of a color TV coupon was 500 yuan, then the effective price of the color TV was 2000 yuan. But when calculating the official price index, the official price 1500 yuan was recorded. Evidently, it underestimated the price level.

The advantage of the market prices is that they are determined by demand and supply. However, there are two shortcomings of the free market price index. First, it is not as broadly based as the official price index. Most commodities in well-established, large scale free markets are food and handcraft industry products. Second, it tends (not necessarily though) to overestimate the real level of inflation due to coexistence with state-owned commerce. For example, suppose that there were 100 tons of pork available, that 90 tons were distributed through government-controlled commerce at a low price (with a rationing coupon), and that the remaining 10 tons were sold in a free market. It is easy to see that the free market price would then be higher than in the scenario in which all 100 tons of pork were sold in the free market, which would be the ideal case to measure the true price level. Although both official and market price indices have their own limitations, at least they provide two polar cases. We can use the official and free market price indices as the lower and upper bounds of the true inflation level respectively. Table 8.1 provides the free market price index as well. Even if we use the market price index, the excessive money still exists. That is, the growth rates of money are greater than the sum of the growth rate of real GNP plus inflation measured by the free market price index for most years of the reform period. This is a sufficient condition for excess money existing in the economy, which could not be fully explained by the downward biased price index hypothesis.

8.3 The Forced Saving Hypothesis

The excessive money stock in the economy and decreasing of the income velocity can be explained by the forced saving hypothesis. Briefly, the forced saving hypothesis asserts that consumers and firms are forced to hold money for two reasons. First, there are very few other alternative ways to hold financial assets. Second, there are not enough goods available in the markets. Let us look at these two reasons in more detail.

Demand for money makes sense when people have alternative ways to invest their wealth. In the West, demand for money reflects people's willingness to hold money as opposed to bonds, stocks, real estate, and other types of investment. In China most of these investment alternatives were not available until recently. By the end of 1988, the total amount of bonds (including government bonds, key projects bonds, local enterprise bonds, and all other bonds) was 86.85 billion yuan. The total amount of outstanding stocks (the book value, not the market value) was 3.5 billion yuan. The sum of bonds and stocks was still less than 10 percent of M2, which was 928.89 billion yuan at the end of 1988 (*Statistical Yearbook of China*, 1989). Obviously, cash and bank deposits were the primary ways to hold financial assets. The rapid development of financial and real estate markets in China is only a recent event.

Does the lack of other financial securities result in forced savings? The answer is "not necessarily." As long as there are enough commodities available in the markets, people still have a choice between money and consumer goods. Forced savings occur only when there is a shortage in the economy, where consumers and firms are forced to save their income because the commodities they want to buy are not available. They hold cash or bank deposits involuntarily and wait to make a purchase. In other words, forced savings result when too much money chases too few goods, coupled with price control. Therefore, forced savings and repressed inflation are two sides of the same coin.

There is much evidence in the literature (Ports and Santorum 1987; Yi 1990b) which confirms that the shortage problem has worsened during the reform in China. As far as shortages are concerned, the problem is how severe it is rather than whether or not it exists. Feltenstein and Ha (1991) estimated the extent to which the price level was repressed in China and showed that the decline in observed income velocity was due to involuntary savings by households. They concluded that there was a monetary overhang in the sense that money was being held by households in excess over the nominal value of transactions. Consequently, there was repressed inflation and forced savings.

There are two questions that the forced savings hypothesis could not explain. The first is why the currency in circulation has increased so rapidly. If everyone is holding money and waiting to buy, they should hold money in the form of bank deposit. In China, there is very little transaction cost to convert the savings deposit into cash. Why did people forgo the opportunity to earn interest by holding cash? The second question that the forced savings theory has not answered is of the relationship between forced savings and people's expectations of future inflation. One observation worth mentioning is that since the economic recession and sluggishness of the market started in the third quarter of 1989, a number of consumer durable goods became available at the 1988 prices or lower, but the demand was still soft. Household savings have soared continuously in this period. It is safe to say that these savings were voluntary rather than forced. This suggests that whether the savings are voluntary or forced largely depends on the real return to the savings and people's expectations of the future price level. Chart 8.1 at the end of this chapter shows the total household savings for the period 1978-1992.

8.4 The Monetization Hypothesis

The other theory that can explain the excess money in the economy is the monetization hypothesis, which is the main theme of this section.

What is monetization? Roughly speaking, monetization refers to the process by which the proportion of economic activities conducted by money (using money for measurement of value and as the medium of exchange) has increased. In a less developed country like China, the economy can be decomposed into two parts, a monetized and a non-monetized part. Usually, the transactions of the monetized part are realized in the marketplace, while the non-monetized part corresponds to the traditional self-sufficient economy with some barter trades. For instance, a farmer consumes his own agricultural products. That part of the output never enters the market and hence belongs to the non-monetized part of the economy. As the economy developed, especially since the economic reform was launched, not only has the total output increased, but also the proportion of the monetized economy has increased as a result of decentralized policies.

A Modified Version of the Equation of Exchange

For a less developed country, we can define the real total national income as

$$y = \lambda y + (1 - \lambda)y \tag{8.4}$$

where λ is the proportion of the economy monetized. Consequently, the appropriate version of the equation of exchange for the partially monetized economy should be

$$MV = \lambda yP \tag{8.5}$$

Equation (8.5) says that nominal money multiplied by its velocity equals the monetized part of the nominal national income. Taking the natural log of equation (8.5) and differentiate, we get

$$\dot{M} + \dot{V} = \dot{\lambda} + \dot{y} + \dot{P}. \tag{8.6}$$

Equation (8.6) differs from equation (8.3) by an extra term $\dot{\lambda}$.

With the notion of monetization, it is easy to explain the excess money. If we assume that the velocity is constant (i.e., $\dot{V} = 0$), then we have $\dot{M} = \dot{P} + \dot{y} + \dot{\lambda}$, which says that money supply should increase not only in proportion to the growth of the economy, but also to accommodate the newly monetized sectors. The price level increases only when $\dot{M} > \dot{y} + \dot{\lambda}$. That is, when the money supply growth is greater than the sum of the income growth and the growth rate of the monetization process. Recall that the excess money is defined as $(\dot{M} - \dot{P} - \dot{y})$, which is equal to $\dot{\lambda}$, the rate of monetization.[2] This means that the excess money is not really "excessive", it is the amount of money needed to accommodate the newly monetized economy.

However, as the last two columns of Table 8.2 (which are calculated by equation (8.2)) clearly indicate, the income velocity of money is not constant. It decreased rapidly regardless of which measure is used. With the monetization framework, at least we can show that velocity calculated by equation (8.2) exaggerated the speed of the velocity decrease. If we take the monetization process into account, the true velocity for a partially monetized economy should be

$$V^* = (P\lambda y)/M \tag{8.7}$$

Since $0 < \lambda < 1$ and is increasing, the income velocity defined in equation (8.7) has not decreased as rapidly as calculated by equation (8.2).

How to Estimate λ

λ, the proportion of the economy monetized, can be estimated at least theoretically by the following ad hoc procedure. According to the Chinese way of classification, the national income consists of six components: agriculture, industry, construction, transportation, commerce, and service. Then, in terms of percentage, we have

$$100 = a + i + b + t + c + s \tag{8.8}$$

where a, i, b, t, c, s are percentages of national income from agriculture, industry, construction, transportation, commerce, and service sectors respectively.[3] If we can estimate the monetized proportion of each sector, then the proportion of the monetized economy as a whole could be calculated by

$$\lambda = a\lambda_a + i\lambda_i + b\lambda_b + t\lambda_t + c\lambda_c + s\lambda_s \tag{8.9}$$

where λ_a, λ_i, λ_b, λ_t, λ_c, λ_s are proportions of the economy monetized in each sector.

Let us look at the agriculture as an example. In 1952, 57.7 percent of the total national income was from agriculture. It was estimated that only about one third of the rural output entered into markets at that time; the remaining two thirds was directly consumed by peasants. By 1985, the share of national income from agriculture decreased to 35.4 percent, and 63.9 percent of the total rural output entered into markets (*Statistical Yearbook of China*, 1989, page 32; The Rural Development Research Center 1987). In the past decade, the introduction of the responsibility system in the rural area and the gradual releasing of controls over the distribution of agricultural products have obviously increased the proportion of agricultural products that entered the market. We would be able to estimate λ_a, providing data are available.

We can do this kind of estimation for each sector. It is obvious that the estimation of λ is not only tedious, but also requires a lot of information. Furthermore, it is very difficult to establish a general rule by which the λ can be estimated systematically, because in the past there have been too many exceptions and drastic institutional changes that caused jumps and discontinuities of the λ.

There is more literature on this topic recently. For example, Yang et al. (1988) estimated the percentage of the monetized economy in China for the period 1978-1986.[4] Xiaoxiang Huang (1988) suggested that the money supply needed to increase 6-8 percent a year to accommodate the newly monetized economy. Unfortunately, none of them provided detailed expositions of their estimations. After all, in a developing country, economic growth and monetization has happened in tandem. It is very difficult to have a precise measurement of the monetization process. The monetization process depends primarily on two things, the degree of economic development, and the institutional or structural change of the economy. In the case of China, both of these factors are changing.

Reforms and the Monetization Process

At the beginning of the reform, the Chinese economy could be classified into three parts according to the degree of monetization. First, the consumer goods market was the most monetized sector despite rationing. People spent their incomes to buy consumer goods in markets and the transactions were conducted in cash. Second, the producer goods market could be regarded as semi-monetized. On the one hand, producer goods were produced for sale, not for self use, and had prices in terms of money; these were attributes of a monetized economy. On the other hand, most producer goods were allocated by the plan, not by the market; this was a feature of a centrally-planned economy. Therefore, we say that the producer goods market was semi-monetized before the reform. Third, the non-monetized economy refers to the traditional self-sufficient economy with some barter trades. The outputs of this part of the economy were mostly for self-consumption and did not enter into markets.

In the centrally-planned economy, the government controlled virtually every sector of the economy. They knew very well what proportion of the economy was monetized and how much currency was needed to facilitate transactions. The government injected currency into the economy when it made the procurement purchases of agricultural products, and paid salaries and wages to urban workers. Then, every transaction consumers made constituted a cash inflow to the government. When people purchased consumer goods, the government received the proceeds, since it controlled all state and collective commerce. All stores had to turn in their cash revenue to local banks at the end of the day. When consumers deposited their savings into banks, that certainly caused an inflow of cash to the government. In this kind of simple centrally-planned economy, there were no other intermediate institutions that could drag or delay cash flowing back to the government.

The goal of the economic reform is to transform the centrally-planned system into a market economy. Associated with the institutional changes is a monetization process. Specifically, the monetization process involves three different phenomena in the reform. First, some economic transactions used to be done by bank transfer money; the economic reforms changed the medium of these transactions into cash. The responsibility system in the agricultural sector that brought millions and millions of farmers into the marketplace is obviously an example. Another example is that more and more producer goods have been sold in the free market and the transactions are conducted by cash. Many state-owned firms have participated in the free producer goods market. This implies a significant part of the semi-monetized economy became fully monetized during the reform and the proportion of economic activities facilitated by bank transfer money has shrunk.

Second, the new non-state institutions and enterprises that emerged during the reform are more market-oriented. They are usually profit driven and have more autonomous management powers. They have no privilege to obtain cheaper raw materials from the government and certainly do not want the banks to check every transaction they make. Consequently, a large proportion of these outside-plan firms (especially the small ones) tend to use cash to conduct their business.

Third, a large proportion of these new enterprises are in retail business, which has been the main channel that allows cash flow back to the government. Now the private retail businesses become the intermediaries between consumers and the government. A significant amount of the currency in circulation went to and settled down in those non-government sectors. That money is out of the government's direct control. This implies that the chain of the currency in circulation is getting longer and more complicated. This is one of the main reasons that the velocity of money has decreased drastically.

From the above analysis, we conclude that the centerpiece of the monetization process is that the demand for currency has increased rapidly during the reform. This is another reason that we focus our discussion on currency in this chapter. The evidence of the monetization process in China will be documented in detail in the next chapter.

Notes

1. This is just the opposite of the experience of the United States. The income velocity of M1 was growing at a stable rate of about 3.2 percent per year from 1960 to 1980 in the United States and the growth trend stopped in the 1980s (Mayer, Duesenberry and Aliber 1987, page 234).

2. Here, the official price index is used, which underestimated the true level of inflation. Consequently, part of the excess money would be the repressed inflation. Nevertheless, the monetization process explained most of the excess money, especially when the market supply condition was good.

3. The *Statistical Yearbook of China* provides the data of the share of national income from agriculture, industry, construction, transportation and commerce each year.

4. Their estimation of the percentage of the monetized economy are 82.4 for 1978, 83.0 for 1979, 83.1 for 1980, 83.2 for 1981, 82.2 for 1982, 82.8 for 1983, 84.1 for 1984, 85.3 for 1985, 85.6 for 1986. The percentages are estimated without taking intangible assets into account. No details are provided on how these numbers were derived (Yang et al. 1988).

Table 8.1
Money Supply, Price Indices, GNP, and Bank Deposits
(All in billion yuan at current price except percentage)

Year	M0	M1	M2	OPI(%)	MPI(%)	GNP	HBD
1978	21.20	94.90	115.91	121.6	221.6	358.8	21.06
1979	26.77	117.70	145.81	124.0	211.6	399.8	28.10
1980	34.62	144.30	184.29	131.4	215.8	447.0	39.95
1981	39.63	171.10	223.45	134.6	228.3	477.3	52.37
1982	43.91	191.40	258.98	137.2	235.8	519.3	67.54
1983	52.98	218.30	307.50	139.3	245.7	580.9	89.25
1984	79.21	293.20	414.63	143.2	244.7	696.2	121.47
1985	98.78	326.20	488.43	155.8	286.8	855.8	162.26
1986	121.84	402.40	626.16	165.1	310.0	969.6	223.76
1987	145.45	459.10	766.45	177.2	360.5	1130.1	307.33
1988	213.40	548.70	928.89	210.0	469.7	1406.8	380.15
1989	234.40	577.30	1092.0	247.2	520.4	1599.3	514.69
1990	264.40	687.50	1390.9	252.4	490.7	1769.5	703.42
1991	317.80	844.60	1755.6	259.7	486.3	1985.5	911.03
1992	432.20	1131.7	2299.9	273.7	498.0	2393.8	1154.5

NOTE:
M0 is defined as currency in circulation at the end of the year;
M1 is equal to M0 plus demand deposits of firms, institutions;
M2 equals M1 plus and passbook saving and term deposits of households;
OPI = official general retail price index (1952=100);
MPI = free market price index of consumer goods (1952=100);
GNP = gross national product;
HBD = total households bank deposits.

SOURCE: *Almanac of China's Finance and Banking*, 1992, Beijing, China; *Statistical Yearbook of China*, 1992, Beijing, China and *Almanac of China's Prices*, 1990, Beijing, China.

Table 8.2
Excess Money and the Income Velocity
(All numbers are in percentage except the velocities)

Year	GM0	GM2	GGNP	OIR	EM0	EM2	VM0	VM2
1978	8.5	4.7	-	0.7	-	-	16.92	3.10
1979	26.3	25.8	7.6	2.0	16.7	16.2	14.93	2.74
1980	29.3	26.4	7.8	6.0	15.5	12.6	12.91	2.43
1981	14.5	21.2	4.5	2.4	7.6	14.3	12.04	2.14
1982	10.8	15.9	8.7	1.9	0.02	5.3	11.93	2.01
1983	20.7	18.7	10.3	1.5	8.9	6.9	10.96	1.89
1984	49.5	34.8	14.7	2.8	32.1	17.4	8.79	1.68
1985	24.7	17.8	12.8	8.8	3.2	-3.7	8.67	1.75
1986	23.3	28.2	8.1	6.0	9.0	13.9	7.98	1.55
1987	19.4	22.4	10.9	7.3	1.1	4.1	7.80	1.48
1988	46.7	21.2	11.3	18.5	17.4	-8.1	6.57	1.51
1989	9.8	17.6	4.4	17.8	-12.4	-4.6	6.82	1.46
1990	12.8	27.4	4.1	2.1	6.6	21.2	6.69	1.27
1991	20.0	26.2	7.7	2.9	9.4	15.6	6.25	1.13
1992	36.0	31.0	12.8	5.4	17.8	12.8	5.54	1.04

NOTE:
GM0 = growth rate of M0;
GM2 = growth rate of M2;
GGNP = growth rate of gross national product in real term;
OIR = official inflation rate measured by general retail price index;
EM0 = (growth rate of M0) - (growth rate of GNP + official inflation rate);
EM2 = (growth rate of M2) - (growth rate of GNP + official inflation rate);
VM0 = GNP velocity of M0;
VM2 = GNP velocity of M2.

SOURCE: All calculations are based on the data from *Almanac of China's Finance and Banking*, 1992, Beijing, China; *Statistical Yearbook of China*, 1992, Beijing, China and *Almanac of China's Prices*, 1990, Beijing, China.

Figure 8.1 Total Household Saving in China

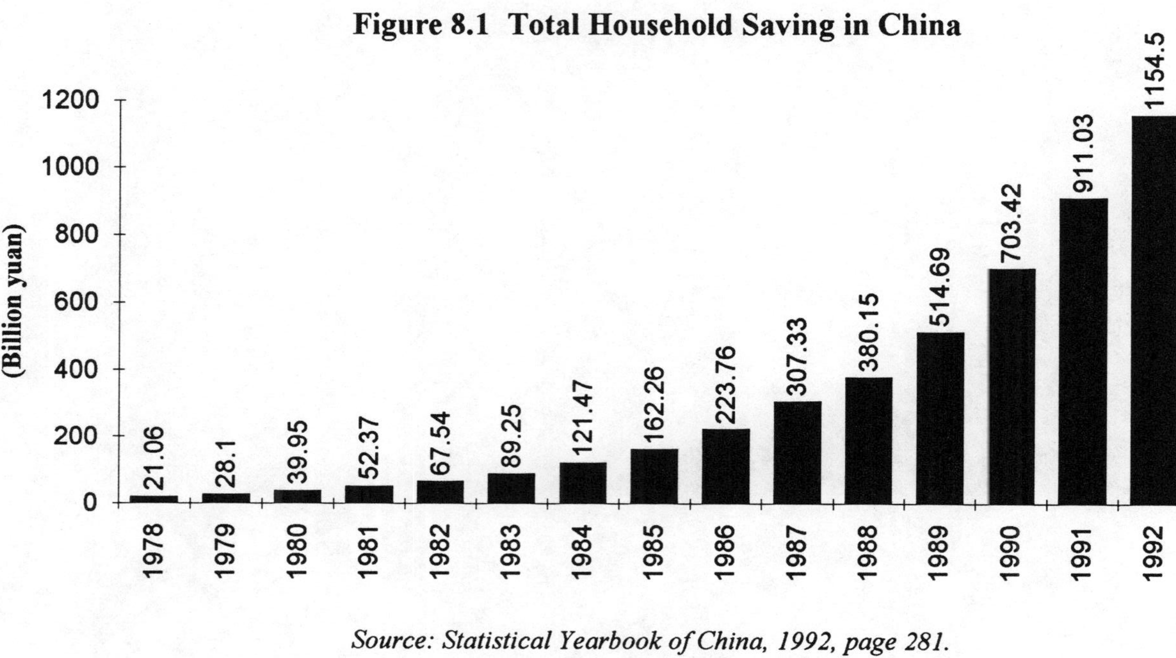

Source: Statistical Yearbook of China, 1992, page 281.

9

Evidence of the Monetization Process

Let us start with two important macro indicators related to the monetization (or financial deepening) process. First, the ratio of broad money to GNP has been increasing monotonically for the reform period, from 0.32 in 1978 to 0.60 in 1985, to above 1.0 in 1992. The same ratio in 1990 was 0.47 for India, 0.67 for the United States, 0.57 for Korea, 1.48 for Taiwan, and 1.89 for Japan (Chang 1994). This ratio has increased at an astonishing rate in China comparing to other developing countries. For example, in 1978, this ratio was 0.32 for China and 0.37 for India. The rapid increase of this ratio reflects the institutional changes during the reform.

Second, the total stock of financial assets has increased rapidly. The composition of the owners of financial assets and the structure of national saving have changed. Before the reform, there was virtually no other forms of financial assets except currency in circulation and bank deposits. In 1978, the total household bank deposit was 21.06 billion yuan, which was only 5.9% of GNP. Most of national saving was from the central government at that time. The total household bank deposit reached 1154.5 billion yuan by the end of 1992, which was about 48% of GNP of that year (2398.8 billion). Households have become the main source of national saving. The control powers of the financial assets have been decentralized. The proportion of financial assets owned and controlled by the central government has declined steadily. The proportions of financial assets owned by households, enterprises, financial institutions and local governments have increased.

There are a number of articles in the recent literature that discuss various aspects of money and the financial sector in China (e.g. Feltenstein and Farhadian 1987, Perkins 1988, Qin 1993, Qian 1993). While most experts accept that there has been a monetization process going on during the reform, so far there is very few detailed documentation on the monetization process of China in the literature, perhaps for the following reasons (Yi 1991). First, the term "monetization" is vague and not well-defined. It is too broad and aggregate. Theoretically and empirically, it is difficult to distinguish monetization from economic growth, since they are developed in tandem. Second, there is a lack of data. A systematic analysis of monetization needs tremendously detailed data for each sector of the economy, which has not been available until recently.

The purpose of this chapter is to provide evidence of the monetization process based on the available information. The method that we will use is to decompose the economy into sectors and trace out where the money went. The preliminary result suggests that in the period 1979-1984, the economy was monetized rapidly due to the introduction of a responsibility system in rural areas and the emergence of numerous nonstate-owned enterprises. The newly monetized economy absorbed most of the excess money supply. Consequently, the inflation rate was moderate in this period. Since 1985, the monetization process has been slowed significantly; the excess money supply has mainly resulted in inflation.

Economic reform caused monetization through at least the following five channels. First, through increase of transaction demands of households and firms. Second, through introduction of a responsibility system in the rural areas which led millions and millions of farmers into the marketplace; they need cash to facilitate their transactions. Third, through numerous township and village enterprises (TVEs) which emerged during the reform. They were usually outside the central plan and had autonomous management powers. Cash became one of the main mediums of exchange for these new institutions. Fourth, through the rapid development of the self-employed and private business. Fifth, through the swift increase of the free market.

In this chapter, we will discuss how these new developments accelerated the demand for currency and how part of the economy was monetized. We limit our analysis within the scope of currency in circulation for simplicity purposes. It is easy to generalized this kind analysis to M2 by focusing on the demand for broad money. As a matter of fact, currency in circulation and M2 are moved basically together during the reform period. Chapter 16 will discuss the financial markets and the composition of the financial assets in detail.

9.1 Distribution of the Currency in Circulation

To answer the question of where the money went, let us start with Table 9.1, which lays out the distribution of the currency in circulation for the period 1978-1986. Cash holders are classified into four groups: rural households, urban households, institutions and enterprises (not including the government), and others (mainly consisting of mobile population). Table 9.1 lists the currency balance for each group in billions of yuan together with the percentage of their balance relative to the total currency in circulation.

The percentage change of each group's cash demand over the period is somewhat interesting. For instance, we see that the largest group of currency holders was rural households. They held 59.01 percent of the total currency in circulation in 1978 and 65.38 percent in 1983. This rapid gain, not only in absolute quantity but also in terms of percentage, reflects that, during this five-year period, farmers' incomes increased more rapidly than other groups, coupled with the institutional changes in the rural areas, which made the demand for currency of rural households grow very fast. However, after 1984, the trend reversed. The proportion of rural households' cash balance has declined.

The percentages of cash demand by urban households and institutions have changed in more or less the opposite direction, because of the time sequence of the reform. The incomes of urban workers lagged behind their rural counterparts in the period of 1978-1983, because the reform had not started in cities at that time. That explains why the proportion of currency demand of urban households first declined and then caught up after 1984.

The reasons for the decline of the percentage of the cash demand of institutions and enterprises in the period 1978-1983 were complicated. The dismantlement of the commune system definitely played a role. It was no longer necessary for production brigades and production teams to hold cash reserves after the responsibility system was introduced. One of the reasons for the later increase (after 1984) of the proportion of the institutions' and enterprises' cash demand was the rapid growth of TVEs.

Table 9.2 provides information on average cash demand per household. From Table 9.2, we see that the cash demand per household in nominal terms increased rapidly, on average 23.23 percent annually, for the period 1978-1986. The cash demand of rural households increased more rapidly than that of urban households. In 1978, the average cash balance per rural household was 15.44 yuan, which was only 63.6 percent that of the urban household. In 1986, the average cash balance per rural household was 85.67 yuan, which was 95.3 percent of its urban counterpart for the same year.

The per capita cash balances in real terms increased 304 percent and 169 percent for the rural and urban population respectively in the period 1978-1986. The real consumption levels rose 95 percent and 62 percent respectively for the rural and urban residents for the same period.[1] If we use the real consumption level as an approximation of the transaction demand, then the increase of real cash balances of both rural and urban households was much higher than the transaction needs. Obviously, just using the transaction demand to explain the tremendous increase in cash balance is not enough. There were other factors besides the income growth that created new demands for currency. What were these factors?

9.2 Institutional Changes in Rural Areas

The economic reform started from the agricultural sector in 1979. The most significant move of the reform in agriculture was the introduction of the responsibility system. Before the reform, under the commune system, rural households did not use currency at all during the agricultural production cycle. The government's procurement purchase of agricultural products was mainly through production teams. A typical production team sold its agricultural products to the government at prescribed low prices usually twice a year (summer and fall) and then distributed the proceeds to their members according to their accumulated working points. Most production teams distributed cash to their members twice a year, a preliminary distribution during the summer and a final distribution at the end of the year. This kind of arrangement enabled most transactions between the government and production teams to be cleared by bank transfer money. The government pumped the bulk of currency into rural areas only immediately preceding the cash distribution of production teams.

The introduction of the responsibility system brought millions of farmers into the marketplace. Under this system, a typical farmer receives the right to use a small piece of land. He is responsible for the entire production cycle. He has the obligation to submit a predetermined amount of output to the government (as a tax or a rent) and to sell a certain amount of the output to the government at prescribed prices. He has to pay a small tax and an administrative fee to the village. The remaining output belongs to himself. He can consume it or sell it in free markets. Because today farmers sell their agricultural products directly to the government and get paid in cash, there is a tremendous increase in cash payments when the government purchases agricultural products from farmers. In 1978, 72.1 percent of the government procurement purchases of agricultural products was cleared by bank transfer money, and only 27.9 percent was paid in cash. The average proportion of government agriculture procurement paid by cash increased quickly during the period 1979-1983, proportions were 33.7 percent, 40.2 percent, 46.6 percent, 52.3 percent, and 60.0 percent respectively for 1979,

1980, 1981, 1982, and 1983 (People's Bank of China 1988). These numbers were national averages, however, they varied from region to region. By the end of 1983, the responsibility system had been implemented in more than 95 percent of the rural areas. The People's Commune system was quietly abolished. This is a typical example of how an institutional change brought in a huge demand for currency and was associated with a monetization process.

9.3 Rapid Development of the Township and Village Enterprises (TVEs)

China has 1.17 billion people; most of them live in rural areas. It is well known that there is a gigantic excess labor force in rural areas. One of the biggest challenges to the economic development of this country is how to transfer this huge agricultural labor forces to non-agricultural sectors. The transformation process was actually started in 1979 and accelerated in the mid-eighties. The main channel of transformation has been the astonishing growth of TVEs.

Table 9.3 summarizes the development of TVEs in the reform decade. The growth rate of TVEs for the period 1979-1988 was 29.25 percent a year on average, much higher than the state-owned industrial sector, which grew 9 percent annually on average for the same period. The proportion of the TVEs output relative to the total industrial and agricultural output[2] has also increased rapidly. In 1979, the TVEs output only accounted for 8.75 percent of the total output. In 1988, it already accounted for 26.97 percent of the total output.

It is very clear from Table 9.3 that TVEs are the major channel by which the agricultural labor force has been transferred to non-agricultural sectors. In 1988, the total employees of TVEs reached 95.45 million, about 25 percent of the total rural labor force. For the ten year period 1979-1988, TVEs absorbed 66.36 million excess rural laborers, whereas all urban areas combined absorbed only 11.20 million rural laborers for the same period (Wu and Zou 1989). Charts 9.1 and 9.2 illustrate the total output of TVEs and the total employment of TVEs for the period 1978-1992.

The rapid growth of TVEs created tremendous demand for money (both in cash and loans). It was an important part of the monetization process. There is no doubt that the development of TVEs needed huge amounts of investment. To support the development of TVEs, banks had to supply more currency and loans to accommodate the demand. For a detailed discussion on the development of TVEs, see Byrd (1990) and Wu and Zou (1989).

Here we focus only on the cash demand of TVEs. Generally speaking, TVEs are market-oriented. They have autonomous management powers and are fully responsible for the bottom line of their operations. They buy inputs from the marketplace at competitive prices and sell products for a profit. Their behavior could be well modeled by profit maximization. Most of their transactions are done by cash, rather than through bank transfer money. First, cash is generally acceptable and subject to less surveillance from the government. Second, credit is not well-developed in China. Cash payments are usually quick and convenient, whereas bank transfers are often delayed by red tape. Demand for cash from TVEs contributed to the increase of the proportion of institutions' cash demand for the period 1983-1986.

Table 9.4 reports the results of a survey done by the People's Bank of China in 1985. It provides the cash flow information of the TVEs in the sample. The sample sizes for 1984 and 1985 were 5,374 and 5,666 respectively. The table reports the total amount of cash revenue and expenditure of the enterprises in the sample. The last row of the table provides the average cash balance of TVEs, which was 1,870 yuan in 1984 and 2,534 yuan in 1985. In 1986, the average cash balance per TVEs was 3,512 yuan (based on a sample of size 12,285). The total number of TVEs was 1.52 million (*Almanac of China's Economy*, 1988, p.XI-42). This means that 5.34 billion yuan currency was held by TVEs, which was about 4.4 percent of the total currency in circulation.

9.4 The Self-Employed and Private Businesses

According to the Chinese government's definition, those privately-owned businesses which hire more than eight employees are called private enterprises (Siying Qiye). Those which hire eight or fewer employees are called self-employed businesses (Getihu). It is estimated that, by the end of 1987, China had 225,000 private enterprises that hired a total of 3.6 million employees. The total number of self-employed businesses was 13.7 million, which employed 21.6 million people by the end of 1987 (*Almanac of China's Economy*, 1988, page XI-158).

A large proportion of the self-employed businesses are in the retail sector. In 1979, the share of state, collective, and self-employed commerce in the total retail sale were 54.0 percent, 43.1, and 2.9 percent respectively. In 1988, the share became 39.5 percent for state, 34.4 percent for collective, and 26.1 percent for self-employed businesses. When analyzing the monetization process, we certainly have to take into account the demand for currency of the self-employed and private businesses.

Most of the self-employed businesses are in the retail, service and handcraft industries, and they are mostly family businesses. These businesses are virtually entirely facilitated by cash coupled with some personal credit relations. A certain amount of cash reserve is necessary for them as working capital. Table 9.5 provides information on the cash position of urban (not including rural) self-employed businesses. This information was obtained from random samples, which were drawn nationwide each year. The sample size for 1981 and 1982 are not available. The sample sizes for 1983, 1984, 1985, 1986 are 7048, 20480, 15376, and 14881 respectively (People's Bank of China 1988). The last column of Table 9.5 provides the average cash balance per business. For example, at the end of 1986, the average cash balance was 2667.75 yuan per business. If the sampling information was accurate and there were roughly 3 million self-employed businesses in the urban area, then about eight billion yuan in currency was in the hands of the urban self-employed businesses alone at the end of 1986, which was about 6.6 percent of the total currency in circulation. No wonder people asked where the money went! The emergence and rapid growth of self-employed and private business have changed the currency demand and circulation picture dramatically. The objective function (which is profit maximization) of these new enterprises determines that they choose whatever medium of exchange to minimize the transaction costs. In China, this medium of exchange is cash for the same reasons as discussed before.

9.5 Development of Free Markets

Most commodities traded in the free markets are agricultural, sideline, and handcraft products. Table 9.6 provides information on the growth of the free markets. We see that the number of free markets in 1988 was more than doubled when compared to 1978. The volume of trade in 1988 was 13 times that of 1978.

As far as the monetization process is concerned, two points are worth mentioning. First, the development of the free markets added another link to the chain of currency circulation. In free markets, currency changes hands among private individuals, instead of from consumers to the governments. In other words, free markets provide an important way by which currency can flow away from the government. Second, a large proportion of trade in the free markets are farmers' sales to urban residents. This provides a channel by which cash can flow from cities to the countryside.

Under the centrally-planned economy, virtually the only way that farmers could get cash was when they sold their products to the government. After that, cash started to flow back to urban areas since a large proportion of farmers' cash income was spent in cities and small towns where they made their purchases of consumer goods. The channel that cash could move from cities to countryside was very narrow until the free markets became significant.

All the evidence provided in this section suggests that there was a monetization process associated with the economic reform, the center piece of which is that the proportion of economic activity conducted with cash has increased.

9.6 Money Flows Among Regions

Now, let's look at the currency distributions among geographic regions. Table 9.7 summarizes the information of moneyflows among regions. The regions listed in the first column are names of provinces, autonomous regions, and the three large cities that have provincial ranking in the administrative hierarchy of China. These provinces can be classified into six regions according their geographic locations: North, Northeast, East, South, Southwest, Northwest in the order listed in Table 9.7.

The second and third columns in Table 9.7 are the stocks of currency in circulation at the end of 1978 and 1986, respectively. The fourth column provides the information of currency injected by the banking system (+) or currency received by the banking system (-) in each region for the period 1978-1986. The number in column 5 is currency net inflow and outflow in each region for the period.

From Table 9.7, the following points are observed. First, the metropolitan areas served as commercial centers, where large amounts of cash net inflow were received. This can be seen from the numbers of cash net inflow for Shanghai, Beijing, and Tianjin. Second, besides the three metropolitan areas, the following provinces received a net cash inflow for the period 1978-1986: Jiangsu, Zhejiang, Fujian, Hunan, Guangxi, and Sichuan. Third, the reason that Jiangsu, Zhejiang, Fujian, and Sichuan were currency net receiving provinces is that the stage of economic development of these provinces is higher than their neighbor provinces. Fourth, Hunan and Guangxi were cash net receiving provinces for the opposite reason. Their economic development was far behind their rich neighbor, Guangdong province. For this reason, their price levels were also lower than Guangdong. As a result, some money in Guangdong flowed to Hunan and

Guangxi to buy relatively cheap raw materials. This explains why Guangdong, the most advanced province in China, was a currency net outflow province for the period. Fifth, all other provinces were cash net outflow provinces, primarily because consumers in those provinces spent a portion of their income in the relatively advanced regions.

The evidence provided thus far suggests that the currency distribution and moneyflows in China have changed significantly in the 1980s. These changes can be summarized as follows: (1) The introduction of the responsibility system, the rapid development of TVEs and free markets, and the growth of the private sector engendered extraordinary demand for currency. (2) The government's share in the national income declined whereas the shares of consumers and the private sector increased. (3) The path of moneyflows became much more complicated than that of the centrally planned economy. One phenomenon that is particularly interesting is called the "outside circulation of money," which is the main theme of the next section.

9.7 The Outside Circulation of Money

Currency in circulation refers to the amount of cash circulating in the hands of the public. By definition currency is circulating outside of the banking system. Nothing is uncommon in this regard. The outside circulation of money refers to two phenomena that appeared in the second half of the 1980s: (1) There were unusually large amounts of cash circulating in the hands of the public. Many transactions, that should be done through bank transfer, were actually conducted by cash. (2) Firms (state owned, collective, and private) started to raise funds by issuing bonds and stocks directly from the public and not through the banking system. In this section, we will discuss the motivation of the outside circulation of money

In China, the ratio of total deposits (households plus institutions) to currency in circulation is often used to indicate if there is too much cash in circulation. This ratio was pretty stable before 1988. The average of this ratio for the period 1979-1987 was 4.80 with a standard deviation of 0.38. By the end of 1989, the currency in circulation was 234.4 billion *yuan* and the deposits to currency ratio decreased to 3.48, which was lower than its mean in the previous period by more than 3 standard deviations. If we use 4.8 as the norm of the ratio, the currency in circulation by the end of 1989 was about 47 billion higher than what it should be.

In the previous discussion, we see that the economic reform brought extraordinary demand for currency. What we have not discussed is that the deposits also increased proportionally. Therefore, the ratio of deposit to currency was pretty steady in the period 1979-1987, during which the Chinese economy was monetized rapidly. Thus the dramatic increase of cash relative to total deposits in 1988 needs further explanation.

The most important factor that triggered the extraordinary demand for cash was the accelerating inflation. In the summer of 1988, the Chinese leaders repeatedly expressed their determination on the price reform. The high inflation expectations led to panic buying and hoarding behavior for both households and firms, which resulted in a drastic decrease of bank deposits (2.6 billion *yuan*) in August 1988 and the inflation rate of that year (officially 18.5%) was the highest in the history of the People's Republic.

In an inflation environment, the incentive of withdrawing cash from the banking system is obvious. First, safety motive. When inflation rate is high, the monetary authority often carries out a tight monetary policy. Those who have money are afraid that some kinds of cash control regulation would prevent them from withdrawing their money in the bank. Consequently, they prefer to hold more cash.

Second, profit motive. Under an inflation situation, it is difficult to get a loan because of the banking system's tight monetary policy. Those who have money can make a profit by lending out their money and charging a high interest.

Third, transaction cost motive. The objective of firms is to maximize profit. They will choose whatever form of payment necessary to minimize the uncertainty and transaction cost. Under a tight monetary policy, the credibility of the banking system is diminished for the following reason. Many branches of the specialized banks are running out of cash and quota of loans. They ask their headquarters and the central bank for help. However, the central bank can not provide enough loans to satisfy the demands for cash and credit. Consequently, specialized banks are forced to delay payments or in some cases even temporarily stop payments. As a result, the uncertainty and transaction cost of payment through the banking system is higher. Firms prefer to hold more cash to facilitate their business. It is plausible to assume that the per dollar transaction cost associated with a payment through the banking system decreases as the amount of payment increases; and the per dollar transaction cost associated with a cash payment increases as the amount increases. Then when the transaction cost of a bank payment is low, cash payment is used for only small transactions. As the transaction cost of a payment through the banking system rises, firms have the incentive to pay cash for larger transactions.

Who holds the most currency in circulation? Zeng (1989) points out that the following three types of economic agents hold a large amount of cash: (1) Private enterprises and self-employed business; (2) those who are in charge of a state-owned or collective enterprises and have signed a contract with the government;[3] (3) those households that became very rich in rural areas through their successful business (usually family business) in agriculture, commerce, transportation, construction, or even manufacture.

The larger amounts of cash held by the above three types of economic agents have the attributes of both capital and income, depending on the cash holders' expectations of future business. If the economy moves to the free-market direction and the government encourages the development of the private ownership, then they will invest those funds as capital and expand their businesses. When the government emphasizes the socialist road and squeezes private businesses, they will stop investing and treat the funds as income. In summary, they can use the currency to invest; to serve as a medium of exchange to conduct their business; to bribe in order to obtain a necessary license; to make loans and earn high interest; to consume if they are pessimistic about their business future; or to convert the cash into hard currencies in the black market and to buy a passport and visa to go abroad.

9.8 Summary

The economic reform of China since 1979 has not changed the fundamental structure of the two-circuit money supply mechanism, although it made the borderline of currency and bank transfer money more obscure. The obvious drawback of this system is that it hinders the intrinsic attribute of money, which requires uniformity and convertibility. The excessive money supplies in 1985 and 1988 are evidence that the two-circuit money supply system does not work very well in a semi-market environment. The problems of the two-circuit money supply mechanism will be faced by the Chinese monetary authority again in the future, because it is deeply-rooted and it reflects the basic contradictions between a market economy and a centrally-planned system.

The monetization discussed in this chapter mainly focuses on the increasing demand for currency, i.e., more and more economic transactions are now conducted in cash. The monetization process has made the chain of currency in circulation longer and more complicated. It created new channels that enable cash to move among individuals instead of flowing back to the government directly. Therefore, it has reduced the velocity of money significantly.

The evidence presented in this chapter indicates that the Chinese economy was monetized rapidly during the period 1979-1984, in which the institutional changes in the agricultural sector, the rapid growth of TVEs, and the self-employed businesses made the demand for currency greatly exceed the normal increase of transaction demand caused by rise in income. Because farmers, self-employed entrepreneurs, and TVEs had little credit in the past, an efficient way to smooth their business transactions and build up their credit was to accumulate their cash balance rapidly. Consequently, the inflation rate was moderate despite that the excess money supply was on average 13.5 percent for currency in circulation in this period. This suggested that most of the excess money supplies were absorbed by the newly monetized economy.

The monetization process has been certainly a function of the institutional changes. For the period 1985-1989, the monetization process was slowed down somewhat. The new institutions created by the reform were stabilized with a more or less normal growth. The inflation rates were much higher even though the excess money supply rates were much lower on average than in the previous period. This indicated that the economy could no longer absorb the excess money supply as rapidly as in the period 1979-1984. The extra money supplies above and beyond the growth rate of real GNP and the rate of monetization resulted in higher inflation. After three years of retrenchment (1989-1991), the monetization and financial deepening process has gained some momentum since 1992, as a new round of economic reform programs launched.

If the monetization process has been mainly the increasing demand for currency, we would expect that the proportion of currency in circulation relative to broad money would increase in this period. However, this has not been the case. In 1978, the currency in circulation accounted for 18.3 percent of broad money, compared with 19.0 percent in 1987 and 23.0 percent for 1988. For most years in this period, the currency in circulation accounted for about 20 percent of broad money. The high proportion in 1988 was an exception. Two factors prevented the cash proportion from growing too high. One was the tremendous increase in bank savings of households. The other was the rapid growth of the bank loans to enterprises. The data in the early 1990s confirmed this observation. The ratio of currency in circulation to broad money was about 19% by the end of 1992.

The basic question that this chapter tries to answer is where the excess money went. We have answered it with a discussion of the monetization process, not because the downward biased official price index and the forced saving hypotheses are inappropriate, but because there has been no detailed discussion on monetization in the literature previously. Actually all these theories are complementary. However, for the period 1979-1984, the monetization process certainly played the major role in absorbing the excess money of the economy.

So far, we have focused our discussion on the currency in circulation. Broader measures of financial deepening, such as the ratio of M2 to GNP (McKinnon 1973) or the ratio of the total financial assets to GNP (Goldsmith 1969), have also confirmed the monetization process in China. Table 9.8 provides the ratio of the total financial assets to GNP for the period 1978-1991, during which the ratio increased from 95.2% to 233.8%.

Further research is needed to estimate the speed of monetization more accurately and to determine how much extra money should be supplied to accommodate the newly monetized sector without causing inflation.

Notes

1. The increase of real cash balance and consumption level are calculated by using a deflator equal to 137.44 in 1986 (based on 1978 = 100). This deflator is a weighted average of the official price index (weight = 0.6) and the free market price index (weight = 0.4) (*Statistical Yearbook of China*, 1989, page 720.).

2. The value of total output is measured by the total value of industrial and agricultural output. It is the sum of the total value of the final products, rather than the value-added. Therefore it has a double-counting problem. On the other hand, it omits the value added of many service sectors in the economy. This measure has been widely used in many socialist countries. It is not comparable with GNP.

3. A typical contract states how many years the contractor controls the firm; how much taxes and profits the firm must pay to the government. The contractor controls the residuals. This is the so-called "responsibility system" in the urban areas, which has been not very successful. Obviously, there are a lot of incentive problems in this kind of responsibility system.

Table 9.1
Distribution of the Currency in Circulation
(All in billion yuan except percentage)

Year	TC	RHC	PR(%)	UHC	PU(%)	IEC	PIE(%)	OC	PO(%)
1978	21.20	12.51	59.01	3.59	16.93	3.82	18.01	1.28	6.05
1979	26.77	16.08	60.07	4.45	16.62	4.69	17.52	1.55	5.79
1980	34.62	21.00	60.65	5.57	15.97	6.10	17.73	1.96	5.65
1981	39.63	24.83	62.64	6.19	15.61	6.53	16.48	2.09	5.27
1982	43.91	28.19	64.19	6.70	15.26	6.72	15.30	2.31	5.25
1983	52.98	24.64	65.38	7.58	14.31	7.99	15.09	2.77	5.22
1984	79.21	50.13	63.29	11.55	14.58	12.76	16.10	4.77	6.03
1985	98.78	59.69	60.42	15.33	15.52	17.44	17.66	6.32	6.40
1986	121.84	72.66	59.64	18.49	15.18	22.46	18.43	8.23	6.75

NOTE:
TC = total currency in circulation;
RHC = total rural household currency balance;
PR = percentage of RHC relative to TC;
UHC = total urban household currency balance;
PU = percentage of UHC relative to TC;
IEC = total currency balance of institutions and enterprises;
PIE = percentage of IEC relative to TC;
OC = currency balance by others (mainly mobile population);
PO = percentage of OC relative to TC.

SOURCE: *Survey of the Distribution of the Money in Circulation, 1979-86*, the People's Bank of China, China Finance Press, 1988.

Table 9.2
Average Cash Balance Per Household
(All in yuan except percentage)

Year	NA	GNA(%)	RA	GRA(%)	UA	GUA(%)
1978	18.14	-	15.44	-	24.28	-
1979	22.74	25.36	19.77	28.04	28.27	16.43
1980	28.99	27.48	25.64	29.69	33.81	19.60
1981	33.23	14.63	30.03	17.12	36.47	7.87
1982	36.79	10.71	33.70	12.22	38.38	5.23
1983	44.07	19.78	41.17	22.17	42.23	10.03
1984	64.49	46.34	59.83	45.32	59.97	42.01
1985	78.13	21.20	71.50	19.50	74.33	23.95
1986	94.00	20.32	85.67	19.82	89.85	20.88

NOTE:
NA = per capita cash balance for the nation as a whole;
GNA = growth rate of NA;
RA = per capita cash balance of rural areas;
GRA = growth rate of RA;
UA = per capita cash balance of urban areas;
GUA =growth rate of UA.

SOURCE: *Survey of the Distribution of the Money in Circulation, 1979-86*, the People's Bank of China, China Finance Press, 1988.

Table 9.3
The Development of
Township and Village Enterprises (TVEs)

Year	Growth rate[a]	Total TVEs employees (million)	Total TVEs output[b] (billion yuan)	As % of total output[c]
1979	11.2	29.09	54.84	8.75
1980	19.8	30.00	65.69	9.28
1981	13.5	29.70	74.53	9.83
1982	14.5	31.13	85.31	10.29
1983	19.2	32.35	101.68	11.04
1984	68.2	52.08	170.99	15.79
1985	59.6	69.79	272.84	20.46
1986	29.8	79.37	345.09	23.28
1987	34.1	87.76	474.31	25.65
1988	22.6	95.45	649.57	26.97
1989	-2.9	93,67	742.84	26.02
1990	11.6	92.65	846.16	26.79
1991	33.5	96.09	1162.17	31.92
1992	44.4	105.8	1768.55	38.54

NOTE:

a. Growth rate of total output of TVEs in real terms deflated by the official price index.

b. Total TVEs output is in current price.

c. The percentage of total output of TVEs relative to the total industrial and agricultural output of the economy (see note No. 2 of Chapter 9).

SOURCE: *Ten Years of Reform*, edited by Tang Mingfong, Beijing Press, 1990, p. 94. *Statistical Yearbook of China*, 1992, Beijing, China, page 54, 389, 390.

Table 9.4
Average Cash Balance of TVEs in 1985
(All in million yuan except the last row)

Item	1984	1985	Growth (%)
Sample size	5374	5666	-
Total cash balance at beginning of the year	5.00	11.15	123.0
Total Cash revenue	569.97	686.62	20.5
Among which:			
Sale revenue	251.05	317.36	26.4
Total cash expenditure	564.92	683.41	21.0
Among which:			
Capital expenditure	233.14	271.10	16.3
Labor expenditure	224.63	315.96	40.7
Total cash balance at end of the year	10.05	14.36	42.9
Average cash balance per enterprise (yuan)	1870	2534	35.5

SOURCE: *Survey of the Distribution of the Money in Circulation, 1979-86*, the People's Bank of China, China Finance Press, 1988, page 407.

Table 9.5
Cash Balance of Urban Self-Employed Business (Getihu)

Year	Urban self-employed workers (million)	Number of business (thousand)	Average cash balance per business[a] (yuan)
1981	1.13	826	330.00
1982	1.47	1132	396.00
1983	2.31	1706	717.37
1984	3.39	2222	1367.44
1985	4.50	2799	1915.99
1986	4.83	2910	2667.75

NOTE:

a. The average cash balance per business was calculated from random samples, which were drawn nationwide. The sample size for 1981 and 1982 are not available. The sample sizes for 1983, 1984 1985, 1986 are 7048, 20480, 15376, 14881 respectively.

SOURCE: *Statistical Yearbook of China*, 1989, Beijing, China, p. 118. *Survey of the Distribution of the Money in Circulation, 1979-86*, the People's Bank of China, China Finance Press, 1988, pp. 345, 405, 514.

Table 9.6
Development of Free Markets

Year	Number of free market	Volume of trade (billion yuan)	Farmers sale to nonfarmers (billion yuan)
1978	33302	12.50	3.11
1979	38993	18.30	4.75
1980	40809	23.54	6.90
1981	43013	28.70	8.94
1982	44775	33.31	11.08
1983	48003	38.58	13.30
1984	56500	45.69	17.00
1985	61337	63.23	29.10
1986	67610	90.65	37.50
1987	69683	115.70	46.10
1988	71359	162.13	59.50
1989	72130	197.36	69.80
1990	72579	216.82	77.33
1991	74675	262.22	90.98
1992	79188	353.00	104.7

SOURCE: *Statistical Yearbook of China*, 1992, page 619.
A Statistical Survey of China, 1993, National Statistics Bureau, Beijing, China, page 97.

Table 9.7
Currency Flows Among Regions, 1978-1986
(All in billion yuan)

Region	Currency at end of 1978	Currency at end of 1986	1978-86 cash issued (+) received (-)[a]	1978-86 cash net inflow (+) cash net outflow (-)[b]
Total	21.203	121.836	100.633	0.00
Beijing	0.310	1.500	-10.183	11.373
Tianjin	0.250	1.225	-0.215	1.190
Hebei	1.390	7.560	9.508	-3.338
Shanxi	0.603	2.550	6.299	-4.352
Neimenggu	0.331	2.250	5.716	-3.797
Liaoning	1.590	6.410	7.271	-2.451
Jilin	0.865	4.050	6.593	-3.408
Heilongjiang	1.180	6.280	8.652	-3.552
Shanghai	0.359	2.157	-15.592	17.390
Jiangsu	1.220	8.530	6.838	0.472
Zhejiang	0.735	4.860	3.183	0.942
Anhui	0.660	4.680	6.053	-2.033
Fujian	0.529	3.120	1.116	1.475
Jiangxi	0.615	2.500	3.220	-1.335
Shandong	1.210	10.570	13.042	-3.682
Henan	1.290	8.610	7.706	-0.386
Hubei	0.984	4.609	4.488	-0.863
Hunan	0.585	4.200	2.508	1.109
Guangdong	1.968	14.501	13.844	-1.311
Guangxi	0.420	2.560	0.334	1.806
Sichuan	1.336	7.400	3.767	2.297
Guizhou	0.470	1.900	2.514	-1.084
Yunnan	0.550	2.700	2.920	-0.770
Tibet	0.051	0.340	0.827	-0.538
Shaanxi	0.660	2.280	1.851	-0.231
Gansu	0.415	1.540	2.087	-0.962
Qinghai	0.125	0.570	1.373	-0.928
Ningxia	0.092	0.484	0.958	-0.566
Xingjiang	0.410	1.900	3.957	-2.467

NOTE:

a. Currency issued by the banking system (+); currency received by the banking system (-).

b. Currency net inflow (+) or net outflow (-) in each region for the period 1978-86.

SOURCE: *Survey of the Distribution of Money in Circulation, 1979-86*, the People's Bank of China, China Finance Press, pp. 20-21.

Table 9.8
The Financial Assets and GNP in China
Data: 1978-1991, in billion yuan except the ratio

Year	Financial assets (FA)[a]	GNP	(FA/GNP)
1978	341.8	358.8	95.2
1979	400.0	399.8	100.3
1980	494.6	447.0	110.6
1981	578.3	477.3	121.1
1982	690.6	519.3	133.0
1983	775.9	580.9	133.6
1984	1054.3	696.2	151.4
1985	1280.9	855.8	149.7
1986	1686.8	969.6	174.0
1987	2093.2	1130.1	185.2
1988	2512.7	1406.8	178.1
1989	3011.7	1599.3	189.2
1990	3723.3	1769.5	210.5
1991	4578.2	1958.5	233.8

NOTE:
a. The total financial assets include all financial claims on financial and non-financial institutions, the composition of which will be defined in Table 16.1.

SOURCE: Xie (1992).

Figure 9.1 The Total Output of TVEs in China

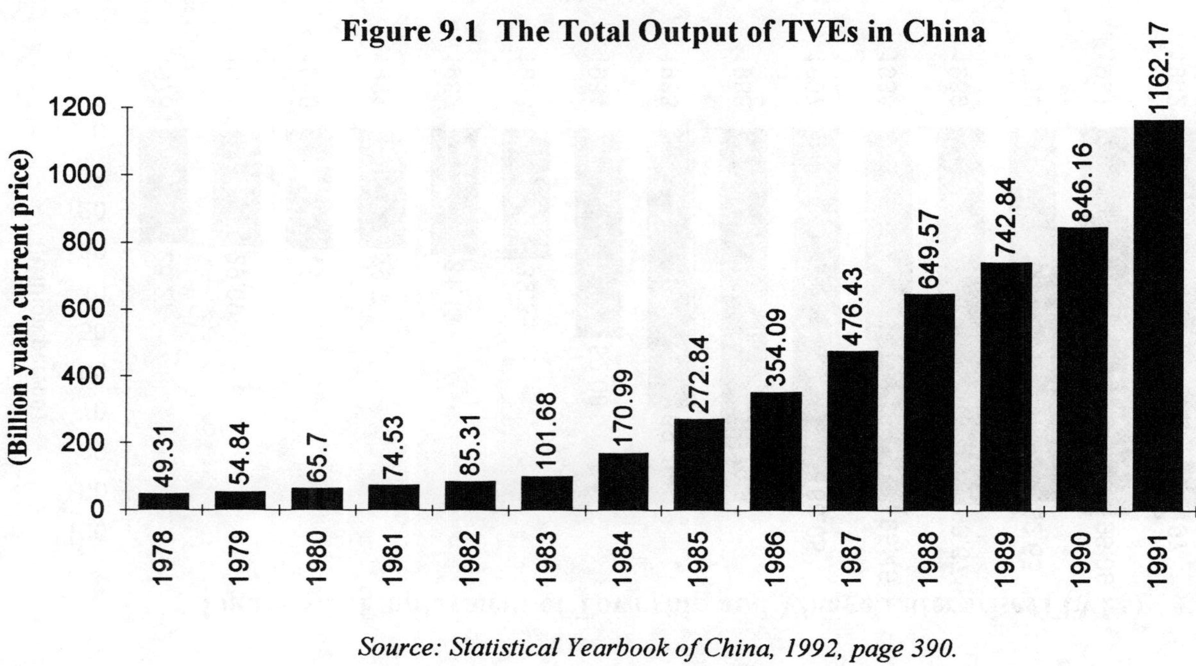

Source: Statistical Yearbook of China, 1992, page 390.

Figure 9.2 Employment of Township and Village Enterprises (TVEs)

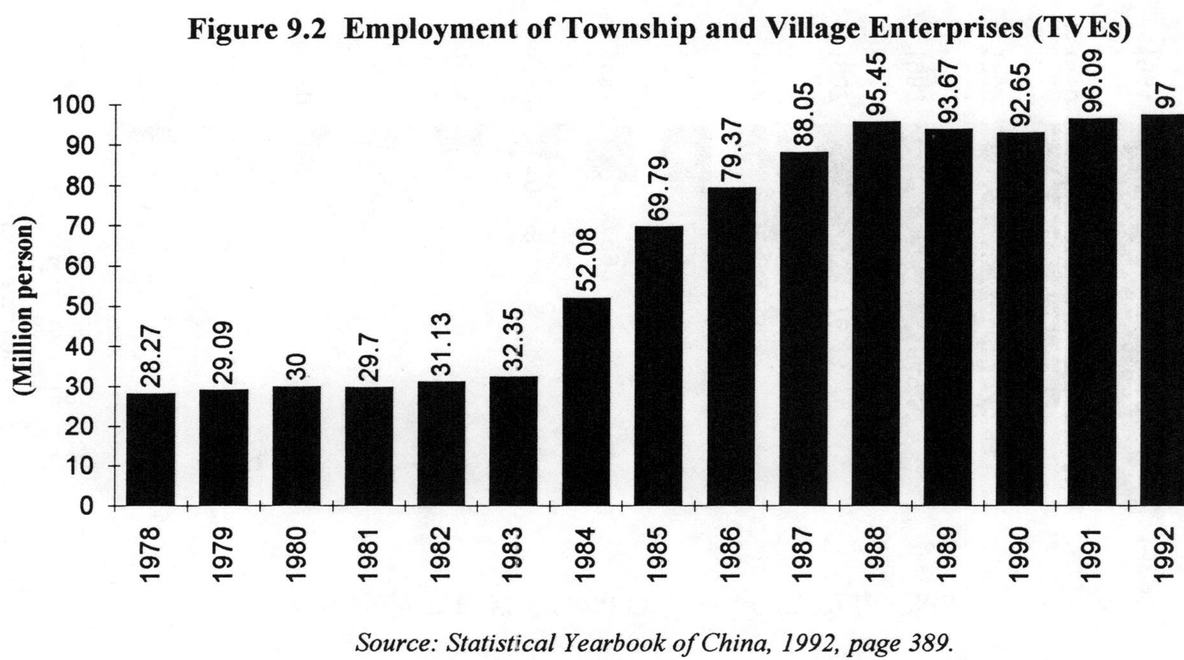

Source: Statistical Yearbook of China, 1992, page 389.

10

Inflation Expectations and Price Instability

The relationship between the level of inflation and its variability has been an active area in the literature (e.g., Okun 1971; Pagan, Hall and Trivedi 1983; Ram 1985). As Friedman (1977) pointed out in his Nobel Lecture, it is its instability, not its level *per se*, that distorts resource allocation and reduces economic efficiency. He related price instability to a lack of predictability of inflation. Undoubtedly this lack of inflation predictability was one of the major reasons that caused the panic buying and hoarding behaviors of both households and firms in China, which resulted in a drastic decrease of bank deposits (2.6 billion yuan) in August of 1988 and made the inflation rate of that year (officially 18.5 percent) the highest in the history of the People's Republic. Chart 10.1 at the end of the chapter shows the rate of inflation for the period 1978-1992.

This chapter tests empirically the hypothesis that the level of inflation is positively related to its variability by using the Chinese data over the period 1953-1991. It contributes to study in this area in the following three ways. First, price instability is traditionally measured by the standard deviation or some moving averages of annual inflation rates. We decompose price fluctuations into two parts: anticipated and unanticipated, and measure price instability by the squared error of inflation forecast, which is defined as the difference between the actual and the expected rate of inflation. Second, the majority of previous results are based on some specific forms of inflationary expectations. We examine the most popular expectation hypotheses, ranging from a very simple static hypothesis to a rational expectation equation estimated by a quite sophisticated sequential model selection criterion (Hsiao 1981) and find that the strong relationship between the level of inflation and price instability is robust under all these inflation expectations. Third, and perhaps more importantly, the level-variability hypothesis is supported by the data from China, where the economic system is very (if not entirely) different from a typical market mechanism. This result certainly increases our confidence in the generality of the hypothesis.

Section 10.1 discusses the measures of price instability and various ways of inflation-expectation formation. Section 10.2 reports the empirical results and provides a diagnostic analysis. Section 10.3 re-estimate the model taking into account of the outlier problem. Section 10.4 offers a brief summary.

10.1 Measurement of Price Instability and Inflation Expectations

There are various ways of assessing price instability, all of which are connected in some way with price dispersion. Traditionally it is measured by the standard deviation and/or some moving averages of the actual rate of inflation (Ram 1985). Glezakos and Nugent (1984) noted that such measures have no theoretical foundation to be related to the level/variability hypothesis. Using some numerical examples, Foster (1978) has shown that even in the hypothetical case where inflation rates lay exactly on a trend line, the standard deviation would rise over time, although it is generally agreed that there has been no increase in variability.

The fundamental drawback of the traditional measures of price instability is that they fail to distinguish the anticipated part from the unanticipated part of inflation. It is well accepted that a fully anticipated inflation would have little real effect. For instance, if everybody could forecast inflation rate perfectly, then the whole economy would adjust accordingly. Consequently, there would be little price instability and loss of efficiency due to uncertainties and distortions. The problem concerned by Friedman and others is the unpredictable nature of the inflation, which is the source of the instability and distortion. Based on this notion, price instability is measured in this chapter by the squared error of inflation forecast, as suggested by Pagan, Hall and Trivedi (1983):

$$Y_t = (p_t - p_t^*)^2 \tag{10.1}$$

where Y_t is the index of price instability, and p_t and p_t^* are the actual and the expected rate of inflation respectively. If we adopt the notion of rational expectations, which asserts that people's guesses about the future must be correct on average, then equation (10.1) simply says that price instability is measured by the variance of the unanticipated part of inflation. It asserts that price instability increases only when a higher rate of inflation is associated with an increase in the variance of the unexpected part of inflation relative to a given information set, from which the expected inflation rate is estimated. The level/variability hypothesis is confirmed if the slope coefficient of the following simple regression is significantly different from zero (positive).

$$Y_t = \alpha + \beta p_t + \epsilon_t \tag{10.2}$$

where ϵ_t is a white noise error term. Notice that the index of price instability Y_t is a function of the actual inflation rate p_t. Of course, they are expected to be related. One may ask whether there is a measure of price instability that is *not* a function of p_t. Generally speaking, the answer is no. Consider the following popular measures of price instability: the standard deviation or some moving averages of the actual inflation rate, the absolute value of the first order difference of the inflation series, and the absolute value of the forecast errors. All of these measures are functions of p_t. The important question here is which among these measures of price instability, is the most appropriate one, and then how Y_t and p_t are related.

Expectation formation is essential to price instability, as the latter is measured by the difference between the actual and the expected rate of inflation squared. If we know the expected rate of inflation, then a price instability index (10.1) can be easily calculated. The question is how people form their expectations. There are many different expectation hypotheses in the literature. Generally speaking, they can be classified into two groups: *ad hoc* expectations and rational expectations. In the remaining part of this section, we discuss some popular expectation hypotheses and how to estimate an inflationary expectation equation based on different model selection criteria (MSC).

Let us first look at three widely used *ad hoc* expectation hypotheses.

$$p_t^* = p_{t-1} \tag{10.3}$$

$$p_t^* = p_{t-1} + \theta(p_{t-1} - p_{t-2}) \tag{10.4}$$

$$p_t^* = p_{t-1}^* + \gamma(p_{t-1} - p_{t-1}^*) \tag{10.5}$$

Equation (10.3) is called static expectations, according to which the anticipated rate of inflation for period t equals the actual rate of inflation in the previous period. If we use (10.3) to forecast, the price instability defined by (10.1) is simply the square of the first order difference of the actual inflation series. Hypothesis (10.4) is known as an extrapolative hypothesis (Turnovsky 1977). It claims that expected inflation equals the immediate past rate of inflation plus a correction that takes into account the trend of inflation over the previous period. If $\theta > 0$, the past trend is expected to continue. If $\theta < 0$, the past trend is expected to reverse. If $\theta = 0$, hypothesis (10.4) collapses to hypothesis (10.3). Equation (10.5) is often described as the adaptive hypothesis (Nerlove 1958), which asserts that the forecast for the current period is equal to the last period forecast corrected by some fraction of the forecast error of that period. In order to calculate the expected rate of inflation based on equations (10.4) and (10.5), we need to know θ and γ. We estimate these two parameters by introducing a wage determination equation. The result is $\theta = -.3687$ and $\gamma = .5585$ (see appendix).

All the preceding expectation hypotheses have systematic errors, which is in direct conflict with the rational expectation hypothesis (Lucas 1972). It is plausible to assume that rational individuals have the incentive to form their expectations by using all information available in order to eliminate systematic forecast errors. Let us now consider several alternative ways to form inflationary expectations that are "rational" in Muth's (1961) sense. To be specific, the rational anticipation of inflation is assumed to be the optimal linear forecasts using the time series model

$$p_t^* = \beta X(t-1) + v_t \tag{10.6}$$

where p_t^* is the expected rate of inflation for period t at period t-1; $X(t-1)$ is the vector of all relevant information available at time t-1, and v_t is a white noise error term. In this study, the information set consists of past rates of inflation and the following lagged macro variables: annual money supply growth (defined as the amount of cash in circulation at the end of year), real national income growth, and the average nominal wage growth. Given the sample size we have, we thought it appropriate to set the maximum lag length to be four years. Therefore, to start with, we have sixteen variables (four variables, each of which has four lags) as possible regressors. We will estimate model (10.6) by a least squares method and use the predicted value as the expected rate of inflation. This approach is consistent with the rational expectation hypothesis, which asserts that on average people's expectations are right.

Now we are facing a typical model selection problem. We start with a higher dimensional space of possible regressors and suspect that some variables in that set might be redundant. The estimates of the model would be more efficient if we were able to eliminate those irrelevant variables. The difficulty is that it is not convincing to exclude any variable in the information set as a possible inflation predictor on an *a priori* theoretical basis. To avoid imposing arbitrary restrictions, we have selected the optimal model by using Hsiao's (1981) procedure, which is based on Granger's notion of causality and Akaike's (1969) final prediction error (FPE) criterion. Hsiao's criterion is a multivariate sequential selection procedure that can determine simultaneously the relevant explanatory variables and their optimal lag length. Its steps can be summarized as follows.

First, all variables must be transformed to stationary series. Roughly speaking, a variable is considered to be stationary if the slope coefficient of its simple regression against time is found insignificant. If time is found significant, then the variable is subjected to first – or higher – order differencing until the time trend coefficient is insignificant. The second step is to determine the optimal lag length of the lagged dependent variable (own lag) by minimizing the FPE criterion, which is defined as

$$FPE(m) = [(T + m + 1)/(T - m - 1)][RSS(m)/T] \qquad (10.7)$$

where T is the number of total observations; m is the lag length (in our case, m = 1, 2, 3, 4), and RSS is the sum of squared residuals. The m^* corresponding to the minimum value of $FPE(m)$ is selected as the optimal own lag.

The third step is to take the optimal own lag m^* as given and to run a bivariate regression that contains the optimal own lag plus one of the remaining explanatory variables. Repeat this step for each explanatory variable in the information set and calculate:

$$FPE(m^*, n) = [(T + m^* + n + 1)/(T - m^* - n - 1)][RSS(m^*, n)/T] \quad (10.8)$$

where n is the lag length of the explanatory variable in the bivariate regression. There is an n^* that minimizes (10.8) for each explanatory variable. As Hsiao has shown, if $FPE(m^*, n^*) > FPE(m^*)$, the underlying regressor is considered not to Granger-cause inflation. Any variable found not to Granger-cause inflation is dropped from the model. The explanatory variable corresponding to the overall minimum of $FPE(m^*, n^*)$ among all the bivariate regressions is the optimal choice of this step.

Fourth, we run a series of trivariate regressions, each consisting of the optimal choice of the previous two steps and a third variable from the remaining regressors. Similar steps as before are taken until all explanatory variables are either included in the model or eliminated.

For comparison purposes, we have also selected the optimal model by the following traditional model selection criteria (MSC): Akaike (AIC) (1974), Schwarz (SC) (1978), Mallow's Cp (1973), Amemiya's PC (1980) and Mean Squared Error (MSE) (Darlington 1968). For detailed discussion of these MSC, see Judge et al. (1985). It is well known that the traditional MSC exhaust all possible combinations of the explanatory variables and then choose the best set of regressors that minimizes the criteria value. By comparison, Hsiao's procedure does the causality analysis for all the explanatory variables in the information set, one at a time, starting with the lagged dependent variable. The order (sequence) in which each potential regressor enters the model depends on which variable is the most "causal" one according to the FPE criterion. It is this sequential causality analysis that distinguishes Hsiao's procedure from the traditional MSC.

From this discussion, we can see that the virtue of the MSC (including Hsiao's) procedures is that they primarily let the data select the optimal model rather than imposing arbitrary restrictions that may lead to a specification error. This is especially important to research on the Chinese economy, about which no mature theory is available. At the same time, we should be very cautious to prevent falling into another trap called "data mining". Because information is sparse, there is no easy solution to this dilemma. In the next section, we shall provide a diagnostic analysis for the optimal models selected by different MSC and also report the results of the level/variability hypothesis testing.

10.2 Empirical Results

China's general retail price index together with indices of money supply, real national income, and nominal average wage are provided in Table 10.1. Table 10.2 summarizes the optimal models selected by different MSC. The regression coefficients for the expected inflation equations are reported in Part A of Table 10.2. Notice that the Schwarz criterion, SC, and Mallows' Cp selected the same model; so did AIC and Amemiya's PC. It is no surprise that the SC picks up the most parsimonious model, while AIC and MSE tend to favor a larger model. As Schwarz (1978) noted, for eight or more observations the SC favors a lower-dimensional model than AIC. For a discussion on the limitations and asymptotic properties of MSC, see Yi and Judge (1988).

Hsiao's procedure also gave us a fairly large model with six explanatory variables. The F-test value and the coefficient of determination R^2 are lower for Hsiao's model than others, reflecting the fact that Hsiao's criterion is subjected to more restrictions. First, as Hsiao's procedure is a sequential one, it could not select the best model from all possible combinations of the regressors. One step's optimum is taken as given for the next step, and it does not allow a backward adjustment. Second, Hsiao's procedure assumes that if a higher-order lag coefficient is non-zero, then all lower-order ones will be non-zero too. This is probably another reason that the model selected by Hsiao's procedure tends to contain more variables.

Because the existence of the lagged variables in these models, multicollinearity might be a problem of concern. The condition index, which is defined as the square root of the ratio of the largest eigenvalue to the smallest eigenvalue of the $X'X$ matrix, is reported. As we can see from Part B of Table 10.2, the condition indices are quite small, indicating that multicollinearity is not a problem for these models.

Another problem that is worrisome is serial correlation among the error terms, as our sample is time series data. Durbin-Watson statistics (DW) are reported. However, since all models contain at least one lagged dependent variable as a regressor, the DW test is not adequate. Durbin's h test is also undefined, because the variance of the lagged dependent variable multiplied by the number of observations is greater than 1 for all models in Table 10.2. Alternatively, we did an equivalent test (Durbin 1970) by estimating the following regression

$$e_t = \alpha + \rho e_{t-1} + \textit{all other regressors}, \tag{10.9}$$

where e_t is the estimated residual of model (10.6). The t ratios of the estimated parameter $\hat{\rho}$ are also reported in Part B of Table 10.2. We can not reject the null hypothesis that there is no serial correlation based on these t ratios, all of which are insignificant. Actually, the evidence is quite to the contrary; it supports the null hypothesis that no serial correlation exists in these models.

One may challenge the models in Table 10.2 by arguing that the structure of the inflationary process might have been changed in China after 1977. To answer this question, the structural stability was also examined by the Chow (1960) test. It is well known that the Chow test is sensitive to the choice of breaking data. We thought it most appropriate to divide the time period under study into two periods: the Mao era (1953-1976) and post-Mao era (1977-1988). As we just have twelve observations in the post-Mao era, it would not be very meaningful to do the Chow test for a regression model with many parameters to estimate. For this reason, we did the Chow test for just the model selected by SC and Cp in Table 10.2. The F statistic with (4, 24) degree of freedom is .436, based on which we can not reject the null hypothesis that the structures of the two periods are the same. A Goldfeld and Quandt (1972) test for heteroskedasticity was also performed for the model, using the same breaking point. The F statistic with (8,16) degree of freedom is 1.07, which again leads to acceptance of the null hypothesis that the error terms are homoskedastic. At first, this result is a bit surprising, because our conjecture was that the post-Mao period is different from the Mao era because of economic reform. However, if we look at the data more carefully, we would find that the situation is quite the way it should be. Basically there are two outliers in the annual inflation rate data that could cause variance to be large. One was in the Mao era (1961), the other was in the post-Mao era (1988). Therefore, as far as the variances of the error term are concerned, it is hard to say that the second period is necessarily different from the first period.

Table 10.3 summarizes the regression results of the effects of the level of inflation on the price instability. For the first three simple regressions in Table 10.3, a complication arises because there is a serial correlation within the unanticipated inflation series when they are estimated from the ad hoc expectation hypotheses. To mitigate this problem, we assume that the error term in model (10.2) falls into a first order autoregressive process AR(1),

$$\epsilon_t = \rho\epsilon_{t-1} + v_t. \tag{10.10}$$

Then the problem is corrected by ρ-differencing, as suggested by Durbin (1960). The estimated serial correlation coefficients (.683, .201, and .189 for the static, extrapolative, and adaptive model respectively) are used in the correction process. The regression results based on the rational expectations are also reported in Table 10.3. It is clear that the slope coefficients of all simple regression models in the table are highly significant, strongly supporting the hypothesis that higher rates of inflation are associated with higher price instability. This result is robust regardless of how people's inflationary expectations are formed. Further, when we replaced the measure of price instability by the magnitude of first-order difference of the annual rate of inflation and the absolute value of the forecast errors, the results were similar to that in Table 10.3.

10.3 The Outlier Problem in the Estimation

(*Background of this section:* The results of the above two sections were published in Yi (1990a). Please notice that the results of Table 10.2 and 10.3 were estimated from the data 1953-1988. This section is from a reply (Yi 1992b) to Professor Hafer's (1992) criticism. In writing this reply, the author re-estimated the model by using the updated data set 1953-1991.)

Professor Hafer (1992) criticizes the results reported in the above section as being not robust. He argues that if the outliers in the data set (the observations of 1960 and 1988) are taken care of, there won't be any significant relationship between the level of inflation and the price instability.

The concern raised by Professor Hafer in his comment over the robustness of the results presented in the previous section is an important one. However, the methodology used by Hafer is inappropriate for the following three reasons. First, it is well known that how outliers should be treated depends on the underlying outlier generating process. If an outlier is generated by a purely random event, then it is useful to model it by using a dummy variable. However, if the outlier indicates some mis-specification of the parametric part of the model, it is preferable to use some kinds of robust estimations. The use of dummy variables suggests that Hafer views the observations of 1961 and 1988 as purely random events. A brief analysis on the inflation in the early 1960s (Chen and Hou, 1986) and in the 1987-1989 period (Yi, 1992a) indicate that in both cases the inflation had some structural background. Furthermore, it is premature to interpret the observation of 1988 as an outlier without looking at the 1989-1991 data. From Table 10.1, it is obvious that if the observation of 1988 were an outlier, so would be the observation of 1989. Anyone who has some knowledge of the inflationary experience in China would agree that treating both 1988 and 1989 as outliers caused by purely random (exogenous) events would misspecifiy the entire dynamics of the inflation process in the 1980s. Therefore, using dummy variables for 1961 and 1988 observations oversimplifies the underlying outlier generating process and is an inappropriate approach to the outliers in this problem.

Second, the estimation of Hafer (1992) has a fundamental conceptual flaw. By using the dummy variable for 1961 and 1988, it violates the basic assumption of formulating expectations: In order to estimate the expected value at time t, one can only use the information up to time $(t-1)$. To be specific,

$$p_t^* = f(I_{t-1}) + v_t \tag{10.11}$$

where p_t^* is the expected inflation rate at time $(t-1)$ for the period t; f is a function; I_{t-1} is the information up to time $(t-1)$. If the function f is linear, equation (10.11) becomes equation (10.6). Using a dummy variable which is equal to 1 for 1961 and zero otherwise is tantamount to say that one knew 1961 was a high inflation year when he estimated the expected inflation for 1961, which makes no sense. Remember the dummy variable is one of the predictors. *Ex post*, it is easy to point out that the inflation rate in 1961 and 1988 are much higher than other years. However, it is problematic to use a dummy variable, which singles out 1961, to predict the expected rate of inflation of 1961. It is not surprising that the two dummy variables are the most important independent variables and have most of the explanatory power in Hafer's estimation.

Third, it is also questionable that Hafer employs the original lag structure (Yi 1990a) while adding the two dummy variables. He justifies this by saying that re-estimating different lag structures would "co-mingle" the issue of lag selection with the effect of outliers. It is skeptical that adding the two dummy variables would change the expectation formulation process significantly and make the original optimal lag structure no longer optimal. The point here is that one should test a hypothesis under the correct specification.

What is the right approach to the outliers in this problem? Well, there are many robust estimation methods in the literature (Koenker 1982). The following is a simple method which is called *bounded influence estimation* (BIE) suggested by Belsley, Kuh and Welsch (1980). This method is used to detect outliers by looking at the change in the fitted value $\hat{y}$ of y that results from dropping a particular observation. Define

$$DFFITS_i = \frac{\hat{y}_i - \hat{y}_{(i)}}{s_{(i)}\sqrt{h_i}} \tag{10.12}$$

where $\hat{y}_i$ is the predicated value when the full sample is used; $\hat{y}_{(i)}$ is the fitted value of y if the ith observation is dropped; $s^2_{(i)}$ is the estimator of σ^2 from a regression with the ith observation omitted; h_i is the ith diagonal of the projection matrix from the predictor space (also called the *hat* matrix), $h_i = x_i(X'X)^{-1}x'_i$; and X is the matrix of the predictors.

Belsley, Kuh and Welsch indicate that $DFFITS$ is a better criterion to detect outliers and influential observations. $DFFITS$ is a standardized measure of the change of the fitted value of y due to deleting a particular observation. Furthermore, they suggest that observations with large $DFFITS$ should not be deleted. Their influence, however, should be minimized by

$$Minimize: \quad \sum w_i(y_i - \beta X)^2 \tag{10.13}$$

where

$$w_i = \begin{cases} (0.34/|DFFITS_i|) & \text{if } |DFFITS_i| > 0.34; \\ 1.0, & \text{otherwise.} \end{cases}$$

Table 10.4 reports the regression results of the inflation expectations models selected by the model selection criteria suggested in Yi (1990a) by using the data for the period 1953-1991. Notice that the lag structures are slightly different from those in Table 10.2. Table 10.4 provides the regression results for both the ordinary least squares (OLS) and the bounded influence estimator (BIE), which is essentially a weighted least squares estimator.

Table 10.5 reports the regression results for testing the level/variability hypothesis. In Table 3, for static, extrapolative and adaptive expectations, which are calculated by using the equations (10.3), (10.4) and (10.5) in the previous section, the level/variability regressions are estimated by the bounded influence estimator. The level/variability regression for rational expectations models (selected by SC, AIC, MSE and Hsiao criteria) reported in Table 10.5 are estimated by the generalized least squares (GLS) for correcting serial correlations.

It is clear that all the slope coefficients reported in Table 10.5 are highly significant, supporting the hypothesis that there is a positive link between the level of inflation and price instability, which is the conclusion of Yi (1990a). It is easy to verify that the bounded influence estimation results also support this conclusion if we use the data for the period 1953-1988. As a matter of fact, the result by using the bounded influence estimator for the data 1953-1988 is qualitatively the same and slightly stronger in terms of the level of significance compared to the results reported in Table 10.4 and Table 10.5.

10.4 Summary

This chapter provides strong empirical evidence to support the hypothesis that there is a positive link between the level of inflation and price instability. This result is robust under different expectation formations. Furthermore, the fact that this evidence is obtained from the time series data of China, where the economic system is quite different from a conventional market mechanism, certainly increases our confidence in the generality of the level/variability postulate. Friedman contends that higher price instability is mainly caused by erratic anti-inflation measures taken by the government. This is more true in China than in the western world, for the Chinese government has more direct central controls over its economy. In fact, the Chinese government did take drastic measures (usually by mandatory administrative orders, rather than through economic levers) to curb inflation several times during the period under study (in 1961, 1985 and 1989-1990), which indeed hindered growth and distorted resource allocation. The policy implication of this study is that a low-inflation, consistent, and stable economic policy is clearly preferable in China.

Appendix to Chapter 10
A Wage Determination Equation

Let us assume that the average nominal wage is determined by the following equation,

$$W_t = a_0 + a_1 N_{t-1} + a_2 p_t^* \tag{10.14}$$

where W_t is the percentage change of money wage and N_t is real national income growth and p_t^* is the expected rate of inflation.

Substituting (10.4) and (10.5) into (10.14) respectively, we get

$$W_t = a_0 + a_1 N_{t-1} + a_2(1+\theta)p_{t-1} - a_2\theta p_{t-2} \tag{10.15}$$

$$W_t = \gamma a_0 + a_1 N_{t-1} - a_1(1-\gamma)N_{t-2} + a_2\gamma p_{t-1} + (1-\gamma)W_{t-1} \tag{10.16}$$

Parameters θ and γ are estimated by ordinary least squares method from (10.15) and (10.16) by using the Chinese data over the period 1953-88. The result is $\theta = -.3687$, which is exactly identified, and $\gamma = .5585$ or .59, which is overidentified. $\gamma = .5585$ is chosen because it has smaller variance. It seems that $\gamma = .5585$ is in the reasonable range of the adaptive expectation literature, yet $\theta = -.3687$ is somewhat odd. Why would people expect the trend of inflation to reverse? Well, maybe they believe the government's promise that China would have lower inflation this year than last year. In any case, we will not argue that this is the right way of inflationary expectation formation. All we claim is that this is one way to do it. Actually, we did use other values of θ and γ in equation (10.4) and (10.5). It does not change the conclusion of this chapter.

Table 10.1
Rate of changes of Price, Money Supply, Real National Income and Nominal Wage in China (All in Percentage)

Year	General retail price	Money supply	Real national income	Nominal average wage
1953	3.4	43.270	14.000	11.211
1954	2.3	4.572	5.789	4.637
1955	1.0	-2.430	6.385	2.890
1956	0.0	42.537	14.108	14.232
1957	1.5	-7.852	4.508	4.426
1958	0.2	28.411	22.026	-13.658
1959	0.9	10.765	8.249	-4.727
1960	3.1	27.698	-1.435	0.763
1961	16.2	31.073	-29.719	1.705
1962	3.8	-15.275	-6.500	10.242
1963	-5.9	-15.586	10.695	8.277
1964	-3.7	-11.012	16.494	3.120
1965	-2.7	13.499	17.002	-1.362
1966	-0.3	19.483	16.962	-2.454
1967	-0.7	12.360	-7.229	-0.943
1968	0.1	10.010	-6.486	-1.429
1969	-1.1	2.237	19.311	-0.483
1970	-0.2	-9.847	23.254	-1.456
1971	-0.7	10.192	6.990	-1.970
1972	-0.2	11.014	2.918	4.188
1973	0.6	9.854	8.290	-1.286
1974	0.5	6.321	1.081	1.303
1975	0.2	3.398	8.305	-1.447
1976	0.3	11.720	-2.677	-1.305
1977	2.0	-4.215	7.799	-0.496
1978	0.7	8.495	12.289	6.977
1979	2.0	26.274	6.995	9.472
1980	6.0	29.323	6.393	13.901
1981	2.4	14.471	4.904	1.121
1982	1.9	10.800	8.296	2.956
1983	1.5	20.656	9.794	3.469
1984	2.8	49.509	13.504	19.538
1985	8.8	24.707	12.705	17.311
1986	6.0	23.341	7.398	16.570
1987	7.3	19.380	9.300	9.335
1988	18.5	41.300	11.400	23.898
1989	17.8	9.841	3.700	13.100
1990	2.1	12.826	4.800	12.700
1991	2.9	20.027	7.200	12.630

SOURCE: The rates of changes in this table are calculated from *Statistical Yearbook of China*, various issue.

Table 10.2 Estimation Results (Data 1953-1988)

PART A: Regression Coeffecients[a]
of the Inflation Expectation Models Selected by MSC

MSC	Constant and Lagged Explanatory Variables				
SC, Cp	C	p_{t-1}	M_{t-1}	W_{t-4}	
	-.833	.529	.103	.301	
	(-.99)	(2.82)	(2.18)	(2.89)	
AIC, PC	C	p_{t-1}	M_{t-2}	M_{t-3}	
	-1.274	.866	-.095	.103	
	(-1.24)	(3.97)	(-1.81)	(2.32)	
	N_{t-2}	W_{t-1}	W_{t-3}	W_{t-4}	
	.153	.151	-.271	.442	
	(2.26)	(1.71)	(-2.57)	(3.83)	
MSE	C	p_{t-1}	p_{t-3}	M_{t-1}	M_{t-3}
	-3.337	.583	.551	.065	.052
	(-2.76)	(2.75)	(2.19)	(1.30)	(1.09)
	N_{t-1}	N_{t-2}	N_{t-3}	W_{t-3}	W_{t-4}
	.102	.114	.151	-.261	.229
	(1.73)	(1.55)	(1.54)	(-2.37)	(1.82)
HSIAO	C	p_{t-1}	p_{t-2}	M_{t-1}	
	-1.717	.437	.207	.104	
	(-1.34)	(1.60)	(.81)	(1.77)	
	N_{t-1}	N_{t-2}	N_{t-3}		
	.071	.111	.041		
	(.78)	(1.17)	(.48)		

PART B. Statistics of the Inflation Expectation Models Selected by MSC

MSC	F-test	Degree of freedom	R^2	Condition index	Durbin-Watson	t ratio of $\hat{\rho}^b$
SC, Cp	11.22	3, 28	.546	2.80	1.81	.06
AIC, PC	7.03	7, 24	.672	4.94	2.11	-1.15
MSE	5.89	9, 22	.707	6.81	1.84	-.17
HSIAO	3.98	6, 26	.479	4.54	1.76	-.68

NOTE:

a. The dependent variable is p_t, the rate of inflation; The explanatory variables are C = constant; p_{t-i} = lagged inflation rate; M_{t-i} = lagged money supply growth; N_{t-i} = lagged real national income growth; W_{t-i} = lagged nominal wage growth. The numbers in parentheses under the coefficient estimates are t-ratios.

b. $\hat{\rho}$ is estimated from equation (10.9).

Table 10.3
Regression Results of the Level of Inflation on Price Instability [Model (10.2)][a]
(Data 1953-1988)

The expected rate of inflation is calculated by	Constant	p_t	R^2	Durbin-Watson
Static	1.870 (.40)	6.710 (6.15)	.542	1.41
Extrapolative	7.769 (.88)	5.324 (2.93)	.217	2.09
Adaptive	4.408 (.62)	6.001 (3.98)	.324	2.08
SC, Cp	3.292 (.98)	3.341 (5.32)	.486	1.79
AIC, PC	4.181 (2.86)	1.607 (5.89)	.536	1.75
MSE	3.870 (3.24)	1.383 (6.22)	.563	2.26
HSIAO	.761 (.19)	5.208 (6.80)	.598	1.63

NOTE:

a. The dependent variable is Y_t, the index of price instability defined as (10.1). The explanatory variable of the simple regression is p_t, the rate of inflation. The numbers in parentheses under the coefficient estimates are t-ratios.

Table 10.4
Inflation Expectations Models Estimated by the OLS and the Bounded Influence Estimator
(Data Period: 1953-1991)

	Ordinary Least Squares				Bounded Influence Estimator			
	SC	AIC	MSE	Hsiao	SC	AIC	MSE	Hsiao
C	-0.960 (-1.10)	-1.195 (-0.94)	-2.129 (-1.91)	-0.910 (-0.90)	-0.824 (-1.40)	-0.752 (-1.03)	-1.612 (-2.46)	-0.689 (-0.97)
p_{t-1}	0.293 (2.02)	0.447 (2.45)	0.273 (1.99)	0.412 (2.77)	0.366 (2.93)	0.522 (3.91)	0.343 (2.90)	0.464 (3.35)
p_{t-3}			0.176 (0.95)				0.213 (1.68)	
M_{t-1}	0.153 (3.31)		0.148 (2.97)	0.139 (3.08)	0.134 (3.83)		0.131 (3.96)	0.114 (3.46)
M_{t-2}		-0.064 (-1.12)				-0.048 (-1.40)		
M_{t-3}		0.115 (2.12)	0.071 (1.33)			0.061 (1.77)	0.022 (0.59)	
N_{t-1}				0.071 (0.97)				0.045 (0.79)
N_{t-2}		0.171 (2.04)	0.099 (1.20)			0.118 (2.15)	0.093 (1.93)	
W_{t-1}		0.169 (1.58)				0.147 (2.28)		
W_{t-3}		-0.235 (-1.92)	-0.192 (-1.67)			-0.116 (-1.33)	-0.115 (-1.24)	
W_{t-4}	0.211 (2.24)	0.274 (2.18)	0.233 (1.97)		0.147 (1.89)	0.186 (2.17)	0.125 (1.43)	
R^2	0.56	0.56	0.63	0.49	0.64	0.66	0.72	0.57

NOTE:
This table reports the bounded influence estimation results for the rational expectations models for the period 1953-1991. It can be regarded as an updated version of the Table 10.2 in this chapter. The dependent variable is p_t, the rate of inflation; The explanatory variables are C = constant; p_{t-i} = lagged inflation rate; M_{t-i} = lagged money supply growth; N_{t-i} = lagged real national income growth; W_{t-i} = lagged nominal wage growth. The numbers in parentheses under the coefficient estimates are t-ratios.

Table 10.5
Regression Results of the Effect of the Level of Inflation on Price Instability
(Data Period: 1953-1991)

Expectation models	Estimated coefficients Constant	p_t	Summary Statistics R^2	DW
Static	6.673 (0.96)	3.880 (2.50)	0.15	1.68
Extrapolative	6.586 (0.90)	3.764 (2.34)	0.14	1.97
Adaptive	2.105 (1.16)	2.087 (3.46)	0.27	1.83
SC, Cp	2.808 (0.87)	3.663 (6.32)	0.51	1.75
AIC, PC	3.826 (1.15)	3.574 (5.95)	0.47	1.69
MSE	1.547 (0.58)	3.618 (7.53)	0.56	1.75
Hsiao	1.503 (0.38)	4.827 (6.64)	0.52	1.82

NOTE:
The dependent variable is Y_t, the index of price instability defined as the predicted error squared, equation (10.1) in this chapter. The explanatory variable of the simple regression is p_t, the rate of inflation. The numbers in parentheses under the coefficient estimates are t-ratios.

Figure 10.1 Inflation in China

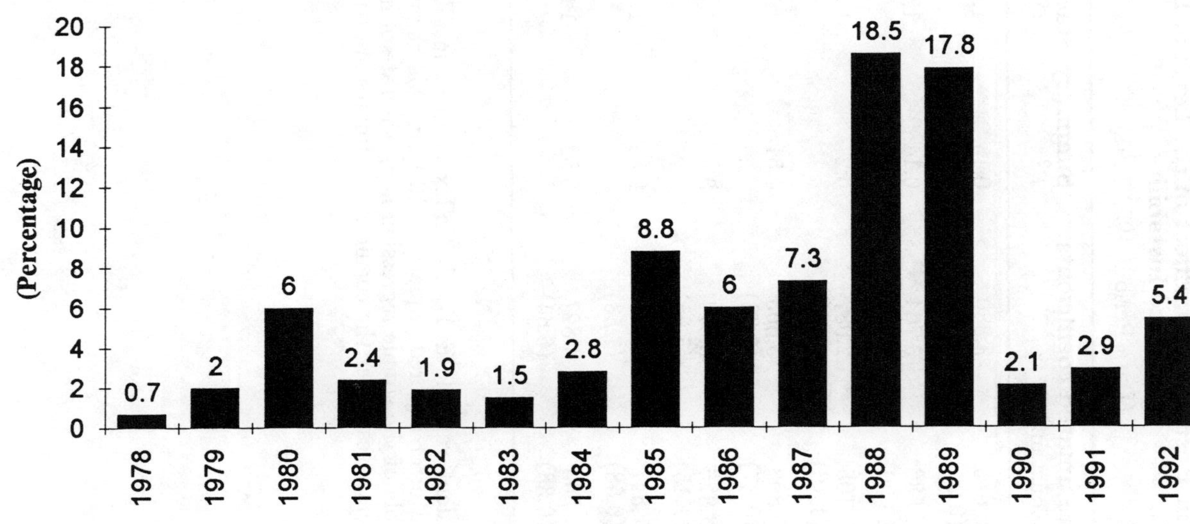

Source: Statistical Yearbook of China, 1992, page 235.

11

The Demand for Money

This chapter estimates the demand for money in China using annual data for the period 1952-1989 and quarterly data for the period 1983-1989. The objective is to find money demand models that would be capable of reflecting the profound institutional changes in the money and banking sector during the economic reform.

The value which this chapter adds to the literature is the following. First, the important characteristics of the demand for money in China are discussed. These "Chinese characteristics" originate from the unique aspects of the Chinese system: a centrally-planned and underdeveloped economy in transition. Second, it is shown that the demand for money has changed profoundly during reform. The monetization process, the establishment of the central bank, and the rapid growth of the private sector provide enough evidence to justify that the demand for money should be estimated separately for the periods before and after the reform. Third, the money demand functions are derived for the semi-reformed economy. Besides the traditional transactions demand variables (Chow 1987), the expected rate of inflation (as a measure of the opportunity cost of holding money) and the monetization process are also incorporated into the demand function. As a result, the explanatory power of the money demand equation has increased significantly. Although this chapter focuses on China only, the problems addressed here are quite common to other centrally-planned and/or developing economies.

Section 11.1 discusses some important characteristics of the demand for money in a centrally-planned, developing economy. Section 11.2 argues that the money demand function has changed in response to institutional changes during the reform. Section 11.3 explains the data set used in this chapter. Section 11.4 derives the money demand functions and presents the estimation results.

11.1 Some Problems Related to Demand for Money in China

In macroeconomics, the demand for money is derived from utility- and profit-maximization by economic agents. In the case of China some assumptions of the maximization process might be questionable. In this section we address some important issues related to money demand in China. These problems are either deeply rooted in a centrally-planned system or in intrinsic aspects of a developing economy.

The Lack of Financial Securities

Demand for money is defined as people's willingness to hold money instead of bonds, stocks, real estate and other types of investments. Financial and real estate markets in China are at a very primitive stage. Most of financial securities and other real investment alternatives were not available until recently. By the end of 1989 the total amount of financial securities (bonds, stock, commercial papers, etc.) held by firms and households was less than 20% of the broad money. Obviously, cash and bank deposits were the primary ways to hold financial assets for consumers and firms. However, bonds and equity stocks appear to be gaining rapidly as a percentage of the total financial asset holdings in the early 1990s.

We discussed the problem of lack of financial securities in Chapter 8 and have asked the question: Does the concept of demand for money make sense, in the face of few other financial securities? To address this question further let us assume, for simplicity, that only two assets exist: money and commodities — no securities (this assumption was close to the reality in China before the reform, and other centrally-planned economies). Under such circumstances the traditional theory of demand for money, such as the transactions and precautionary demand for money, are still relevant. A typical consumer faces a decision of how to allocate his wealth between money and consumer goods. Transaction demand for money is a function of income, and precautionary demand is a function of interest rate or some other measures of the opportunity cost of holding money. The fact that money is the only financial asset does not spoil the analysis as long as people have consumer goods as an alternative. The lack of financial securities becomes problematic when consumer goods are not available and there are forced savings. During the reform, more and more financial securities and real investment opportunities became available. The connotation of demand for money in China is getting closer to the standard definition in the West.

Is There A Monetary Overhang in China?

Feltenstein and Ha (1991) have estimated the extent to which the price level was repressed in China and have shown that the decline in observed income velocity of money was due to involuntary savings by households. They constructed a "true" price index, by which they were able to demonstrate that the "true" velocity of money is statistically constant. By the end of 1988 the true price index was 114 percent higher than the official index, assuming that the two were equal at the beginning of 1979. They concluded that there was a monetary overhang in China in the sense that excess money was being held by households over the nominal value of transactions. Consequently there was repressed inflation and forced saving.

The results derived by Feltenstein and Ha are not surprising except that the fact that the monetization factor is not significant in their paper. If we do not believe the official price index, and postulate that the "true" price is higher, we would get similar results. However, other studies indicate that it is premature to conclude that there is a persistent shortage in the consumer goods market in China (Portes and Santorum 1987) .

Here we argue that, although forced savings existed to different degrees over the period under study, forced savings do not explain the bulk of the changes of broad money for two reasons. First, before reform, the money supply was tightly controlled. Low incomes, combined with high job security, gave households little incentive to save. People did not have much to save to begin with, even if they wanted to. The average saving rate as a percentage of households' income was less than 5 percent on average for the period before the reform (Qian 1988, Bei 1989). Notice that the domestic saving rate as a percentage of national income was very high: 27.8 percent on average for the period 1952-1978. Most of savings were directly from the government. There was hardly any "monetary overhang" before the reform, except for the period 1959-1961, and the price level was frozen stable. Second, household savings have become more and more important since the economic reform started in 1979. At the same time, the consumer goods markets have been in a relatively good shape. Therefore, it is hard to argue that the bulk of the rapid increase of the household saving has been forced.

In this regard one observation is worth mentioning here. During the economic recession for the period 1989-1991, consumer goods market became a buyers' market to a large degree. Most consumer durable goods became available at a better quality and reasonable prices. The inflation rates were 2.1%, 2.9% and 5.4% respectively for 1990, 1991 and 1992. However, aggregate demand was still stagnant until the second quarter of 1991.

During this period, household savings soared continuously. By the end of 1992, the total household savings (in the banking system) reached 1154.5 billion yuan compared to 380.2 billion at the end of 1988. It is safe to say that these savings were voluntary rather than forced.

Which Price Index Should Be Used: Official or Market?

Generally speaking, the demand for money refers to the demand for real money balances. We then have to consider the problem of which price index should be used to convert nominal money into a real balance. Some different conclusions in the literature (e.g. Feltenstein and Ha 1991, Szapary 1989) can be explained (at least partially) as the results of using different price indices.

There are many price indices in China; among them the general retail price index and the free market price index are commonly used. For convenience, we adopt terms which are widely used in the literature — calling the former the official price index (OPI) and the latter the market price index (MPI) — although both of them are calculated and published by the National Bureau of Statistics, an official agency under the State Council.

We discussed the advantage and disadvantage of the two price indices in Chapter 8. The OPI is calculated as a weighted average of official prices, negotiated prices, and market prices. The advantage of the official price index is that it is calculated on a broad basis. Obviously, the advantage of market prices is that they are determined by demand and supply. However, it is not as broadly based as the official price index. Most commodities in free markets are agricultural and light industrial products. And also the MPI tends to overestimate the price level.

Although both official and market price indices have their own limitations, at least they provide two polar cases.[1] The real price level could be somewhere in between. A natural alternative is to create a mixed price index, which is a weighted average of the two price indices. Of course the weights are different from time to time. Generally speaking, at the early stage of the reform, the official price index should be given a larger weight. As the reform progresses, the market price index should be more and more important. A mixed price index is constructed in Appendix A of this chapter.

11.2 Demand for Money with "Chinese Characteristics"

The demand for money in China has changed significantly in the 1980s due to economic development and institutional changes during reform. Consequently, the demand for money function should be estimated separately for the periods before and after the reform. So far, many systematic econometric studies have been done on the Chinese economy at the aggregate level. While all of them reveal some truth, they have a common shortcoming—their econometric models are not estimated separately for the periods before and after reform.[2] If the above claim is valid, then we have to reconsider the econometric results that pool the data in both periods. This is a typical example of Lucas' (1976) critique. It shows that it is crucial to take economic development and institutional changes into full account in building economic models.

Although a book could be written to document the profound changes in the economic system during the reform, as far as the demand for money is concerned, the following three points are important to consider. They are the monetization process (Chapter 8 and 9), people's inflationary expectations (Chapter 10) and the establishment of the central bank and the continuous shaping up of the banking system. Let us discuss them in order.

The Monetization Process

In a developing country like China, the economy can be decomposed into two parts: monetized and nonmonetized. When we consider the demand for money in China, there is an extra demand for money, besides the regular transaction and precautionary demand, caused by the *monetization* process. The term "monetization" here refers to the process in which the proportion of economic activity conducted using money as the medium of exchange increases. As an economy develops not only does the total output increase, so too does the proportion of the economy that is monetized. Consequently, the money supply should increase not only in proportion to the growth of the economy, but also to accommodate the newly monetized sectors. With this in mind, we can define real total national income as $y = \lambda y + (1 - \lambda)y$, where λ is the proportion of the economy monetized.

The monetization process depends primarily on two factors — the degree of economic development, and the institutional or structural change of the economy. In the case of China, both of these factors are changing. There are many alternative ways to estimate λ, the proportion of the economy monetized. Unfortunately none of them is very systematic. After all, in a developing country, economic growth and monetization are often interwoven together. It is difficult arrive at a precise measure of the monetization process.

The previous discussions (Chapter 8 and 9) suggest that the Chinese economy was monetized rapidly during the period 1979-1985, as the introduction of a responsibility system in the agricultural sector, and the proliferation of private businesses and of township and village enterprises engendered an extraordinary demand for currency. Consequently, most of the excess money was absorbed by the newly monetized economy and inflation was moderate in this period. However, since 1985 the monetization process has slowed down somewhat. The economy could no longer fully absorb the excess money. The excess money supplies above and beyond the growth rate of real GNP have mainly resulted in inflation. There has been an other wave of reforms together with a wave of monetization since 1992, triggered by Mr. Deng Xiaoping's talk in Southern China.

Estimating Inflation Expectations

In a traditional money demand model, the interest rate serves as an explanatory variable to measure the opportunity cost of holding money. Interest rates in China have not reflected the opportunity cost of holding money because they were fixed at arbitrary levels that were below market equilibrium rates. One alternative is to use the expected rate of inflation as a measure of the opportunity cost of holding money.

Figure 11.1 shows the natural log of the official and market price indices for the period 1952-89. From Figure 11.1, we see that the official retail price level had been virtually frozen during the period 1952-1978. The market price level was also relatively stable before economic reform except for the period 1960-1963. The inflation rate was extremely low before the reform. Since economic reform started, the Chinese economy has been haunted by rampant inflation.

A detailed discussion on inflation in China is available in Perkins (1988), in Naughton (1991), and in Yi (1990b). Here it is worth emphasizing two points. First, inflation is not only an economic problem, but also a political problem in China. The older generation (who are now policy makers) still remember vividly the hyperinflation in the period of 1947-1949, which certainly contributed to the demise of the Nationalist government. While a 20 percent inflation rate may be acceptable for some developing countries, it is definitely not in China. Second, inflation and inflationary expectations influence the demand for money of households and firms significantly. In 1988, inflation (officially 18.5 percent) in China caused panic buying and hoarding by both households and firms, which resulted in a dramatic decrease in bank deposits (2.6 billion yuan) in August of 1988.

Since the interest rate has been virtually fixed and inflationary expectations are an important factor that influences the demand for money, it would be natural to include the inflationary expectation as an explanatory variable in the money demand equation. In Chapter 10, we have classified different expectations hypotheses into three general categories: ad hoc expectations, rational expectations, and autoregressive process expectations. We have estimated and evaluated various ways of forming inflation expectations using annual data from China and concluded that the rational expectation model and the second-order autoregressive process out-perform other expectation hypotheses in terms of prediction errors. It is also found in Chapter 10 that the static (naive) expectation (Turnovsky 1977)

$$\pi_t = P_{t-1} \tag{11.1}$$

performs fairly well in terms of prediction error, where π_t is the expected rate of inflation and P_{t-1} is the actual inflation rate in the previous period.

The Establishment of the Central Bank

The establishment of the central bank and the reserve system in 1984 brought fundamental changes to the money and banking sector in China. Before reform, the money supply was basically endogenously determined. Money was an accounting tool to accommodate the physical allocation of resources. After the establishment of the central bank and the reserve system, the money supply process has gradually become a money creation mechanism through the multiplier effect. The central bank tries to tune macroeconomic conditions by controlling the money supply. It is obvious that the central bank's control through monetary policy works only when the demand for money of households and firms are responsive to the change of policy instruments (such as the interest rate, open-market operations). These changes have certainly influenced the money demand in China.

When we study the demand for money of China, we should keep the above "Chinese characteristics" and the institutional changes in mind. Before the estimation of the money demand equation, we will first describe the data set to be used.

11.3 Data

The amount of economic information available from China has increased exponentially in recent years. However, due to the difference in economic systems and statistical measures, the Chinese economic data need to be explained before econometric modeling. There are roughly three main sources of data: Chinese official sources, the International Monetary Fund (IMF), and data sets collected by different authors. As far as the money and banking sector is concerned, examples of authoritative publications of the first type are *Statistical Yearbook of China* and *Almanac of China's Finance and Banking*; an example of the publications from the second source is *International Financial Statistics*; examples of the third source are Chow (1987) and Chen (1989). Given the multiplicity of data sources and their disparate measurement techniques, it is common to see different authors use different measures for the same variable in both Chinese and Western literature. In this section, we define and explain the data set used in this chapter. While experts may not agree with our definition, at least it is clear how the variables used in this chapter are defined and measured.

As discussed in Chapter 4, there are at least three ways of measuring M2: the official M2 published by the People's Bank of China in its money survey (Table 4.1); the M2 calculated from the consolidated balance sheet of the state-owned banking system (Table 4.2); and the "money plus quasi-money" series published by the IMF in *International Financial Statistics* (Table 4.3). The first M2 series is available since 1985 and the third M2 series is started from 1977. The only complete M2 series for the period 1952-1992 is the second measure, which is calculated from the consolidated balance sheet of the state-owned banking system by using the following formula:

M2 = (all deposits + currency in circulation - central government's deposits)

Notice that this M2 does not include the financial activities of rural credit co-ops. From Chapter 4, we see that the three measures of M2 are different somewhat, but they are highly correlated. In this chapter, we will use the second measure of M2 to estimate the demand for money. Figure 11.2 illustrates the natural log of real per capita M2 (second measure), deflated by the official and market price indices respectively.

Figure 11.3 displays the natural log of real per capita national income, deflated by the official and market indices respectively. Per capita national income will be used as an explanatory variable in the money demand equation to measure the transaction demand for money. An alternative measure would be per capita gross national product (GNP), which is available since 1978.

The proportion of urban population is shown in Figure 11.4 and will be used as a proxy of the monetization process. The State Bureau of Statistics of China has changed the definition of "urban population" at least a couple of times in the past decade. The proportion of urban population used in this chapter is the data published in *Statistical Yearbook of China* 1990. This definition of urban population was used by the National Bureau of

Statistics for six consecutive years from 1985 to 1991. As we can see from the data appendix of this chapter, the proportion of urban population was unbelievably high according to this definition (51.7% in 1989). Perhaps this definition included all the population in the newly established townships into the category of "urban population," even though those people do not have the official urban resident registration card (*chengshi hukou*). Since 1992, the State Bureau of Statistics has changed the definition of urban population again, which is very close the old definition before 1984. According to the data published in *Statistical Yearbook of China* (1992), the proportion of the urban population was 26.21% in 1989 and 26.37% in 1991. Nevertheless, in this chapter we use the proportion of urban (and township) population data published by the State Bureau of Statistics (*Statistical Yearbook of China* 1990, page 89).

Figure 11.5 demonstrates the nominal seasonally adjusted per capita M2 and retail sales for the period 1983.1-1989.4. The seasonal effect is eliminated by dividing the original series by the seasonal index (Newbold 1984), which are 98.84, 97.83, 97.57, and 105.75 for the M2 series, and 102.47, 97.36, 93.86, and 106.31 for the retail sales, respectively. Retail sales are used in the money demand equation for the period 1983.1-1989.4, because quarterly data for national income are not available and the estimation of quarterly national income is an *ad hoc* and tedious process due to the calculation for the value added of the agricultural sector. Figure 11.6 provides the log of the quarterly official and market price indices for the period 1983.1-1989.4. All the data used in Figure 11.1 to 11.6 are provided in Appendix B.

Although significant progress has been achieved in the data collection process, the limitations of data are still obvious and remain one of the most difficult obstacles of empirical research for China. The data used in this chapter are the best data available and their definitions are explicitly given. Problems such as seasonal effects, nonstationary series, conversion from the monthly data to quarterly data have been carefully dealt with and will be discussed in detail in the next section when the empirical results are presented. Notice that the implication of potential problems due to the use of an imperfect measure of a true variable (errors in variables) is applicable here (although almost all economic data suffer from these problems to a certain degree).

In the next section, we will derive the money demand functions that reflect the characteristics of the Chinese economy. In particular, we will incorporate inflationary expectations and the monetization process into the money demand functions.

11.4 Money Demand Functions and Empirical Results

"The important consideration for money theory and policy is whether the demand for money can be treated as a reasonably stable function of a fairly small number of variables and whether this function can be empirically specified with reasonable accuracy". Friedman (1966) made the above eminent comment twenty-five years ago, the main point of which can still serve as the guideline of estimating the money demand in China today.

In this section, we first discuss alternative money demand models based on the theoretical exposition of the previous sections. We then estimate the money demand functions by using annual data for the period of 1952-1989 and quarterly data for the period 1983-1989.

Deriving the Money Demand Models

The discussion of Section 11.1 suggests two points. First, lack of financial securities does not spoil the analysis of money demand, provided that people have consumer goods as an alternative. Second, there has been no persistent forced saving for the period under study. Consequently, we assume that money demand is by and large equal to the money supply. Therefore, the models discussed below are more or less equilibrium models rather than disequilibrium models.[3] The discussion of Section 3 indicates that the monetization process and inflationary expectations were most significant developments during reform and played important roles in determining the demand for money in China. These two factors will be incorporated in the money demand models in an estimable manner.

With these discussion in mind, let us start with the simplest version of the exchange equation:[4]

$$MV = Py \tag{11.2}$$

or alternatively,

$$m = (1/V)y = ky \tag{11.3}$$

where y is the real national income, $m = (M/P)$ is real money balance and $k = (1/V)$ is the Cambridge k. Notice that the exchange equation is true for both aggregate and per capita data. If k is constant, then it is easy to show that the income elasticity for real money balance is equal to 1. To test whether the income elasticity is equal to unity, we have our first model, which is derived by taking the natural log of equation (11.3) and adding a dummy variable at the end to distinguish the period before reform (1952-1978) from the reform period (1979-1989).

$$Model\ I: \quad ln(m) = C + ln(y) + D \tag{11.4}$$

where $C = ln(k)$. If we believe that the modified exchange equation discussed in chapter 8 is more appropriate (equation 8.5), then we have

$$Model\ II: \quad ln(m) = C + ln(y) + ln(\lambda) + D \qquad (11.5)$$

Equation (11.5) is similar to equation (11.4), except that it has an additional variable, λ, which is the proportion of the monetized economy.

The most difficult task of estimating equation (11.5) is to find a proper λ. There are two ways to tackle this problem. The first is to estimate λ. Because the monetization process is very complicated and many factors have been involved, it is extremely difficult to find an estimator that could mimic the entire monetization process for the whole country. Even if there is an acceptable formula, it would be a formidable task to estimate it due to the data availability problem. The second way is to find an observable variable that can reasonably approximate λ. It is plausible to use the urban percentage of the population (UP) to approximate the monetization process, since it is generally accepted (Yi 1991) that urbanization is highly positively correlated with the monetization process. However, one difficulty is that the term "urban" was redefined in 1984. Therefore, the urban population series published in *Statistical Yearbook of China* is not really consistent. Nonetheless, it is still one of the better proxies, since other series suffer more or less the same problem. For simplicity, we will use the urban percentage of population to approximate λ in this chapter. Alternative measures that could represent the monetization process are the total volume of transactions in free markets, the number of free markets, the total retail sales by farmers to city dwellers, etc. The total value of transactions in free markets has also been used as a proxy of the monetization process in the money demand equation and the result of the estimation is qualitatively the same.[5]

We can regard equations (11.4) and (11.5) as the conditional probability of the dependent variable given independent variables. In other words, there is an unobservable stochastic error term attached to each model.

The Estimation Method

In a provocative study, Nelson and Plosser (1982) find evidence that most macroeconomic time series behave like random walks. Plosser and Schwert (1978) also argue that with most economic time series it is usually better to work with differenced data rather than data in levels. They show that the risk associated with an underdifferenced model is much larger than that of an overdifferenced model. To investigate whether the data used in this chapter are random walks, some kind of unit root test should be performed. Both from visual inspection of the data plots and from the reform experience in China, it is obvious that the structure of demand for money has changed since reform. Perron (1990) suggests a test for a unit root in a time series with a changing mean, which allows a one-time change in the structure of the series at time T_B; note that $(1 < T_B < T)$, where T is the sample size. Part A of Table 11.1 reports the results of the Perron test. In our study, the break point is chosen to be 1978, when reform started. Hence, the ratio between T_B and T, λ, is equal to 0.73. The critical value (Perron, 1990) for $T = 50$ and $\lambda = 0.70$ at the 5 percent significance level is -3.39 for the distribution of $t_{\hat{\alpha}}$. By looking at $t_{\hat{\alpha}}$ in Part A of Table 11.1, it is clear that we cannot reject the null hypothesis that there is a unit root for all the series under consideration at the 5 percent significance level. The standard Dickey-Fuller (1981) test is biased toward nonrejection of the hypothesis of a unit root when the full sample is used and there is a structural change. The correct way of using the Dickey-Fuller test is to test a series in which no structural change is assumed. Part B of Table 11.1 provides the F statistic of the Dickey-Fuller test for the periods 1952-1978 (annual data) and 1983.2-1989.4 (quarterly data), respectively. Once again, the standard Dickey-Fuller test for the separate periods fails to reject the null hypothesis that the time series have a unit root. Recall that the critical values of the Dickey-Fuller test are higher than those of the commonly used F test. The 5 percent critical values are 7.24 and 6.73 for sample sizes equal to 25 and 50, respectively.

From the results in Table 11.1, we cannot reject the null hypothesis at the 5 percent level that they are random walks for all the time series data described above. On the contrary, the evidence strongly suggests that most time series under consideration behave like random walks (the estimated coefficient for the time trend is close to zero and the first order correlation coefficient is close to one). Since a random walk does not have a finite variance, a regression of one against another can lead to spurious results. The Gauss-Markov theorem would not hold and ordinary least squares (OLS) would not yield a consistent parameter estimator.

To mitigate the nonstationary nature of the data set, we use the general differencing approach (Box-Jenkins 1976, transfer function model), which is analogous to generalized least squares (GLS). Harvey (1981) calls this method the two-step full transform method. For expository purposes, we can rewrite the two money demand models, equations (11.4) and (11.5), in the standard matrix form

$$y = X\beta + \epsilon \tag{11.6}$$

where y is the dependent variable, X is the design matrix, β is the parameter, and ϵ is the error term and is assumed to have a first order serial correlation structure. In the first step, ordinary least squares (OLS) is applied to equation (11.6) and the estimated error terms are obtained by $\hat{\epsilon} = y - Xb$, where b is the OLS estimate of β. The first order correlation coefficient of the error terms is estimated by an iterative process until it converges from the following equation

$$\hat{\epsilon}_t = \rho\hat{\epsilon}_{t-1} + v_t \tag{11.7}$$

where v_t is white noise. In the second step, the variance-covariance matrix of ϵ, $\sigma^2 W$, is computed and the GLS estimator

$$\hat{\beta} = (X'W^{-1}X)^{-1}X'W^{-1}y \tag{11.8}$$

is obtained. The GLS estimates, and the estimated first order correlation coefficient, $\hat{\rho}$, are reported in Tables 11.2, 11.3 and 11.4. The t-ratios of the regression coefficients are given in parentheses. If the estimated $\hat{\rho}$ is close to unity, then the above procedure and first-differencing approach should yield similar results. For all GLS estimates obtained in this chapter, we can reject the null hypothesis that the residual term is non-stationary at the 5 percent significance level. In other words, it is highly likely that the residual terms for all the final money demand models are stationary.

The Demand for Money, 1952-1989

Table 11.2 summarizes the regression estimation results for the two models discussed above by using the annual data for the period 1952-1989. Each model is estimated by using the official, market, and mixed (Appendix A) price indices, respectively as deflators.

The following points can be observed from Table 11.2. First, Model I provides a first-step approximation by using income as the only explanatory variable. In Model I, the coefficients of income elasticity are close to unity, indicating that the growth of real per capita income and per capita money demand have increased at the same pace. The dummy variable D in Model I is significantly different from zero, suggesting that the demand for money is different for the periods before and after the reform.

Second, if we add the monetization factor into the model, then the income elasticity decreases (from about unity in Model I to about 0.75 on average in Model II). This is quite natural since part of the money demand increase is explained by the monetization process. Here, the urban percentage of population is used as a proxy of the monetization process.

The estimated urban population elasticity in Model II suggests that a 1 percent increase in the urban percentage of the population would cause a 0.81 percent to 0.95 percent increase in demand for real money, depending on which price index is used.

Third, from Table 11.2 we see that the parameters estimated by the official price index and the market price index serve as two polar cases of the estimation. It is logical to infer that the "true underlying parameter", if there is one, would lie somewhere in between. The parameters estimated by using the mixed price index are usually in between the two polar cases, although not always.

Fourth, it is not surprising to see that the dummy variable in Model II has lower t-ratios than those of Model I. One explanation might be that in Model I, the dummy variable mitigates the misspecification bias of omitting a true (monetization) variable. Part of the variations due to the monetization process are captured by the dummy variable in Model I. Nonetheless, the dummy variables in Model II are all significant at the 15 percent level, suggesting again that the demand for money is different before and after the reform. In summary, the two models in Table 11.2 together shed light on the long-run money demand trend in China.

Another way to confirm that the demand for money has changed during the reform is to apply a Chow (1960) test to Model I and Model II, using 1952-1978 as the first period and 1979-1989 as the second period. We have conducted the Chow test, the F statistic for Model I is 23.0 with (2, 34) degrees of freedom; the F statistic for Model II is 22.5 with (3, 32) degrees of freedom. In both cases, the null hypothesis that the demand for money is the same for the two periods is rejected. Next, we will estimate the demand for money for the two periods separately.

The Demand for Money, 1952-1978

Table 11.3 reports the estimation results of the demand for money (Model II) for the period 1952-78. A comparison with the estimation result for the entire period 1952-1989, yields the following two points. First, the estimated income elasticity in Table 11.3 is quite similar to that in Table 11.2. The intercepts in Table 11.3 are much smaller (bigger in absolute value) compared to those in Table 11.2. Second, the estimated elasticity of the urban percentage of population in Table 11.3 is much greater than that in Table 11.2. The economic interpretation is that the urban percentage of population series had first increased rapidly in the period 1952-1960 and had remained fairly stable for the period 1961-1978. This pattern fits the per capita M2 series very well up to a constant, keeping other variables fixed.

This constant is the estimated elasticity of the urban population. The high value (approximately equal to 2) of the elasticity of urban population explains the rapid growth of per capita M2 in the period 1952-1960. It was true that for a 1 percent increase in urban population, there was a roughly 2 percent increase in per capita M2, keeping other variables constant in the period 1952-1960. For the period 1961-1978, the urban population series had little variation, coinciding with the fact that the monetization process was frozen during this period. The main explanatory power of the variation of M2 came from the per capita national income series for the period 1961-78. These patterns can be seen by comparing Figures 11.2, 11.3 and 11.4 at the end of this chapter.

The Demand for Money, 1983.1-1989.4 (Quarterly Data)

The money demand functions in Tables 11.2 and 11.3 ignored the measure of the opportunity cost of holding money. As we discussed before, interest rates in China have been strictly controlled and virtually fixed at a level that was far below the equilibrium level. Consequently, interest rates could not reflect the opportunity cost of holding money. One alternative is to use inflationary expectations as a proxy for the measure of the opportunity cost of holding money. However, as the economic system changes, the way that people form their inflationary expectations also changes. It is hardly convincing to estimate inflationary expectation from 1952 to 1989, due to drastic institutional changes after 1978. In fact, there was very little inflation before 1978, except in the period 1959-1961.

Fortunately, we have quarterly data for the period 1983.1-1989.4 (in Figures 11.5 and 11.6), thanks to a series of publications of economic information in the 1980s, including periodicals such as *The Monthly Bulletin of Statistics of China* and *China Finance*.

If we use the last period's actual inflation rate as the expected rate of inflation in the money demand function as an explanatory variable to measure the opportunity cost of holding money, we have

$$ln(m) = C + ln(rs) + \pi + ln(UP) \tag{11.9}$$

where (rs) is retail sales in real term, which is a proxy of income variable, π is the expected rate of inflation defined by equation (11.1), and UP is the urban percentage of population. Again, the stochastic error term attached to the end of equation (11.9) is omitted.

Equation (11.9) deserves more discussion. The retail sales, rs, is used because quarterly national income data are not available.[6] The static expectation is chosen in equation (11.9) for the following reasons. First, using the static expectation for this period is intuitively plausible. Inflation is a new phenomenon for the People's Republic. Most people (including a lot of government officials) do not understand the mechanism of inflation very well. They are fairly "naive" in a sense captured by static expectations. Second, the empirical evidence (the panic buying behavior in 1988 and massive saving behavior in 1989 and 1990) in China supports the static expectation formulation. Static expectations mimic the public's inflationary expectations reasonably well in terms of the mean squared error of prediction, especially when we consider the quarterly data. Third, use of static expectations is simple. We would like to use the simplest approach to convey the main points of the chapter without falling into the complications of how inflationary expectations are formed. For instance, if one uses adaptive or extrapolative expectations, then the question is why adaptive and why extrapolative. If one uses rational expectations, then the question is of how to select the model — why use this model selection criterion instead of an other one? Fourth, static expectations make sense by themselves in the money demand equation. They say that people's demand for money of this quarter depends (inversely) on the actual inflation rate of the previous quarter.[7] Equation (11.9) is estimated by the GLS method and the result is summarized in Table 11.4.

Equation (11.7) assumes that the error term is a first order autoregressive process. For the quarterly data, we are also concerned with the possibility of higher order serial correlation. Breusch (1978) and Godfrey (1978) propose some simple tests for higher order serial correlations in a fairly general setting. These tests are derived from the Lagrange Multiplier (LM) principle. The LM test is conducted for the residuals terms estimated by GLS for the quarterly data 1983-1989. Because of the limited degrees of freedom in our sample, we believe that going back four quarters is sufficient. The possible error structure is

$$\epsilon_t = \rho_1 \epsilon_{t-1} + \rho_2 \epsilon_{t-2} + \rho_3 \epsilon_{t-3} + \rho_4 \epsilon_{t-4} + v_t \qquad (11.10)$$

We are interested in testing the null hypothesis $H_o : \rho_1 = \rho_2 = \rho_3 = \rho_4 = 0$. The test statistic is distributed as a Chi-square distribution with four degrees of freedom (Maddala 1992) for a detailed discussion of the testing procedure). The χ^2 statistics are summarized in last column of Table 11.4, from which we cannot reject the null hypothesis (the critical value of the χ^2 distribution with four degrees of freedom is 9.49). In other words, the LM test result does not indicate that higher order serial correlation is a problem for the quarterly data.

The remaining results in Table 11.4 are self explanatory. If we use the mixed price index case as an example, the estimated elasticity for per capita retail sales is 0.65, the estimated elasticity for urban population is 0.51, and as the expected inflation rate increases, the per capita demand for real balances of money drops by a small fraction. It is worth mentioning that the coefficients of the inflationary expectation variable have the right sign (negative) and are significant at the 5 percent level for all three cases, although they are quite small in magnitude.

The parameter estimates in Table 11.4 seem plausible. The result that the coefficients of the inflation expectation variable are highly significant in all three cases indicates that inflationary expectations have played an important role in money demand. On the other hand, the small magnitude of these coefficients reflects the fact that although the inflationary expectation is a significant factor that influences money demand, it is still a small one compared to the transactions demand and the monetization process for the period.

11.5 Summary

Both the theoretical analysis and statistical evidence (Chow test) indicate that the demand for money in China has changed significantly before economic reform. Consequently, the demand for money is estimated separately for the two periods. The results of the Dickey-Fuller test indicate that most time series data used in this chapter behave like random walks or have random walk components. An appropriate differencing transformation must be performed before the money demand equation is estimated. In this chapter, general ρ-differencing is used to the original data and the final money demand equation is estimated by GLS. For all the GLS estimates obtained, we can reject the null hypothesis that the residual term is nonstationary at the 5 percent significance level. The LM test results do not indicate that higher order serial correlation is a problem for the quarterly data used in the chapter.

The monetization process and the inflationary expectations are incorporated in the money demand functions in this chapter. Since economic reform started, the introduction of a responsibility system in the agricultural sector and the astonishing growth of the township and village enterprises and private businesses have engendered an extraordinary demand for currency. The monetization process is certainly an important factor in estimating the demand for money. The preliminary results of this study indicate that including a monetization variable in the money demand function has increased its explanatory power significantly.

The expected rate of inflation provides a feasible alternative to estimating the opportunity cost of holding money. However, there is no consensus on how to estimate inflationary expectations empirically. One way to mitigate this problem is to estimate equation (11.9) by using inflationary expectations calculated from different models and see how robust the result is. In our investigation, the estimated coefficients of the inflationary expectation variable are statistically significant for various expectation formations. These results strongly suggest that inflationary expectation is a significant factor that influences money demand, although its magnitude is still small compared to the influence of transactions demand and the monetization process.

The results of this chapter have clear policy implications. First, it suggests that the growth rate of the money supply should accommodate both GNP growth and the monetization process. Each important reform step is associated with a monetization consequence. In the past, the introduction of the responsibility system in the rural area and the change of the investment scheme from the fiscal allocation method to bank loans caused extraordinary demand for money. Future reform in the housing sector and increasing the size of the stock and bond markets will certainly have monetization consequences, perhaps different ones. The central bank should anticipate the demand for money changes caused by a reform and formulate its monetary policy accordingly. Second, low inflation and consistent monetary policy are clearly preferable since inflationary expectations are very important in determining the money demand, and a high inflationary expectation would cause instabilities in the economy. Maintaining a low level of inflation is particularly difficult when the central government has a huge deficit. Discipline in the money supply require a more developed financial market — especially the bond markets — and a relatively independent central bank. Third, the control over interest rates should be gradually relaxed so that interest rates can be used in the money demand equation to reflect the true opportunity cost of holding money in the future. Without market equilibrium interest rates, it is impossible for the financial market to function properly. A market interest rate is also a necessary condition for an effective and feasible reform in the housing sector.

The present discussion should be regarded as a first step towards estimating the money demand in China. Future research is needed in the area of the monetization process and in how to estimate with more accuracy the proportion of the economy that is monetized. More sophisticated econometric techniques (error correction models and the cointegration approach) are worth exploring with this data set. The autoregressive conditional heteroskedasticity (ARCH) and generalized ARCH (Engle 1982) models are also attractive if one believes that the variance is time dependent for the period 1983-1989.

Notes

1. From Figure 11.1, it is clear that the *price level* measured by the market price index is always higher than that measured by the official price index since 1957. However, this is not always true for the inflation rate. The inflation rate measured by the MPI is not necessarily always greater than that measured by the OPI.

2. For example, Chow (1987) estimates the demand for money in China by using the data for 1952-1983; in Feltenstein and Farhadian (1987), the money supply and repressed inflation are estimated for the period 1954-1983; Chen (1989) examines the causal relationship between the monetary and other macroeconomic variables for the period 1951-1985; Portes and Santorum (1987) estimate the excess demand in China by using the sample period 1955-1983.

3. There is only one observation for money, we assume that it is the money supply as well as money demand.

4. Chow (1987) uses a similar model based on the quantity theory of money except he does not have monetization and inflationary expectation variables in his model. For a detailed discussion on the general functional forms of a money demand equation, see Hendry and Ericsson (1991) and Friedman and Schwartz (1991).

5. If one accepts that estimating λ is not feasible due to the lack of available data, then using an observable variable to approximate the monetization process is the only alternative. The disadvantage of using this approach is that no matter which variable is selected, it can only mimic part of the monetization process and some important aspects would be left out. Here we choose the urban percentage of population as the proxy without claiming that it represents the entire monetization process. What we can say, at least, is that including the urban percentage of population in the money demand equation makes sense by itself: Urbanization creates a demand for money.

6. Because agricultural products still account for a large proportion of the national income and their production cycle is a year, estimating the quarterly national income is tedious and less rewarding. We therefore use retail sales to approximate the transaction demand for money.

7. Alternative ways to estimate the expected rate of inflation have been also tried (e.g. second order autoregressive process, rational expectation models selected by information model selection criteria (Hsiao 1981)), the results are very similar to those presented in Table 11.4. Readers are encouraged to use other expectational formulations to check the robustness of the estimation.

Table 11.1
Testing For Unit Roots

PART A
Perron's Full Sample Unit Root Tests with Changing Mean for 1952-1989 Annual Data

Series (y_t)	$\hat{\mu}$	$t_{\hat{\mu}}$	$\hat{\gamma}$	$t_{\hat{\gamma}}$	$\hat{d}$	$t_{\hat{d}}$	$\hat{\alpha}$	$t_{\hat{\alpha}}$
M2O	0.38	2.94	0.16	2.64	0.03	0.36	0.92	-2.65
M2M	1.14	2.83	0.45	2.68	-0.10	-0.39	0.69	-2.74
NIO	0.51	1.47	0.09	1.34	-0.03	-0.28	0.90	-1.42
NIM	2.42	3.32	0.35	2.52	-0.12	-0.41	0.48	-3.31
$ln(UP)$	0.18	1.42	0.08	2.57	-0.03	-0.55	0.94	-1.37

NOTE:
M2O = log of the real per capita M2 deflated by official price index;
M2M = log of the real per capita M2 deflated by market price index;
NIO = log of the real per capita national income deflated by official price index;
NIM = log of the real per capita national income deflated by market price index;
$ln(UP)$ = log of the percentage of urban population.
The regression is:

$$y_t = \mu + \gamma D_t + dD(TB)_t + \alpha y_{t-1} + \sum_{j=1}^{k} c_j \Delta y_{t-j} + v_t$$

where $D_t = 0$ if $t \leq T_B$ and 1 otherwise; T_B is equal the year 1978 (the 27th observation), in which the change occurred; $T = 38$; $D(TB)_t = 1$ if $t = (T_B + 1)$ and 0 otherwise; $\Delta y_{t-1} = (y_{t-1} - y_{t-2})$ and $k = 1$.

All the t statistics are for testing the null hypothesis that the parameter is equal to zero except $t_{\hat{\alpha}}$, which is the t statistic for testing the null hypothesis that $\alpha = 1$. Thr critical value for the distribution of $t_{\hat{\alpha}}$ for $\lambda = 0.7$, $T = 50$ at 5 percent significant level is -3.39 (Perron 1990).

Table 11.1 continues

Table 11.1 continues from the previous page

Table 11.1
Testing For Unit Roots

PART B
F Statistics of the Dickey-Fuller Test

	1952-1978 Annual Data				
Time series	M2O	M2M	NIO	NIM	UP
$F(2,21)$	4.16	6.25	7.02	4.16	2.89

	1983.1-1989.4 Quarterly Data				
Time series	M2O	M2M	NIO	NIM	UP
$F(2,22)$	1.81	3.36	2.78	2.45	4.77

NOTE:

The critical values for the Dickey-Fuller test are higher than the regular F test. The 5% critical values are 7.24, 6.73 for sample sizes equal to 25 and 50, respectively.

Table 11.2
Estimation of Money Demand Function
Annual Data: 1952-1989

PART A: Estimation of Model I (equation 11.4)

Money demand	C	$ln(y)$	D	R^2	DW	$\hat{\rho}^a$
M2O	-2.269 (-2.59)	1.235 (7.42)	0.273 (1.95)	0.722	1.268	0.805 (7.91)
M2M	-0.397 (-0.92)	0.864 (9.89)	0.419 (3.25)	0.791	1.322	0.793 (7.63)
M2W	-0.944 (-1.46)	0.981 (7.88)	0.360 (2.68)	0.718	1.311	0.808 (8.01)

PART B: Estimation of Model II (equation 11.5)

Money demand	C	$ln(y)$	$ln(UP)$	D	R^2	DW	$\hat{\rho}$
M2O	-2.365 (-3.24)	0.719 (3.76)	0.949 (3.96)	0.185 (1.55)	0.814	1.285	0.802 (7.72)
M2M	-2.427 (-4.65)	0.792 (11.76)	0.810 (5.01)	0.188 (1.75)	0.882	1.356	0.803 (7.75)
M2W	-2.327 (-3.88)	0.752 (7.06)	0.869 (4.64)	0.164 (1.47)	0.824	1.340	0.826 (8.41)

NOTE:

C = intercept; M2O, M2M and $ln(UP)$ are defined as in Table 11.1; M2W = log of the real per capita M2 deflated by the mixed price index; $ln(y)$ = log of the real per capita national income; D = dummy variable, D = 0 for the period 1952-1978, D = 1 for 1979-89; R^2 = coefficient of determination of the transformed (GLS) model; DW = Durbin-Watson test for the transformed (GLS) model. The t-ratios of the regression coefficients are in parentheses.

a. $\hat{\rho}$ = the estimated first order correlation coefficient from the original (untransformed) data. $\hat{\rho}$ is used to estimate the variance-covariance matrix of the error term, which is used in the generalized least squares (GLS) estimation.

Table 11.3
Estimation of Money Demand Function
From Annual Data: 1952-1978

Money demand	C	$ln(y)$	$ln(UP)$	R^2	DW	$\hat{\rho}$
M2O	-6.606	0.899	2.129	0.809	1.202	0.496
	(-5.99)	(4.82)	(4.76)			(2.74)
M2M	-5.137	0.772	1.805	0.840	1.322	0.581
	(-4.90)	(9.67)	(5.17)			(3.42)
M2W	-6.145	0.834	2.078	0.815	1.168	0.529
	(-5.57)	(6.71)	(5.30)			(2.99)

NOTE: Notations in Table 11.3 are the same as in Table 11.2.

Table 11.4
Estimation of Money Demand Function
Quarterly Data: 1983.1-1989.4

Money demand	C	$ln(rs)$	π	$ln(UP)$	R^2	DW	$\hat{\rho}$	$\chi^2_{(4)}$
M2O	1.152	0.657	-.004	0.530	0.932	1.552	0.660	7.63
	(3.16)	(5.03)	(-1.97)	(5.08)			(4.12)	
M2M	1.015	0.822	-.002	0.355	0.927	1.400	0.429	7.13
	(2.62)	(6.94)	(-1.96)	(5.18)			(2.26)	
M2W	1.231	0.653	-.004	0.511	0.933	1.507	0.605	6.87
	(3.13)	(4.64)	(-2.12)	(5.07)			(3.57)	

NOTE:
$ln(rs)$ = log of the real per capita retail sales; π = expected rate of inflation; the remaining notations are the same as in Table 11.2. Notice that the 5% critical value for χ^2 distribution with 4 degree of freedom is equal to 9.49.

Figure 11.1 The Log of the Official and Market Price Indices (1952=100)

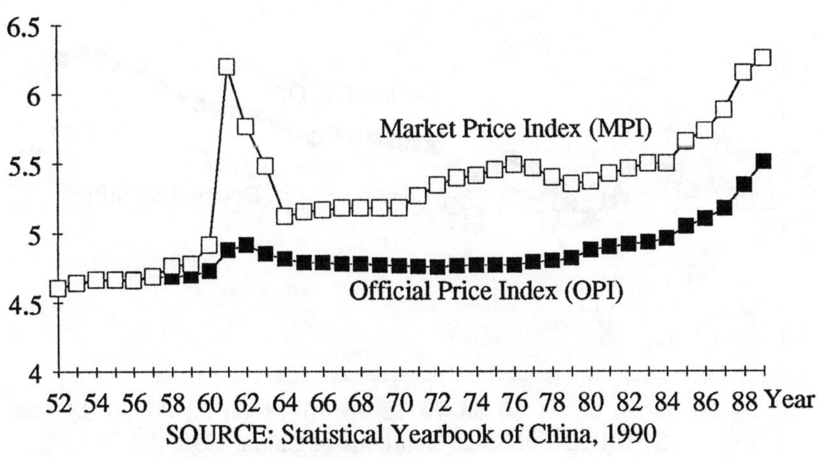

SOURCE: Statistical Yearbook of China, 1990

Figure 11.2 The Log of Real Per Capita M2 (in 1952 yuan)

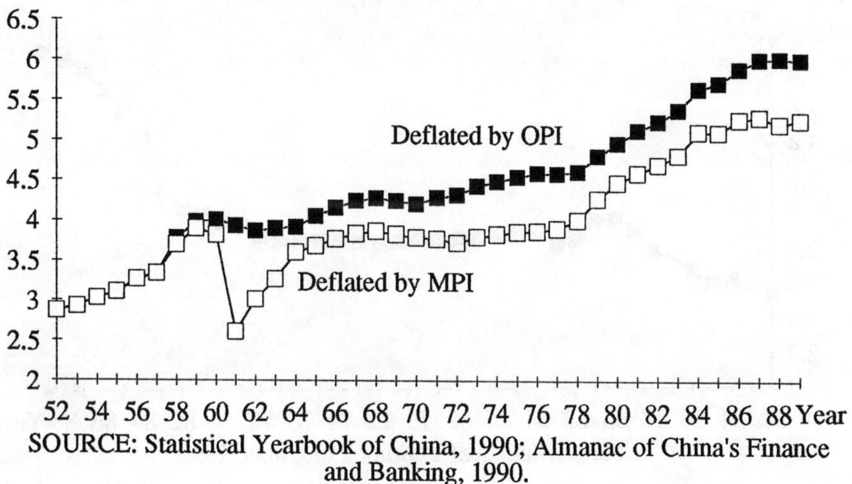

SOURCE: Statistical Yearbook of China, 1990; Almanac of China's Finance and Banking, 1990.

Figure 11.3 The Log of the Real Per Capita National Income (in 1952 yuan)

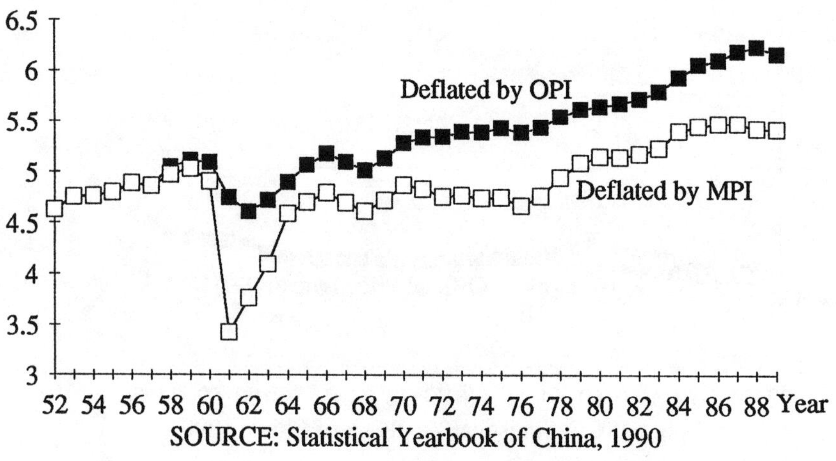

SOURCE: Statistical Yearbook of China, 1990

Figure 11.4 The Log of the Percentage of Urban and Township Population, 1952-89

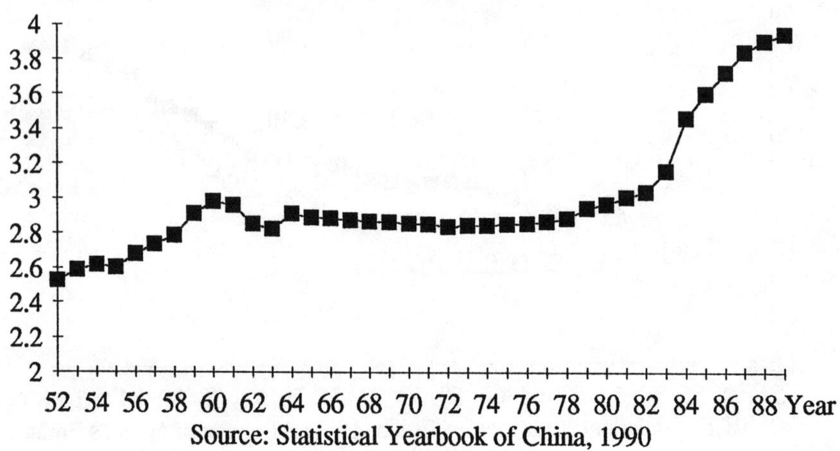

Source: Statistical Yearbook of China, 1990

Figure 11.5 The Log of the Nominal Per Capita M2 and Retail Sales, Seasonally Adjusted Data, 1983.1-1989.4

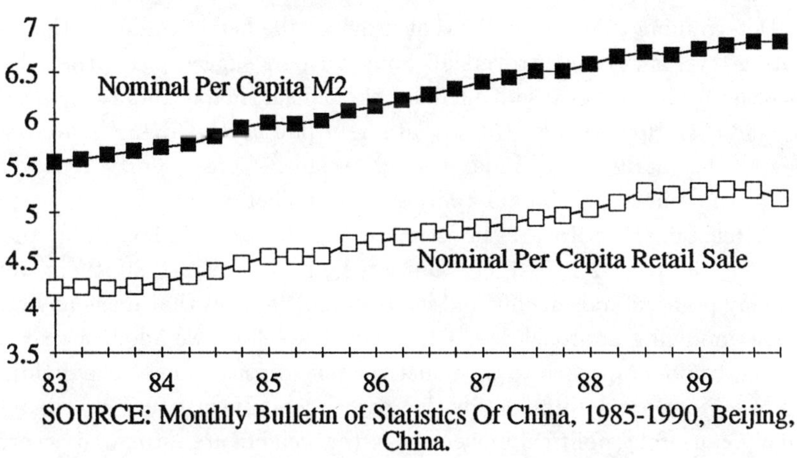

SOURCE: Monthly Bulletin of Statistics Of China, 1985-1990, Beijing, China.

Figure 6. The Log of the Official and Market Price Indices (1982=100)

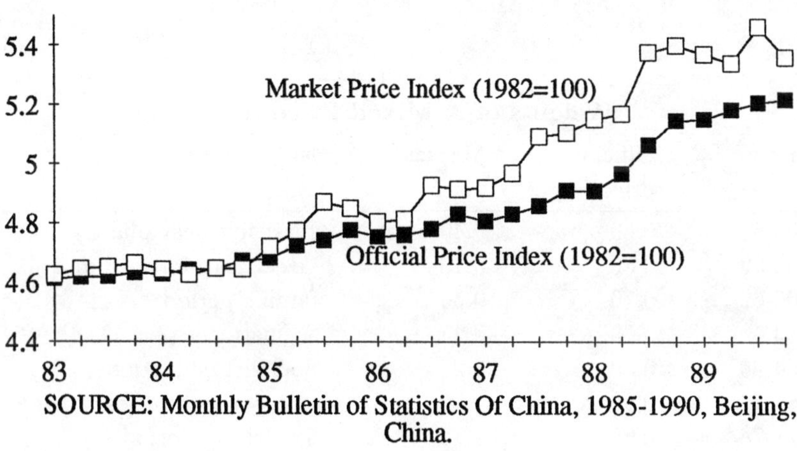

SOURCE: Monthly Bulletin of Statistics Of China, 1985-1990, Beijing, China.

Appendix A to Chapter 11
Mixed Price Index: An Example

Determining the price index that provides the best estimate of the real inflation level is quite controversial. Some authors suggest using the urban cost of living index because it includes the official, market, and negotiated price indices. However, we think that the urban cost of living index does not give the market price index enough weight. Consequently, it is very close to the official price index (only slightly higher).

Feltenstein and Ha (1991) estimate a "true price index" from their model for the period 1978-1988. During the period 1952-1989, there were too many political movements and institutional changes that make any systematic modeling approach less attractive. Therefore, we adopt a year by year fine-tuning approach to construct the mixed price index. The dividing lines of periods are determined by the major economic institutional changes (usually caused by political movements), the weights are estimated according to the share of the planned and market economy in each period. At the same time, we also consider the scope of black markets (transactions not recorded) and the difference between the official and market price indices, which reflects the degree of repressed inflation. Here we construct an *ad hoc* mixed price index, which is a weighted average of the official and market price indices. The weights are as follows.

Table 11.5
Weights of A Mixed Price Index

Period	Official price	Market price	Note
1953-57	0.60	0.40	First five year plan
1958-59	0.80	0.20	Great leap forward and
1960-62	0.70	0.30	famine period
1963	0.75	0.25	Adjustment period
1964-66	0.80	0.20	Socialist education
1967-76	0.90	0.10	Cultural revolution
1977-78	0.85	0.15	Transition period
1979-89	0.75	0.25	Economic reform

In Table 11.5, for those periods when economic data are available, the weights are estimated to reflect the share of the planned and market economy. For example, scattered data on the spending pattern of consumers and firms can be found from Liu (1980), *The Great Ten Years*, and Cheng (1982) for the period 1952-1957 and Yang *et al.* (1987) for the period 1978-1985. For those periods when economic data are not available, the weights are estimated based on historical knowledge. For instance, during the cultural Revolution period (1966-1976), free markets were criticized as "capitalism" and the number and size of free markets were reduced significantly in that period. Consequently, a 90 to 10 split is assigned between the official and market price indices.

As argued in the paper, the official price index tends to underestimate the true inflation level whereas the free market index tends to overestimate it. The true price index, which was unobservable, should lie somewhere in between. The mixed price index constructed above is merely a proxy of the underlying latent variable. Although it is a fact that almost all economic variables are measured with errors, we would like to warn readers that the consequence of a latent variable (in the errors in variables context) in standard econometric analysis is applicable here (see, e. g. Maddala, 1992, Chapter 11).

It is very easy to criticize this mixed price index. For example, within each period, there were subperiods; the weights are estimated to represent a national average, but a particular region might be quite different. Notice that we are not promoting this mixed index as "the true index;" rather, it is just one way of estimating the true inflation level. In the estimation of the money demand equations, we see that the parameter estimated by using the mixed price index are usually (but not always) between those estimated by the official and market price indices.

Appendix B to Chapter 11
Data

Table 11.6
Annual Data of Money Supply, Price Indices, National Income and Population
(M0, M2 and NI are in billion yuan, population is in million)

Year	M0	M2	OPI	MPI	NI	UP(%)	POP
1952	2.75	10.13	100.0	100.0	58.9	12.5	574.82
1953	3.94	11.37	103.4	103.9	70.9	13.3	587.96
1954	4.12	13.24	105.8	106.3	74.8	13.7	602.66
1955	4.03	14.59	106.9	106.1	78.8	13.5	614.65
1956	5.73	17.50	106.9	105.9	88.2	14.6	628.28
1957	5.28	19.77	108.5	108.9	90.8	15.4	646.53
1958	6.78	31.32	108.8	117.5	111.8	16.2	659.94
1959	7.51	39.17	109.7	119.0	122.2	18.4	672.07
1960	9.59	40.91	113.1	136.6	122.0	19.7	662.07
1961	12.57	43.98	131.5	491.8	99.6	19.3	658.59
1962	10.65	43.62	136.5	319.6	92.4	17.3	672.95
1963	8.99	43.66	128.4	241.2	100.0	16.8	691.72
1964	8.00	43.47	123.7	167.8	116.6	18.4	704.99
1965	9.08	49.76	120.4	173.2	138.7	18.0	725.38
1966	10.85	56.63	120.0	175.3	158.6	17.9	745.42
1967	12.19	62.97	119.1	178.2	148.7	17.7	763.68
1968	13.41	66.69	119.2	178.2	141.5	17.6	785.34
1969	13.71	65.92	117.9	178.1	161.7	17.5	806.71
1970	12.36	65.11	117.6	178.1	192.6	17.4	829.92
1971	13.62	71.49	116.7	193.8	207.7	17.3	852.29
1972	15.12	75.49	116.5	209.6	213.6	17.1	871.77
1973	16.61	87.03	117.2	220.7	231.8	17.2	892.11
1974	17.66	93.68	117.8	224.8	234.8	17.2	908.59
1975	18.26	101.75	118.0	233.8	250.3	17.3	924.20
1976	20.40	108.46	118.3	243.1	242.7	17.4	937.17
1977	19.54	110.73	120.8	237.2	264.4	17.6	949.74
1978	21.20	115.91	121.6	221.6	301.0	17.9	962.59
1979	26.77	145.81	124.0	211.6	335.0	19.0	975.42
1980	34.62	184.29	131.4	215.8	368.8	19.4	987.05
1981	39.63	223.45	134.6	228.3	394.1	20.2	1000.72
1982	43.91	258.98	137.2	235.8	425.8	20.8	1016.54
1983	52.98	307.50	139.3	245.7	473.6	23.5	1030.08
1984	79.21	414.63	143.2	244.7	565.2	31.9	1043.57

Table 11.6 Continues on the Next Page

Table 11.6 Continues from the Previous Page

Year	M0	M2	OPI	MPI	NI	UP(%)	POP
1985	98.78	488.43	155.8	286.8	704.4	36.6	1058.51
1986	121.84	626.16	165.1	310.0	789.9	41.4	1075.07
1987	145.45	766.45	177.2	360.5	936.1	46.6	1093.00
1988	213.40	928.89	210.0	469.7	1173.8	49.6	1110.26
1989	234.40	1092.0	247.2	520.4	1317.6	51.7	1127.04

NOTE:
M0 is defined as currency in circulation by the end of the year;
M2 is the broad money defined in Table 4.2 in Chapter 4;
OPI = official general retail price index (1952 = 100);
MPI = free market price index of consumer goods (1952 = 100);
NI = national income in current price;
UP = percentage of urban population in total population;
POP = total population at the end of year.

SOURCE: *Almanac of China's Finance and Banking*, 1990, Beijing, China; *Statistical Yearbook of China*, 1990, Beijing, China and *Almanac of China's Prices*, 1988, Beijing, China.

Table 11.7.
Quarterly Data for the Period 1983.1-1989.4
(M2, Rsale are in billion yuan)

Quarter	M2	Rsale	OPI	MPI	UP(%)	SAM2	SARS	OPIC	MPIC
1983.1	255.1	68.9	100.7	101.8	21.4	258.5	67.2	100.7	101.8
1983.2	260.3	66.3	101.2	104.0	22.1	266.1	68.1	101.2	104.0
1983.3	273.5	63.2	101.4	104.8	22.8	280.9	67.3	101.4	104.8
1983.4	309.4	73.3	102.7	106.2	23.5	291.6	69.0	102.7	106.2
1984.1	300.9	74.5	101.6	102.0	25.6	304.9	72.7	102.3	103.8
1984.2	310.8	75.0	102.6	98.2	27.7	317.7	77.0	103.8	102.1
1984.3	336.4	76.7	102.7	99.5	29.8	345.5	81.7	104.1	104.3
1984.4	401.2	94.4	104.3	97.9	31.9	378.1	88.8	107.1	104.0
1985.1	397.4	98.8	105.6	108.1	33.0	402.7	96.4	108.0	112.3
1985.2	388.8	94.1	108.5	115.8	34.2	397.4	96.7	112.7	118.3
1985.3	401.7	91.5	110.0	125.2	35.4	412.6	97.5	114.6	130.6
1985.4	489.3	118.6	110.7	122.8	36.6	461.1	111.6	118.6	127.7
1986.1	480.7	117.1	107.5	108.6	37.8	487.2	114.3	116.1	121.9
1986.2	511.0	117.5	103.5	104.1	39.0	522.3	120.7	116.6	123.1
1986.3	544.1	119.8	104.0	105.8	40.2	558.8	127.6	119.1	138.1
1986.4	628.9	140.1	105.5	106.6	41.4	592.6	131.8	125.1	136.1
1987.1	633.7	138.3	105.2	112.4	42.7	642.2	135.0	122.2	137.0
1987.2	659.8	138.1	107.3	116.6	44.0	674.4	141.9	125.1	143.6
1987.3	709.6	141.3	108.1	117.8	45.3	728.8	150.6	128.8	162.7
1987.4	772.0	164.2	108.4	121.1	46.6	727.5	154.5	135.6	164.8
1988.1	779.4	170.2	110.8	125.6	47.4	789.9	166.1	135.4	172.1
1988.2	837.6	174.3	114.6	122.3	48.1	856.2	179.0	143.4	175.6
1988.3	881.7	190.3	122.6	132.7	48.9	905.5	202.8	157.9	215.9
1988.4	928.9	209.2	126.3	134.0	49.6	875.3	196.8	171.3	220.9
1989.1	928.6	208.7	127.1	124.5	50.1	941.1	203.7	172.1	214.2
1989.2	961.3	203.3	123.9	118.7	50.7	982.6	208.8	177.6	208.4
1989.3	1000.9	195.5	115.2	109.1	51.2	1027.9	208.3	181.9	235.6
1989.4	1092.0	202.9	107.4	96.0	51.7	1029.0	190.9	184.0	212.1

Table 11.7 Continues on the Next Page

Table 11.7 Continued from the Previous Page

NOTE:
M2 = broad money;
Rsale = total retail sales;
OPI = official general price index (the same period last year = 100);
MPI = free market price index (the same period last year = 100);
UP = percentage of urban and township population.

SAM2 = seasonally adjusted M2;
SARS = seasonally adjusted retail sales.
The seasonal index calculated for M2 is 98.84, 97.83, 97.57, 105.75. The seasonal index calculated for retail sales is 102.47, 97.36, 93.86, 106.31.

OPIC = quarterwise continuous official price index, which is constructed by multiplying the OPI of year i by the quarterwise continuous price index of year $(i-1)$. The quarterwise continuous price index of the base year (1982) is equal to 100.
MPIC = quarterwise continuous market price index.

SOURCE: *The Monthly Bulletin of Statistics of China*, State Bureau of Statistics, Beijing, 1985-1990, various issues. *Almanac of China's Economy*, Beijing, 1984-1990.

PART FOUR

Money and Inflation

12

Price Reforms and Inflation

The nature of the Chinese economic reform in the past decade is to build an economy where the allocation of resources is determined primarily by the market.[1] A side effect of the economic reform has been rampant inflation. To a large degree, whether the reform can continue depends on whether the Chinese government can successfully control the inflation. An important question to ask here is that whether inflation is avoidable in the transition from a centrally planned economy where mandatory prices were basically accounting tools, to a market economy where prices are determined by demands and supplies.

The purpose of the present chapter is two-fold. First, to provide a brief review on the price reform in China in the past decade, with an emphasis on historical background. Second, to decompose the elements of the upward price pressures and show the intimate relationship between the price reform and inflation. The price reform experience of China suggested that in the transition from a planned economy to a market economy, it is virtually impossible to adjust the relative price without increasing the general price level; i.e., an inflation is inevitable. There are basically two main sources of inflation. One is triggered directly by price reform; the other is caused by decentralization, which leads to an investment fever and subsequently, to an overheating economy. Once the inflation process is started, the rational responses of firms and individuals based on their inflationary expectations would reinforce the upward price pressures, exacerbate the shortage and accelerate the inflation. Although we focus on the experience of China, the analysis is also instructive to other centrally-planned economies. This chapter discusses the reasons and objectives of the price reform, provides a chronological review of price reform in China in the past decade, and analyzes the causal factors of the inflation, especially the link between the price reform and inflation via price subsidies, government deficits and increased money supply.

12.1 Reasons and Objectives of the Price Reform

Throughout this chapter, the term "price" is used primarily in its narrow sense, referring mainly to prices of consumer and producer goods. It does not include wages (price of labor), interest (price of capital), rent (price of land), etc.

The Chinese economy, before the economic reform, can be regarded as a typical centrally-planned economy (CPE), in which the industrial sector was dominated by the state-owned enterprises and the agriculture was organized by communes. Accordingly, consumers were classified into two blocks, rural and urban. Peasants in the communes were strictly restricted in the countryside. They simply could not go to cities to work, let alone share the rationing privileges of the city dwellers. Virtually all prices had been set by the government through a hierarchy of pricing bureaus. Resource allocations were primarily determined by administrative channels, rather than by demands and supplies through the market place. Consequently, prices only played a limited role in resource allocation; even consumer goods were partially allocated by rationing.[2] Nevertheless, the planned price system had the following important functions in a CPE. First, since all industrial, commercial and agricultural profits were calculated by such prices, it significantly influenced the profitability of an enterprise. Second, it played an important role in income distribution. The relative prices of industrial and agricultural products determined the living standards of the urban and rural consumers. Third, it was certainly the main allocation device for the commodities outside the mandatory plan.

Characteristics of the Planned Price System

Before the reform, the planned (or controlled) price system in China had the following characteristics.

The price system was distorted, they were disequilibrium prices. There were three major distortions: First, the planned general price level was lower than the equilibrium price level, and subsequently there had been a persistent excess demand. Second, prices in most energy, raw materials and transportation sectors were too low, whereas the prices of products of processing industries were relatively high. This can be clearly seen from Table 12.1, which gives the profit rates of the state-owned industrial enterprises in 1979, the beginning year of the price reform. Third, the procurement prices of agricultural products were too low relative to industrial products. This reflected a long overdue problem that the government had taken too much away from the countryside through the scissors movement of the prices of agricultural and industrial products. In a backward agricultural country like China, industrialization needed huge amounts of capital. The main source of the accumulation, of course, was from the contribution of peasants. The exploitation of peasants in China was mainly through the arbitrary low prices of agricultural products relative to industrial products. It has been estimated that from 1949 to 1979, the Chinese peasants' contribution through the unequal exchange was more than 600 billion yuan (The Rural Development Research Center 1987). The peasants had no way to resist this exploitation, because the government had virtually monopolized all channels of buying and selling agricultural products. If we decompose the cost of agricultural production into three parts: (1) the fixed cost (land, irrigation system, durable machinery, etc.), (2) labor cost and (3) other variable costs (like utility bills, fertilizers, pesticides, and seeds), then the selling prices of agricultural products could not even cover the third part of the cost in some areas of China before 1979.

It was a multiple price system. The prices of the centrally controlled materials were set by the national price bureau. The prices of commodities produced by local plan were set by local governments. Most price calculations were based on the costs of production. Enterprises controlled by the central plan were usually bigger and more efficient. They could produce better quality products at lower costs. Consequently, prices of their products were low. The efficiency of the firms controlled by local governments were usually low; higher production costs resulted in higher prices of their products. It was not uncommon that the better quality cement produced by larger firms sold for 51-56 yuan per ton, while lower quality cement produced by small firms sold for 70-80 yuan per ton (Price Reform Research Group of Chinese Academy of Social Sciences, 1986). Both were planned prices. Why would somebody want to pay more for the lower quality cement? The answer is that in a CPE, goods are allocated by the plan (or quota). Those who could not get the better cement at a lower price from the planning bureau were willing to pay a higher price. Hence, the existence of the excess demand and shortage was the major reason that the multiple price system was viable.

The allocation power provided an opportunity for the officials to make a monetary profit for themselves at the expense of the state-owned properties. And furthermore, there were many loopholes which resulted in enormous waste, regardless of the government's tremendous efforts on rationing. For example, grain was rationed in the urban areas by issuing coupons per person/month to city dwellers. They were able to buy the rationed amount of grain at low planned prices. It was easy to see that the rationing coupons had a value equal to the difference between the market prices and the low rationing prices. There was a huge amount of the rationed grain that flowed back to rural areas, because peasants bought grain rationing coupons from city residents and then bought grain and shipped the grain to the countryside. Imagine how much transportation costs this operation wasted, let alone the transaction costs of the rationing efforts and the costs of policing the illegal trade in the rationing coupons.

The price level had been essentially frozen. From 1952 to 1978, the general price level increased only 0.7 percent annually. This super-stable price policy made it extremely difficult to respond to any external or internal shocks. The government had been obliged to maintain the low price level, and obviously this would almost certainly result in a huge price subsidy program. In summary, the centrally planned price system distorted the signals of resource allocation, punished more efficient enterprises, protected the less-efficient producers, and created an environment in which both individuals and firms had little incentive to innovate and to be more efficient. These are the main reasons for the price reform.

Objectives of the Price Reform

Although there has been some controversy and debate over the objectives and methods of the price reforms, most economists in China have agreed that the final objective of the price reform is to change the price determination system to a market mechanism, rather than to adjust the relative prices within a planned system. Specifically, the following objectives are important: (1) To provide incentives to firms and individuals; to change from a situation in which an efficient firm pays extra taxes while an inefficient firm enjoys its subsidy, to one in which an individual's income should be closely related to contribution to value-added. (2) To establish a competitive market, so that firms and individuals have an equal opportunity to compete; to change from the current situation in which the profitability of a firm is primarily determined by the parameters set by the government (such as the prices and quantities of firms' inputs and outputs), to one in which firms and individuals are independent economic agents, who are responsible for their own actions — enjoying the rewards of their successes and bearing fully the costs of failures. (3) To reduce the share of the resources allocated by the plan and increase the market share of allocation. (4) To reduce the government's price subsidies.

As far as the methods of the price reform are concerned, "adjust" and "release" are the two key words. *Adjust* means to bring prices in the current planned system closer to equilibrium prices. Increasing the procurement prices of the agricultural products several times during the reform belongs to this category. *Release* means to abandon controls over the prices of certain commodities and let the market decide. For example, the prices of most everyday life consumer goods were released in middle 1980s. In practice, the approach of the price reform has been a combination of these two strategies. It is not feasible to decontrol all prices at once, because that could lead tremendous inflation, which would be beyond the acceptable range of the society. Besides, decontrolling prices in an environment where the property rights of state-owned enterprises are not clearly defined could result in firms' irrational (or rational, depending on how you look at it) behavior, which would lead to a chaotic situation, rather than to a unified competitive market. Adjustment alone without any release is not a good strategy either. The rationale of the adjustment itself has some logical problems. For instance, if the objective is to adjust planned prices toward equilibrium prices, then how would the equilibrium price be known without a market? One could never reach an equilibrium price by adjusting the planned price, simply because the equilibrium price is the result of actions in the market place rather than of the calculation of planners. This view is also shared by western observers. Byrd (1989) pointed out that changes in planned prices will be ineffective in improving efficiency or expanding the role of markets.

12.2 A Brief Review of the Price Reforms in China

The Price Reforms: 1979-1987

We can regard the third plenary meeting of the eleventh central committee of the CCP, which was held in December of 1978, as the starting point of the economic reform in China. The first important move of the price reform was that the state council decided to raise the procurement prices of 18 main agriculture products (a 24.8 percent increase on average) in March, 1979. Later, the government tried to decontrol food prices gradually. In 1985, food prices (except grain) were basically decontrolled in major urban areas of China. The procurement prices of agriculture products in 1985 were 67 percent higher on average than those of 1978. It turned out that this was a brilliant decision. Together with the responsibility system, it made possible the miracle of the rapid growth of Chinese agriculture in the period 1979-1984.

Following the example of the agriculture, the relative prices of other sectors were also adjusted. For instance, in early 1980s, there was a comprehensive price adjustment in the entire textile industry; prices of polyester fibre were decreased and prices of cotton fibres were increased. In 1984, railroad freight fares were increased; the passenger and freight fares of water transportation were also increased. Short-distance railroad passenger and freight fares went up further in 1985.

Since 1979, prices of some important heavy industrial products (such as coal, iron, steel etc.) have been adjusted upward or partially released. The national planning bureau had reduced its mandatory targets for industrial products to 60 categories in 1987, as opposed to 120 categories in 1984. The producers' goods rationed by the central government were also reduced to 26 categories in 1987, compared to 256 categories in 1984. The proportion of important materials rationed by the government has declined since 1979. In 1986, for example, 53.1 percent of steel, 42.3 percent of coal, 16.2 percent of cement, and 30 percent of lumber were rationed by the government (*People's Daily*, 7/18/1987). In order to reduce the share of the resources allocated by the plan, commodities have been classified into at least three categories: mandatory plan, directory plan, and outside plan. The government controls only the prices within the mandatory plan, allowing prices of the directory planned commodities to float within a certain range, while completely released commodities' prices are outside of the plan. The market's share of the economy has steadily increased. By 1987, it was announced that, overall, 50 percent of resources were allocated by the market (*People's Daily*, 11/9/1987). However, this trend was interrupted (possibly reversed somewhat) by the worsening situation of inflation since the summer of 1988 and especially by the suppression of the mass demonstrations in June, 1989.

The "Two–Tier" Price System

The prices of products in light industries, textile industry and everyday consumer's goods have been gradually decontrolled. A so-called "two-tier" price system was introduced in heavy-industry sectors. Under the two-tier (or perhaps multiple-tier) price system, market prices were assumed to be higher than the planned prices. A typical firm faces a vector of planned targets, which may include a compulsory procurement of output, and an input allocation. All input purchases and output sales beyond the target level take place in the market at flexible prices. Generally speaking, a firm's privilege of getting input at low planned prices is proportional to its compulsory procurement output obligations. If a firm is completely outside of the plan, it has neither input purchase privileges nor procurement output obligations.

One example of the two-tier system worth mentioning is to be found in the producers' goods market of Shijiazhong (a city to the south of Beijing), where all producer's goods are sold at market prices. The city government abandoned the old in-kind allocation plan. Instead, it gives firms a monetary compensation according to the historical quota of the rationed input. In other words, the government gives a firm the amount of money which is equal to the difference between the planned price and market price multiplied by the quantity of the previous planned input allocation to the firm. Then it is totally up to the firm as to how to use this money. Under this arrangement the firm is at least as well off as the old in-kind allocation plan. However, now the firm has more choices, this arrangement certainly improves the efficiency of the resource allocation. As a matter of fact, it is almost equivalent to single-tier market price mechanism. The only difference is that the historical allocation quota system is carried over, according to which the amount of compensation is determined.

As we mentioned before, the planned price was a multiple-tier price system. It is natural to use the two-tier system as a device in the transition to the market mechanism. The original intention of the two-tier price system was to freeze the existing planned allocation quotas, and any new incremental would be through the market. And (it was hoped) the dynamics would lead to an increase of the market share and gradually phase out the old planned system. However, this proved not to be the case. The two-tier price system was good enough to break down the old system, but it could not lead to a unified competitive market. The main reason is that the two different prices (planned and market) are created by two conflicting forces: administrative power and market mechanism. Under the two-tier price system, how to allocate, and who could get the resources at low planned prices are quite arbitrary and totally in the hands of the allocation officials, so that it is very easy for them to convert their power into monetary profits. A typical firm pays primary attention to the government, because it is probably easier to bribe an official than to improve efficiency in order to compete in the market. Another consequence of the two-tier price system is that it reduces the share of resources allocated by the planning bureau and, consequently, the power of the direct control of the central government over the economy. The traditional government policy instruments are now resisted by market forces, and at the same time, the market has been intervened in and distorted by the administrative power. The old system is about to break down, but the new system cannot grow up from the two-tier prices due to the corrupt officials. It seems that it is the consensus of most economists in China that the disadvantages of the two-tier price system outweighed its advantages. However, like it or not, the two-tier price system will continue to play an important role in the Chinese economy. It is something that is deeply rooted in the Chinese economic system. For further discussion on the two-tier price system, see Byrd (1987) for pros and Shi and Liu(1989) for cons.

The Price Reforms: 1988-1993

The price reform in China in 1988 was probably the most dramatic. In May, it was announced that the price subsidies would be changed from invisible to visible.[3] Then the prices of four basic food items (vegetables, eggs, pork and sugar) were decontrolled. In June, the top leaders of China repeatedly expressed their determination to overcome the barriers of price reform and were about to launch a full-scale price reform including the abolition of the two-tier price system (*People's Daily* , 6/23/1988). In July, the government tested the water by decontrolling prices of brand-name cigarettes and liquor. The consequence of this series efforts was disastrous. People were in panic; rumors swept the country, especially in major cities. Bank deposits decreased 2.6 billion yuan in August. The official inflation rate was 18.5 percent in 1988.

To calm people down the government had to take a series of measures to fight the inflation. (1) In September the People's Bank raised interest rates for almost all bank deposits and introduced the so-called guaranteed-value saving deposit, the yield of which is tied to the official rate of inflation. (2) The government also announced that they would not decontrol the prices of important materials (mainly producers' goods) in 1989, and that they would not introduce new price reform programs in the near future. (3) The government also reduced basic construction investment. By the end of November, more than 10,200 projects were stopped or postponed, estimated to be worth 33.4 billion yuan. (*People's Daily* , 1/14/1989). (4) The government determined to curb consumption by institutions, to inspect the controlled prices nationwide, and to investigate and trim companies, especially those newly established ones who had some sort of connection with government branches.

As a result, saving deposits have recovered since September, 1988. Prices continued going up, but at a slower rate. There is no doubt that the Chinese government has the experience of controlling prices by administrative measures.

There are two main results from the austerity policy for the period 1988-1991. One is expected, the other one is unexpected. The expected result is that the economy was in recession for three years. The costs of the tightening measures were tremendous: The economy suffered from the drastic policy. It was difficult to get a loan after the tightening. The reduction of investments and loans was an across the board cut: it was very difficult to distinguish which enterprises were efficient since the market was very distorted and there was no objective price to judge which project should be preserved. The growth rates of GNP for 1989-1991 were 4.4%, 4.1% and 7.7% respectively, which were much lower than the average of the reform period. The income for the rural area was even worse. The average increase of income for the rural population was only 0.7% for this three year period.

The unexpected result is that during the recession, the aggregate demand was sluggish for a long time. For the first time in the history of the People's Republic, there were persistent excess supplies for many consumer and producer goods. Consequently buyers markets appeared. Firms started to worry that they were unable to sell their products. They had to improve the quality of the products and lower the prices. The most important and unexpected consequence of the austerity policy is that most prices have converged to the equilibrium prices during this period. Economists in China joked about this result: We tried everything to conquer the price reform and failed. We stopped the price reform and did nothing during the period 1989-1991, when the price reform was succeeded to a large degree.

According to the official statistics, more than 90 percent of consumer goods were allocated by markets at equilibrium prices in 1993. There were more than 4000 producer goods markets in China and the estimated total value of transactions of these markets was over 160 billion yuan in 1993. It is estimated that more than 90% of producers goods are purchased from producer goods markets for firms in the coastal areas. For the state-owned large scale enterprises, about 75% of their input materials are purchased from the markets (*People's Daily*, 11/20/1993).

To sum up, The price reform started from the controlled price system, which was distorted and inefficient. The price system has been moving towards a market equilibrium. A negative side effect of this process was the rampant inflation. Because the economy and society could not tolerate the inflation, the central government controlled the inflation by a set of austerity policies for the period 1989-1991, which was basically the price and credit control method used in the centrally planned economy. Perhaps because the semi-competitive environment created by the reform, most prices of consumer and producer goods converged to the market equilibrium during the recession period 1989-1991 due to the relative abundant supply and sluggish demand. However, the factors prices were still largely controlled and distorted by the end of 1993. The price reform is far from over in China.

12.3 Analysis: The Causal Factors of the Inflation

What are the main factors that caused the inflation? Of course, inflation is always and everywhere a monetary phenomenon. We can always say that the inflation was caused by excessive money supply. We have discussed the money supply mechanism and the monetization process in the previous chapters and provided the evidence that the growth rate of money supply has been consistently faster than the sum of the growth rate of GNP and the inflation rate during the reform period. Even if we have considered the monetization process, there has been still an excess money supply for most years in the reform period. This excess money supply has certainly fueled the upward pressures on the general price level, which has led either to a repressed inflation under the controlled price system or to a real inflation when the price control was released.

Here we are going to ask: Why has the central bank of China supplied so much money into the economy? Why did every step of the price reform cause inflation? Is the inflation avoidable? In this section, we shall decompose the causal factors of the inflation and analyze the major elements that contribute to the inflation most.

The Controlled vs. Equilibrium Prices

Suppose that the Chinese economy before the reform was a typical CPE that had suppressed inflationary pressures. Under fixed, planned prices, aggregate demand was greater than aggregate supply and there was a persistent shortage. Kornai (1980) described a typical socialist planned system as "a shortage economy". It is generally accepted that the CPE have suffered from sustained, significant repressed inflation (Grossman 1966; Bush 1973). Although Portes's and Santorum's (1987) study on the Chinese consumption goods market suggested that the excess demand in China was not dominant, we have plenty of empirical evidence that there existed a prolonged shortage in China (Chinese Economic System Reform Research Institute, 1985).

Figure 12.1 illustrates this situation, where P_1 is the planned price, and P is the equilibrium price. Under P_1, the excess demand is $Q_2 - Q_1$. At Q_1, buyers are willing to pay P_2. The difference between P_2 and P_1 is the value of the rationing devices. Since the rationing plan was controlled by the planning bureau, the rectangular $P_1P_2E_2E_1$ provides a monetary measure of the power of the planning bureau.

If the goal of price reform is to reach the equilibrium price, then the ideal path would be to eliminate the excess demand by increasing the general price level to P. Therefore, even for this most ideal case, it is impossible to accomplish the task of price reform without increasing the general price level. Notice that at the equilibrium price, the nominal general price level has increased, but the real full price level has decreased. This seemingly contradictory phenomenon happens because the planned price represents only part of the price, the other part is the value of the rationing devices, whereas the equilibrium price represents the full price. In the process of converging to the equilibrium price, the value of the rationing devices is embodied into the equilibrium price. Since the inflation rate is calculated by comparing the nominal general price levels before and after the reform, it is very natural to have some inflation after the reform for the latter is closer to the equilibrium price and depends less on the rationing devices.

Subsidies and the Cost Push Inflation

If the increase of the price level had really eliminated the excess demand and led to equilibrium, that would have been a great success for price reform. Unfortunately, this was not the case. The increase of the price level did not lead to equilibrium, nor reduce the shortage. This can be clearly seen from the example of raising the prices of agricultural products in China. It was pretty much the consensus that the prices of agricultural products were too low relative to industrial products before the reform. As far as the magnitude of the inflation is concerned, there are at least three alternative ways to correct this distortion: (1) a zero-inflation approach, adjusting relative prices without raising the general price level — simultaneously increasing the prices of agricultural products and decreasing the prices of industrial products. (2) Raising the prices of agricultural products while keeping the prices of industrial products unchanged. (3) A moderate inflationary approach, increasing prices in both sectors, but increasing the prices of agricultural products more than industrial products.

The first alternative is obviously not feasible, because of the price rigidity of industrial products. Lowering the price level of industrial products implies that workers' wages have to be decreased, assuming the productivity and technology are fixed.

Is the second alternative feasible? The answer is no. Consider a scenario in which the retail prices of food were increased, while urban employees' wages and salaries were not. This was definitely not feasible, because the city dwellers would be worse off. It is worth noting that wage and salary earners in cities are the most powerful political force in the Chinese society. For more than 40 years, the government has been emphasizing that the working class is the leading force of the country. A reform plan which hurts the interest of the leading class is obviously not feasible.

What the Chinese government did in 1979 was more or less the third alternative. It raised the procurement prices of the agricultural products. As a result, the retail food prices also increased in cities. To compensate for this the government had to engage in huge amounts of invisible price subsidy, and at the same time start a visible subsidy program: giving each urban employee and college student a 5 yuan/month subsidy. In 1985 and 1988, the government repeated this strategy. Figure 12.2 offers a simple illustration that might fit what has happened in China. There were three consequences of the Chinese government's approach. First, the costs of industrial products were increased due to higher labor costs, since the subsidy now became part of the wage bill. Therefore, the aggregate supply curve shifted to the northwest direction (in Figure 12.2, from S_1S_1 to S_2S_2). Second, the subsidy increased consumers' money income, so that the aggregate demand curve shifted in the northeast direction (from D_1D_1 to D_2D_2). Third, the general price level increased as a result of the interaction between the demand and supply curves. Accordingly, demand for money was also increased and the central bank had to issue more money to accommodate the need. After one round of price reform, the new demand and supply curves were D_2D_2 and S_2S_2, and the new shortage was $Q_4 - Q_3$. The main result of the price reform was inflation, rather than the adjustment of the relative price. Now industrial sectors faced a cost-push inflationary pressure, the prices of their products would increase sooner or later to cover the costs. After the increase of the prices of industrial products, the original benefits of peasants from raising the procurement prices of the agricultural products have been reduced. This is the so-called "price regression" phenomenon (Kornai 1980). Therefore, the price rigidity and the interest of the urban wage and salary earners made it extremely difficult (virtually impossible) to adjust the relative price while maintaining the general price level unchanged.

The Role of Government Deficits

Before 1979, the government's budgets were pretty much balanced; there were some surplus years, and some deficit years. From 1959 to 1978, the Chinese government had neither domestic nor foreign debts. In 1979, the official deficit was 17.06 billion yuan, the largest in the history of the People's Republic. The general retail price level rose 6 percent in 1980, although not very high, this increase signaled that the era of stable prices was over.

Notice that the official government deficit published in the *Statistical Yearbook of China* does not include borrowings. There, borrowings have been counted as part of government revenue. Therefore the real deficit should be the official deficit plus borrowings. Does this mean that the official deficit is the amount of the deficit financed by printing money? Well, roughly speaking, yes. However, there is another detail in the Chinese budget management system. That is that the surplus of a local government belongs to itself. But when the official deficit is calculated, it does count the local governments' surplus as revenue. Therefore, the amount of the central government's deficit financed by printing money might be greater than the official deficit figure. For example, in 1986, the official deficit was 7.06 billion, the real deficit (plus the borrowings 13.84 billion) was 20.90 billion. The local governments' surplus was 2.36 billion. So that the central government's deficit financed by printing money was 9.42 (7.06 plus 2.36) billion. (Tian Yinong, The Report on the Final State Accounts of 1986, *People's Daily* , 6/25/1987).

After raising the procurement price of agricultural products, while continuing to maintain the low retail prices in cities, the burden on the government was getting larger and larger. From 1953 to 1960, the price subsidies of the government amounted to 720 million yuan, only 0.26 percent of the total government revenue of that period (Qiao 1986). From 1979 to 1987, price subsidies were 263.15 billion yuan, accounting for about 19.3 percent of the total revenue of that period. Table 12.2 summarizes the price subsidies and government deficits in the period 1978-88. Notice that these numbers include just the invisible subsidies, which occurs when the government's procurement purchase prices are higher than the retail prices. The so-called visible subsidies, which are monetary payments to city employees every month in addition to their wages and salaries, are not included in Table 12.2. This explains why there was a significant decrease in price subsidy from 1984 to 1985: part of the invisible subsidies were changed to visible in 1985 (The retail food prices increased in 1985, subsequently the invisible price subsidies decreased, and each city employee received an 8 yuan/month compensation from the government).

It appears that the macro link between the price reform and inflation can be summarized as follows. The objective of the price reform is to adjust relative prices, to correct the distortion. However, the adjustment of the relative prices is tantamount to income redistribution. Since it is not feasible to make the urban wage earners worse off, this would inevitably lead to a price subsidy. Given the revenue of the government, the increase of subsidies means a large deficit. There are three ways to finance a deficit: domestic borrowing, foreign borrowing or printing money. Both domestic and foreign borrowings are limited; printing money has to make up the rest. The rapid increase in the money supply is the direct reason for the inflation. However, it is superficial to criticize the central bank of China for pumping too much money into the economy, because the central bank of China does not have an independent monetary policy. It is almost like the cashier of the government (Zhou and Zhu 1987).

Economic Structure and the Bottleneck Shortage

The leaders of China often have incentives to overheat its economy with a so-called "leap forward" campaign. Perhaps they always want to show the socialist system is superior to the capitalist system and the ultimate way to show that is to prove that its economy is developed more rapidly in the socialist system. Once a leap forward campaign fever creates famine and shortage and drives the economy to the brink of bankruptcy, the government has to adjust to the direction of obeying economic laws, such as providing material incentives and respecting the invisible hand, etc. After the economy has recovered from the disaster, the government is ready to start another great leap forward campaign. This kind of movement happened several times in the 40 years history of the People's Republic under different slogans, most notoriously in 1958 (the Great Leap Forward), in 1978 (Four Modernization), and in early 1980s (Quadrupling the Total Output by the Year 2000) and perhaps in 1988 under some new slogans. Although China has repeatedly suffered the ill-effects of investment fever, this problem is still haunting its economy, because the incentives for such fever remain. One thing that is worth mentioning is that before the economic reform, only one economic agent, namely the central government, was capable of overheating the economy, given its tight control over local governments and firms. After decentralizing reform, local governments and numerous firms have also been infected by this investment fever disease. The economic reason behind this is simple. Facing a soft budget constraint, it is rational for a firm — or a local government — to invest more when it has the authority to do so. The relationship between the interest of the investing agent and the result of the investment is asymmetric. It enjoys the success of the investment (in terms of gaining power, material rewards and promotions, etc.), but does not bear fully the cost of a failure. It is often said by Chinese government officials to excuse a failed investment that "this is the tuition we have to pay to learn".

Table 12.3 provides investment information for the period 1984-1988, during which total fixed capital investment increased at an average rate of 26.1 percent per year. After correcting for inflation, it is still 17.4 percent, which is much higher than average real national income growth (10.9

percent) over the same period. The consequence of this kind of flood of investments is that it creates tremendous excess demand in both consumers goods and producer's goods, increases the government deficits and puts upward pressures on the general price level. The existence of excess demand pressure is also confirmed by Portes and Santorum (1987), all indices they used in their study suggested significant excess demand under recent reforms. Furthermore, the pressure of the excess demand is unevenly distributed across the economy, it generates so-called "bottlenecks". The most obvious bottlenecks in China now are in the infrastructure sectors, such as energy, raw materials and transportation. From Table 12.3, we see that energy production and freight turnover by railroad increased on average 6.0 percent and 8.3 percent respectively over this period, much lower than the investment rate. Without the proper support from the energy and transportation sectors, there is no way that investment can keep growing in the long run. Because total investment has exceeded the growth of the infrastructure sectors, the latter became more and more scarce. This would certainly exert inflationary pressure, starting from these bottleneck products. Since most of them are important inputs, this upward price pressure would easily generate a new round of inflation.

An important question is whether the government could avoid these investment fevers. The answer is "unlikely" for the following reasons. First, moving from a planned economy to a market economy, decentralization is absolutely necessary. Second, investment fever results from the combination of decentralization (giving firms the power of making an investment decision) and ill-defined property rights. (Who owns the property? A firm, a local government or the central government?) Third, it takes time to define property rights. Even if the government could promulgate a law to define such property rights overnight (which is unlikely), it still needs time to build credibility. This is particularly difficult in China because frequent political movements and changes of government policy in the past have severely damaged people's trust in government policy. This mistrust is reflected in a popular Chinese saying: "The policy of the Communist Party is like the moon, it looks different on the first of a month from the 15th." This intangible psychological damage would definitely prolong the process of establishing property rights. Fourth, property rights cannot be established in advance of decentralization because "property rights " without decentralization (decision power) are at most dummy rights. In short, in the transition from a planned economy to a market economy, there is a period of time, in which the decision making power is decentralized and the property rights are not well defined. During this period, there are tremendous incentives for leaders of firms and local governments to over invest. This is another reason why inflation in the transition is virtually inevitable.

Inflationary Expectations and Firms' Behavior

The Economic Institute of the Chinese Academy of Social Sciences did a survey on firms' responses to the inflation in September, 1988 (Du et al. 1989). According to the firms in the sample, the rate of increase of the producer's goods had been in a tolerable range before 1988. Table 12.4 summarizes the rate of price increase of producer's goods faced by the firms in the sample in 1988. It is not difficult to see that a rational firm's behavior based on its inflationary expectation in this kind of environment would exacerbate the already existing shortage and accelerate the rampant inflation. First, a high price could not decrease the demand if firms are expecting the prices will go even higher. Second, because of the shortage, it is more difficult for the planning bureau to deliver the amount of raw materials at planned prices. Firms could use this as an indisputable excuse to refuse to sell their products to the planning bureau at planned prices. There is a domino effect once this process is started. Third, the existing sellers' market goes to its extreme. Sellers become lords, and buyers are turned into beggars. Consequently, there have been barter trades, conditional selling and buying. The market becomes chaotic and less transparent. Uncertainty and transaction costs have increased drastically. Fourth, firms inventory behaviors are also changed. If the price increase over time is large enough to cover the inventory cost, a rational firm would prefer more inventories. On the other hand, a rational seller would prefer to delay its sale and wait for further price hikes. All of these would intensify the shortage and push the price level even higher.

Wages and the Inflation

Wages and salaries had been essentially frozen in the period 1957-1978. The average annual wage was 637 and 644 yuan in 1957 and 1978 respectively. The average labor industrial productivity (based on total personnel) of the state-owned enterprises went up 75 percent and price level increased by 12 percent during the same period (computed from the *Statistical Yearbook of China* , 1983, p. 297 and p. 455). The real wage was actually lower in 1978 than that of 1957 in absolute terms, not even counting the improvement of the productivity. The relationship between the rate of inflation and wage increase was rather weak (random) in this period, the correlation coefficient was only 0.03.

Table 12.5 compares the wage increase with the average labor productivity improvement for the period 1978-87. We see that the nominal wage increased rather fast, on average 10.4 percent a year in this period. The rapid growth of nominal wages increased money costs and consequently the price level. It is easy to see that the rapid growth of nominal wages played a significant role in the inflation. As expected, there is an obvious positive association between the growth rate of nominal wage and the inflation, the correlation coefficient was .60 for this period. However, the percentage increase of the real wage was pretty much in line with the productivity increase. In this period, the real wage increased 53.7 percent, while the labor productivity increased 51.7 percent.[4]

12.4 Summary

During the reform, two main sources have contributed to rampant inflation. One was triggered by price reforms, the other was the eagerness of the central and local government for a rapid growth, which led to investment fever and an overheating economy. From the above analysis, we conclude that if the objective of the price reform is to complete the transition from a controlled price system to a equilibrium price system, then inflation is virtually inevitable even in the most ideal case. The main reason is that the change of the relative prices is equivalent to the income redistribution. Price rigidity and the interests of urban wage earners would make some sort of price subsidy unavoidable. Theoretically, it is possible that the gain from the price reform is sufficiently large that it allows the government to tax the gainers and compensate the losers and make everybody better off. Practically the government is unlikely to make that kind of arrangement, because in a large developing country like China, how to establish a tax system, which is feasible for a population that has a low education level, is still an open question. Under the political pressure from different interest groups, the easiest way for the government to solve the problem was to finance price subsidies by borrowing and printing money, the latter would certainly contribute to inflation.

The second source of inflation is excess demand generated by an overheated economy. We see that the decentralizing reform in an economy where the property rights of the state-owned enterprises are not clearly defined, would almost surely lead to an investment fever, which would aggravate the existing shortage and accelerate the inflation. The rampant inflation is probably the number-one enemy of economic reform in the transitions for the former CPEs. However, stopping the reform is not the solution, because it would imply going back to the old planned system. The task of economic research is to find out how to minimize the pain of the inflation in this process, what is the optimal path to accomplish the transition, and how much inflation a society could tolerate.

Notes

1. Notice that there is a distinction between marketization and privatization. According to the Report unanimously adopted at the thirteenth party congress of the Chinese Communist Party (CCP), the ultimate goal of the economic reform is to establish a socialist market economy based primarily on the public ownership with planning as a guidance (Zhao 1987). The 14th party congress of CCP reconfirmed more clearly that the goal of the economic reform is to establish a socialist market economy. The meaning of the "socialist market economy" is not clearly defined and the debate over this concept is less significant. The important fact is that the Chinese economy is indeed moving towards a market economy during the reform. The connotation of the socialist market economy is more and more like a real market with less and less socialist elements.

2. Before the reform in China, most producer's goods were allocated by quota (plan); and important consumer goods were allocated by rationing coupons. A typical household in a major city had about a dozen different rationing coupons, each of which looked like a stamp and usually had a specific valid date and the amount of the specified commodity one could purchase by the coupon. These rationing coupons were very popular before the economic reform, but their popularity declined in the 1982-86 period due to better supply conditions together with an increase of the price level. They came back to every household in major cities in the battle with the rampant inflation fro the period 1988-1990. At beginning of 1989 in Shanghai, for instance, there were many kinds of rationing coupons for important basic consumer goods, such as rice, flour, sugar, cigarettes, soybean products, pork, eggs, matches, soaps, edible oil, etc. These rationing coupons have been less and less used since 1992.

3. "Invisible price subsidies" refers to the subsidies when the government's procurement purchase prices are higher than the retail prices for maintaining stability purposes. It is invisible in the sense that an ordinary buyer might not know that the government is subsidizing this commodity. The visible subsidies refer to the monthly monetary payment that an employee

received from the government to compensate the loss of the price increase. For example, to compensate the loss of food price increases, the government gave each city employee a monthly subsidy, 5 yuan in 1979, 8 yuan in 1985 and 10 yuan in 1988. They are obviously visible.

4. The average labor productivity is measured by the average output per unit of labor (based on total personnel). Actually, the marginal labor productivity is a more relevant measure for our purposes here. Yet, one could argue that since the average productivity is increasing, the marginal productivity curve should be above the average productivity curve. The real problem here, however, is that the capital and other factors are not fixed. We do not know whether the increase of the average labor output is due to the newly added capital, or to the improvement of the labor productivity.

Table 12.1
Profit Rates of the State-owned Industrial Enterprises in 1979

Coal	2.1%
Iron ore	1.6%
Cement	4.4%
Chemical raw materials	3.2%
Lumber	4.8%
Rubber processing	44.9%
Paint and dyestuff	38.4%
Watch	61.1%
Bicycle	39.8%
Chemical drugs	33.1%

SOURCE: The Price Reform Research Group of the Chinese Academy of Social Sciences, 1986.

Table 12.2[a]
Price Subsidies and Government Deficits

Year	Inflation rate[b] (%)	Price subsidy	Gov't deficit	Total borrowing	Real deficit	Total revenue	Percentage[c] (%)
1978	0.7	9.386	(1.01)[d]	0.0	(1.01)	112.11	8.37
1979	2.0	18.071	17.06	3.531	20.591	110.33	16.38
1980	6.0	24.207	12.75	4.301	17.051	108.52	22.31
1981	2.4	32.772	2.55	7.308	9.858	108.95	30.08
1982	1.9	31.836	2.93	8.386	11.316	112.40	28.32
1983	1.5	34.166	4.35	7.941	12.291	124.90	27.35
1984	2.8	37.000	4.45	7.734	12.184	150.19	24.64
1985	8.8	29.947	(2.16)	8.985	6.825	186.64	16.05
1986	6.0	25.748	7.06	13.825	20.885	226.03	11.39
1987	7.3	29.405	8.03	17.020	25.050	234.66	12.53
1988	18.5	31.700	7.86	26.120	34.150	262.82	12.06

NOTE:

a. Except the percentage, all numbers in this table are based on the current value in billion yuan.

b. This is the official inflation rate, which is measured by the general retail price level.

c. The percentage of the price subsidy relative to the total government revenue.

d. The numbers in parantheses are surplus.

SOURCE: *Statistical Yearbook of China*, Beijing, 1987 and 1988.

Table 12.3
The Rate of Increase of the Total Fixed Capital Investment, Energy and Transportation

Year	Invest-ment(I)[a]	Growth of I (%)	Energy output[b]	Energy growth (%)	Freight turnover (FT)[c]	Growth of FT(%)
1984	183.300	33.9	778.47	9.2	724.8	9.1
1985	254.319	38.7	855.38	9.9	812.6	12.1
1986	301.962	18.7	881.35	3.0	876.5	7.9
1987	364.100	20.6	912.67	3.6	947.2	8.1
1988	434.100	18.5	951.00	4.2	987.6	4.3
Average	307.556	26.1%	875.77	6.0%	869.7	8.3%

NOTE:

a. The total fixed capital investments in billion yuan (current price).

b. The total energy production in terms of million ton of the standard fuel.

c. The total freight turnover by railroad (billion ton/kilometer).

SOURCE: *Excerpt of Statistical Yearbook*, Beijing, 1988 and *Statistical Yearbook of China*, Beijing, 1987. The last observation (1988) is from the Annual Report of the National Statistics Bureau of China (*People's Daily*, 3/2/1989).

Table 12.4
The Price Increase of Some Important Producer Goods in 1988

Producer's goods	Unit	Price at beginning of 1988 (yuan)	Price in Sept. 1988 (yuan)	Percentage increase
Steel plate	ton	2200	5800	163.6
Steel wire	ton	7000	15300	118.6
Pig iron	ton	280	790	182.1
Lead	ton	2650	7000	164.2
Nickel plate	ton	30000	120000	300.0
Aluminum	ton	4000	13000	225.0
Imported wood pulp	ton	3000	5500	83.3
Silkworm cocoon	dan[a]	310	840	171.0
Coal	ton	135	250	85.2
Cement	ton	110	250	127.3
Titanium Dioxide	ton	1300	8180	529.2

NOTE:

a. *dan*, a Chinese unit of weight (1 *dan* = 50 kilograms).

SOURCE: Du, Haiyan et al (1989).

Table 12.5
Wages vs. Productivity

Year	Average wage[a] (yuan)	Nominal wage index	Real wage index[b]	Productivity /labor[c] (yuan)	Productivity index
1978	644	100.0	100.0	11131	100.0
1979	705	109.5	107.6	11838	106.4
1980	803	124.7	114.1	12081	108.5
1981	812	126.1	112.6	11863	106.6
1982	836	129.8	113.5	12133	109.0
1983	865	134.3	115.1	13049	117.2
1984	1034	160.6	136.5	14070	126.4
1985	1213	188.4	140.4	15080	135.5
1986	1414	219.6	153.0	15809	142.0
1987	1546	240.1	153.7	16889	151.7

NOTE:

a. The average annual wage (in current value) of the employees in the state-owned enterprises and non-profit organizations.

b. Adjusted by Zhigong Shenghuo Feiyong Zhishu (the Urban Consumer Price Index) in *Statistical Yearbook of China*, 1988.

c. The average industrial labor productivity per person (based on total personnel) in the fixed (1980) price of the state-owned enterprises.

SOURCE: *Statistical Yearbook of China*, Beijing, 1988.

Figure 12.1
The planned price vs. the equilibrium price

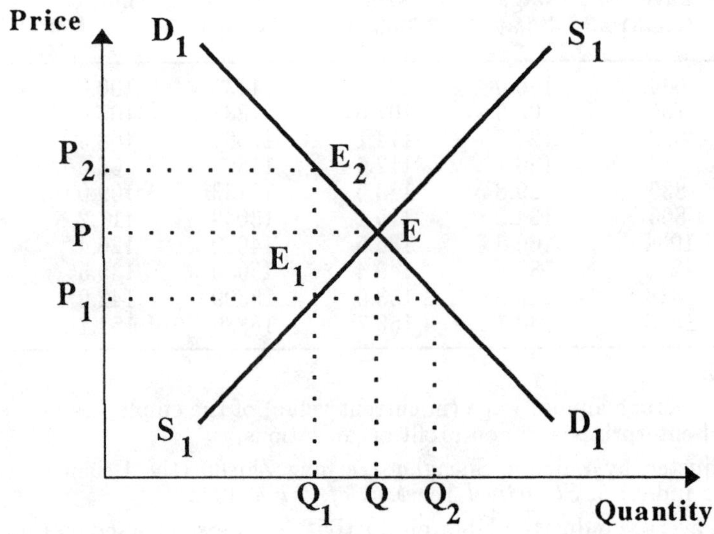

Figure 12.2
The impact of price subsidies on the supply and demand

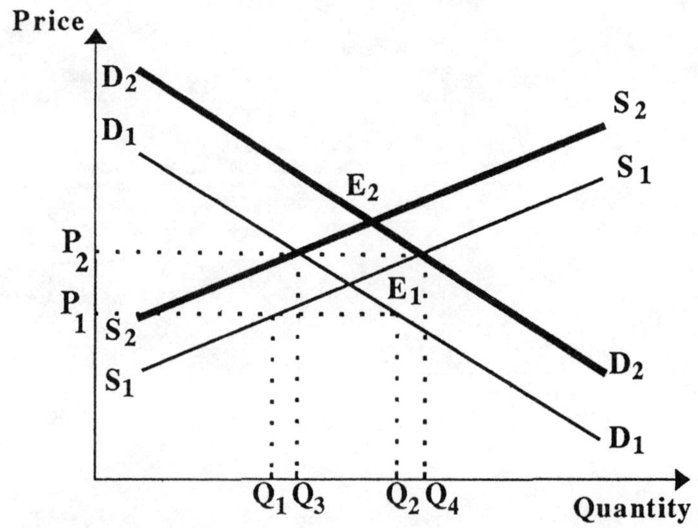

13

Models of Inflation in China

In the previous chapter we discussed the causation of inflation in China during the reform period. The focus of this chapter is on some theoretical models that aim at explaining inflation in China.

Before starting our discussion, we reemphasize that *inflation* refers to the condition of a continually rising price level at a rapid pace. By this definition, a once-and-for-all upward price adjustment is not an inflation, nor is a steady price increase at a slow rate, say 1-2 percent a year. In the history of the People's Republic of China up to this point, there was rampant inflation in two periods: during 1960-1962 and during the reforms period. Causation of the inflation in the two periods was quite different.

In his famous declaration, Milton Friedman asserted that inflation is always and everywhere a monetary phenomenon. He postulates that the source of all inflation is a high growth rate of the money supply. The policy implication of this proposition is that by restricting the growth rate of the money supply to relatively low levels, inflation can be prevented.

A more difficult question is why the monetary authority conducts an inflationary policy in China. Who has forced the central bank to supply money at an abnormal rate? In this chapter, we will discuss several theoretical models that may provide a clue to answer the above questions.

There are many well-known economic models that attempt to explain the mechanism of inflation, for a summary, see Hall (1982). In this chapter, we will focus on some useful models specifically constructed from the Chinese experiences. The first one is a simple descriptive model which provides a basic framework for analyzing inflation in China. The second model, proposed by Naughton (1991) explains a macroeconomic mechanism that causes the inflation. The third model, suggested by Wang (1991) provides microeconomic analysis of inflation. The last model, constructed by Feltenstein and Ha (1991), regards the inflation in China as a repressed one, which resulted from the lack of coordination between monetary policy and price controls.

13.1 A Descriptive Model of Inflation

Most economists agree with Friedman's proposition and conclude that large continuing upward movements in the price level (inflation) can only occur if there is a continually increasing money supply.

Figure 13.1 demonstrates the inflation process by using the interaction of the aggregate supply and demand curves. Suppose that an economy is initially at equilibrium with a natural rate of employment, point A with output level Y_n and price level P_1 in Figure 13.1 where AS_1 denotes aggregate supply and AD_1 aggregate demand. If the money supply increases, the aggregate demand curve shifts right to AD_2. At first, for a brief time, the economy may move to point A' and output may increase above the full-employment level to Y'. However, this above-full-employment output level is unsustainable. Wages and other factor prices will rise and aggregate supply will quickly begin to shift in until it reaches AS_2, at which the economy has returned to the natural-rate level of output. At the new equilibrium, Point B, the price level has increased to P_2.

If the money supply increases again, the aggregate demand curves will shift to the right again to AD_3 and aggregate supply will shift to the northwest from AS_2 to AS_3; the economy will move to B' and then to C, where the price level has risen to P_3.

Generally speaking, a centrally-planned economy is a resource restraint economy, the production capacity of which can not be stretched easily to a higher level. Consequently, the assumption that the economy is near the natural-rate level (basically, that output is at the full employment level) is very close to reality. Yi (1990) provides an analysis for the case where the full employment assumption is relaxed. He gets a very similar result except that the output level also increases in the process of a spiral rising of the price level. In other words, his analysis has a Keynesian flavor which leads to more or less the same conclusion. Here we focus on the model illustrated in Figure 13.1, because it's a polar case analysis and the full employment assumption is close to reality.

Given that inflation is defined as a process of continually increasing prices, it is easy to see that price reform, budget deficit, and supply shock can cause a once-and-for-all price-level increase, but cannot cause inflation.

Can Price Reform by Itself Cause Inflation?

The objective of price reform is two-fold: to adjust relative prices and to raise the market equilibrium price level in order to eliminate distortions and shortages. This argument is based on the assumption that the controlled price level is below the market equilibrium level, which is plausible.

The fact that the price level is controlled and that supplemental coupons and other rationing devices have market values indicates that the controlled price is below the market clearing level. Figure 12.1 in the previous chapter illustrates this point.

In Figure 12.1, Q and P represent the equilibrium quantity and price. P_1 is the controlled price level. If the price reform brings the economy from E_1 to E, then it leads to only a temporary increase in the price level, not an inflation in which the price level is continually rising.

It is not very accurate to say that price reform increased the price level even temporarily. Because the controlled price level P_1 does not represent the full price level, the real price level under the controlled regime is P_2. The distance between P_1 and P_2 is the rent associated with the rationing device. If we define the full price level as the sum of the controlled level and the rent of the rationing device, then the market equilibrium price level P is actually lower than the full price level under the controlled regime, P_2. From this point of view, the price reform lowers the full price from P_2 to P.

Therefore, under the controlled-price system, the real price level is much higher than the nominal price level. The difference is equal to the market value of the rationing devices. It is true that going from the controlled-price to a market-price system would increase the nominal price level. However, generally speaking, the real price level is actually decreased under the market equilibrium price because there are no rationing devices.

Can Fiscal Policy by Itself Cause Inflation?

To answer this question, let us look at Figure 13.2, which illustrates the effect of a one-shot permanent increase in government expenditure on aggregate output and the price level.

Initially the economy is at the natural rate level of output Y_n and price level P_1. The increase in the government expenditure shifts aggregate demand from AD_1 to AD_2 and moves the economy to point A', where the output level is higher than Y_n. The higher-than-normal output level bids up the labor cost and factor prices and the aggregate supply curve shifts inward, eventually reaching AS_2, where it intersects AD_2 at point B. Output is at the natural rate level again at point B and the price level has risen to P_2. The net result of a permanent increase in government expenditure is a one-shot permanent increase in the price level. If we define inflation as an continual increase in the price level, then we have to conclude that a once-and-for-all increase of government expenditure can only cause a once-and-for-all increase in price level, not inflation. This conclusion is valid no matter how the government finances its one-shot increase in expenditure. It could be financed by issuing bonds, or by printing money, or by a combination of the two, the above conclusion is essentially the same except that the level of the one-shot increase in price level would differ.

However, if government spending increased continually, we could have a continually rising price level. Then we would conclude that a rapid growth of government expenditure causes inflation. The problem with this argument is that an unlimited increase of government expenditure is not feasible. A government has only four ways to finance its expenditure: tax revenue, domestic borrowing, foreign borrowing, and printing money. There is always a limit to the first three ways. For example, the absolute limit for tax revenue is 100 percent of GNP; domestic and foreign borrowing have obvious limits. It seems that the government can always print money to finance its deficit. But if that is the case, then we are back to Friedman's proposition that inflation is caused by a continually increasing money supply.

Can Supply-Side Shocks or Inflationary Expectations by Themselves Cause Inflation?

Now the Chinese economy is essentially an open economy. The total value of trade (total exports plus total imports) has accounted for more than 30 percent of GNP in recent years. Part of its exports depend on imported parts. Suppose that there is a negative supply shock—say an increase in prices of imported parts. As demonstrated in Figure 13.3, the negative supply shock shifts the aggregate supply curve inward from AS_1 to AS_2. If the money supply and the aggregate demand curve are unchanged, the economy will move from point A to point B.

At point B, output is below the natural-rate level and the price level is at P_2, which is higher than the equilibrium level. It is obvious that point B is not a steady state. The price level tends to adjust downward and the aggregate supply curve would shift back in the southeast direction gradually. If the supply shock has a long term real effect on production capacity, then the new supply curve would end up somewhere in-between AS_1 and AS_2. If the supply shock has no long term effect on the economy, the new supply curve would eventually return to AS_1, where it intersects AD_1 at point A. The net result is the following: In the case where the supply shock has no long term effect on resources, the economy returns to its full employment at the initial price level and the price increase is only temporary; no inflation results. In the case where the supply shock reduces the capacity of the economy permanently, there would be a one-time price increase.

How about inflationary expectations? There is no doubt that inflationary expectations play an important role in the process of inflation. As discussed in the previous chapter, if inflationary expectations are high, consumers would run on banks and engage in panic buying while firms hold their product and wait for higher prices. This has happened in almost all hyperinflation cases in the past of many countries with different economic systems. It also happened in China in 1988. The question is whether inflationary expectations by themselves cause inflation. It seems plausible to say that inflationary expectations are self-generating and self-reinforcing. But it is hard to imagine that inflationary expectations can go very far without the company of a rapid growth of money supply. In almost all hyperinflation cases, high inflationary expectations are accompanied by high money supply growth. Various economic studies (Milton Friedman, *Studies in the Quantity Theory of Money*, 1956; R. Hall, *Inflation: Causes and Effects*, 1990) seem to suggest that rapid money supply growth rates causes inflation and high inflationary expectations. Notice that because of the possible pitfall of reverse causation, it is difficult to argue conclusively whether rapid growth of the money supply causes high inflationary expectations, or vice versa.

China's experience confirms the direction of causation argued for in the monetarist literature. The rapid money supply growth rate for the period 1985-1988 preceded the inflation and high inflationary expectations in 1988. If inflation expectations could be or become self-generating and self-reinforcing, then inflation would have been continually high in the following years. The fact that tightened monetary policy in 1989 and 1990 brought the inflation rate down significantly to only about 2.1 percent in 1990 indicates that the direction of causation is such that tightening money supply brought down the inflation rate and dampened out the inflationary expectations. That personal saving in China soared in the 1989-1991 period provides solid evidence that inflationary expectations died out.

To sum up, an analysis of aggregate demand and supply in this section suggests that price reform, fiscal policy, negative supply shocks, and inflationary expectations have a temporary effect on the price level, but cannot cause inflation. High inflation can occur only with a high rate of money growth.

The remaining question is: Why does inflationary monetary policy occur, or why does the central bank let the money supply grow so rapidly?

13.2 Naughton's Macroeconomic Interpretation

In the previous chapter, we discussed the causation of inflation in the late 1980s in China. Naughton (1991) offers another view to explain inflation in China. He argues that the economic reform caused a substantial erosion in government revenue while the central government tried to maintain a large investment program. To finance the large investment project, the government ordered the banking system to print money and increase credit limits, which led to a high growth rate of money supply. Here is why.

In a centrally-planned economy, although prices did not play an important role in resource allocation, the price system was a crucial instrument for resource mobilization. The most important characteristic of the government-controlled price system was the so-called "scissors movement of prices" between the modern industrial products and agricultural products and most services. This highly distorted price structure guaranteed huge profits in the state-owned modern industrial sector, which was the main source of the government revenue. The central government actually used the distorted price system as a effective tax system, which allowed the government to collect about one-third of GNP on average before the reform. The government was also the major player for national savings and investment. In 1978 the percentages of the government, enterprises, and households in total saving were 51 percent, 34 percent, 15 percent respectively. (Qian 1988) Most of government savings went directly to large investment projects of the central government.

Before the reform, the vast majority of national savings came from modern industry. In 1978, modern industry employed only 12 percent of the labor force, but it generated a net financial surplus (total profits plus taxes) that was equal to 25.4 percent of GNP, accounting for about 80 percent of national financial saving. Furthermore, only a small proportion (0.7 percent of GNP) was retained by enterprises, the remaining 24.7 percent of GNP was remitted to the government. Households paid no direct taxes and household financial saving was only 1.3 percent of GNP. Therefore, the modern industrial sector was the major source of both national saving and the government's fiscal revenue.

Profound institutional reforms changed the centrally-planned price structure fundamentally in the following ways. First, agricultural products prices have increased, the so-called scissors price difference has converged consequently, high prices in raw materials were passed to urban residents and processing industries, which have resulted in low profit margins in those industry. Second, depreciation charges and interest payments have soared.

Third, the industrial sector is facing increasing competition, since barriers to entry were lowered significantly. Therefore, the profit margin for most industries have decreased with only a few exceptions.

As a result, financial surpluses generated by modern industry have declined rapidly since 1978. By 1988, total profit and tax of modern industry had decreased to 16.7 percent of GNP, of which 3 percent of GNP was retained by enterprises, and 2 percent was used to pay back bank loans. Thus the government budget revenue from modern industry declined from 24.7 percent to 11.6 percent of GNP, the total government budgetary revenue had also declined drastically from 35.4 percent in 1978 to 19.8 percent in 1988. Eighty-four percent of the decline in budgetary revenues is attributable to declining remittances from the predominantly state-owned modern industry.

In response to the decrease of government revenue as a percentage of GNP, the central government reduced its expenditures. The overall spending of the government declined from 35.4 percent in 1988 to about 22 percent in 1988. Consequently, the budgetary deficit remained modest, about 2 percent of GNP on average for the 1980s.

Naughton points out that the budgetary deficit does not fully reflect the effect of the government on the economy. Budgetary financing of fixed investment declined sharply, but the central government investment was not reduced accordingly. Completed investment projects under the central plan were equal to 9 percent of GNP in 1978, and about 8 percent in the late 1980s. Notice that less than half of the central investment plan was funded by budgetary revenues, which implied that the government needed to borrow about 5 percent of GNP in order to cover a gap between its central investment plan and the allotment from the budget to finance the plan. In other words, the central government's investment plan was much larger than the fund allocation from the budget to finance it. Consequently, total government borrowing is equal to the sum of the budgetary deficit and the deficit in the central investment plan, which amounts to a total of 7 percent of GNP in 1988 (of which 2.3 percent was the budgetary deficit and 4.7 percent was of the deficit in the investment plan). The government deficit was the main source of inflationary pressure and rapid growth of money supply in the 1980s. Total government borrowing exceed 50 percent of total credit creation by the banking system.

Naughton's model of inflation in China can be summarized as follows: First, significant progress was made in liberalizing product prices and introducing market forces into the economy. Lower entry barriers in industry resulted in a rapid growth of small scale firms, especially township and village enterprises in the rural area. Consequently, competition has increased and profits of government-owned (large scale) firms have decreased. Second, virtually no progress was made in restructuring the tax system, or clarifying property rights and obligations for use of assets. The lack of a modern tax system eroded the government revenues. Third, although total government spending as a percentage of GNP declined consistently throughout the 1980s, the central investment plan was not reduced in the same fashion. As the central government's borrowing requirements increased, it threatened to crowd out new decentralized investment. The large total government deficit forced the central bank to increase the money supply and was one of the main sources of the inflation. The government deficit data during the reform period are provided in Figure 13.4.

13.3 Wang's Model

Wang (1991) provides a formal model which explains why the reform inevitably caused inflation. As Barro and Gorden (1983) point out, it is unsatisfactory to regard a systematic public policy as irrational. Extensive repetition that inflation is everywhere and anywhere a monetary phenomenon is not of much help, because it does not explain why the government persistently fails to control the money supply.

In an extensive study, a group of young economists at the Institute of Economic System Reform (IESR, 1988) observe the following relationship:

Fixed capital investment expansion → High growth rate of money supply → Inflation.

They also point out that the main difference between the current expansion and those in the past is that the local government and firms have replaced the central government as the initiators. The next problem is how to explain the expansionary incentive of local government and firms.

Fan (1989) argues that there is a cost of real resources in the process of economic reform because it involves economic structural changes. Consequently, the aggregate production possibility frontier (PPF) shrinks inward. However, the government policy and its growth target are based on the previous PPF. To achieve its growth goal, the government adopts a expansionary policy through increasing the money supply, which leads to inflation. In spite if its obvious attractiveness, Wang points out this argument has several drawbacks. First, it implicitly assumes an irrational government systematically pursuing a growth policy beyond its means. Second, Fan's interpretation fails to explain why the local government and firms became the main initiators of the expansion.

Wang constructs a behavioral model to explain the inflationary mechanism in China, in which he assumes that the government is rational. The model suggests that the decentralizing reforms gave local government and firms incentive to expand their fixed capital investment. The government has to use an inflationary monetary policy to shrink the real value of the committed fixed capital investment in order to bring the ratio of fixed to circulating capital toward its efficient level.

Wang's model has the following plausible features: (1) It assumes that both the government and firms are quantity maximizers. (2) The central government, local governments, monetary authority, and firms are rational. (3) Both investment expansion and inflationary monetary policy can be explained. (4) The result is positive so that it is empirically testable.

The model assumes that the economy has only one output, Q, that is produced by using two inputs: fixed capital K, and circulating capital L. "Fixed capital" refers to plants and machinery, and "circulating capital" refers to such inputs like energy, raw materials, and labor. There are N identical firms in the economy that are of equal size, have equal amounts of initial fixed capital and have identical production functions. Total output is the aggregation of the output of all firms,

$$Q = \sum_{i=1}^{N} Q_i \tag{13.1}$$

where Q_i is the output of firm i.

The basic assumption of this model is that both the government and firms are quantity maximizers. The only difference is that the government maximizes the aggregate Q whereas individual firm i maximizes Q_i.

Money is used in the economy for resource allocation. The system is assumed to work as follows: First, output is bought and sold in the market and the price is market-determined. The exchange equation holds

$$PQ = MV \tag{13.2}$$

where P = price, M = money supply, and V is velocity. If we assume that $V = 1$ and total monetary revenue is R and the non-inflationary budget is equal to B, then we have

$$PQ = M = R = B \tag{13.3}$$

Second, a substantial part of total revenue is controlled by firms, hence the total budget of firms is $B^f = \sum B_i^f$. The rest of the revenue goes to the government as its budget B^g . The real resources corresponding to B^f and B^g are $Q^f = B^f/P$ and $Q^g = B^g/P$, respectively, at price P. For the economy as a whole, both real resources and total revenue have to satisfy

$$Q = Q^f + Q^g$$

$$B = B^f + B^g$$

$$P(Q^f + Q^g) = B^f + B^g$$

Third, each firm determined how to divide ${B_i}^f$ into I_i and $(B_i - I_i)$ in order to produce Q_i, where I_i is the investment in the fixed capital and $(B_i - I_i)$ is the budget for circulating capital.

Fourth, the government controls financial resources, B^g, and deposits them in a bank. Firms can go to the bank to apply a credit for circulating capital only. If we denote the part of B^g granted to firms i as PB_i^g , then $\sum B_i^g = B^g$.

Given the above description of the model, Wang shows that the individual firm's optimal level of fixed capital investment in any equilibrium is higher than the one that would maximize social output, because (1) firms and local governments' powers are based on the size of their operation; (2) public ownership makes the firms' investment behavior biased toward over-expansion since their gain from profitable projects and loss from bad investment are not symmetric; (3) the less the amount of circulating capital, the higher the marginal productivity of $(B_i - I_i)$, and if the marginal productivity is one of the main criteria for the bank to determine the priority of making a loan, then it is more desirable for the firm with less $(B_i - I_i)$ to get a credit as circulating capital.

Since the rational choice of fixed investment for each individual firm is greater than the socially optimal solution, resources are misallocated; aggregate output is smaller than the optimal level even if all resources are fully employed.

To alleviate this misallocation, the central government's rational choice is to carry out an inflationary policy. By increasing the price level from P to P', the central government effectively reduced the real resources committed by firms to fixed investment, $Q^f = B^f/P$. For given amount B^f, an increase in price level will result in a reduction in Q^f. Through inflationary policy, the government actually takes part of the real resources away from firms. Consequently, Q^g is increased. Since Q^g is allocated to provide circulating capital for firms, it will mitigate the misallocation problem, and make the ratio between fixed capital and circulating capital close to its optimal level.

13.4 Feltenstein and Ha's Model

Feltenstein and Ha (1991) develop an analytical model which derives a "true" rate of inflation on the basis of the different rates of change of the stock of money in circulation and the nominal value of retail sales.

There are two different opinions on the saving behaviors in China. Naughton (1987), Qian (1988), and Yi (1991) argue that saving in China is essentially voluntary and is not a forced outcome of repressed prices. Feltenstein and Ha assert that in most planned economies, prices are controlled at least to a certain degree. Furthermore, foreign trade and foreign exchanges are also distorted. Consequently, an increase in money supply may not be accompanied by an adjustment in price and exchange level which would lead to a disequilibrium in the financial and goods markets and a repressed inflation. The purpose of Feltenstein and Ha's model is to estimate a measure of the extent to which the price level is repressed. The model consists of the following equations.

First the consumers money demand is a function of his real income and expectations of the rate of inflation.

$$log\ qm^d = a_0 + a_1 log\ y + a_2 \pi_t^e \qquad (13.4)$$

where qm is the households demand for real quasi-money balances $qm = (QM)/P_t$, QM = normal quasi money balance. Here quasi-money refers to interest-bearing deposits of consumers, and P_t is the true price index. y represents real income and π_t^e is the expected rate of inflation measured by P_t. log denotes the natural log.

Second the rate of inflation is given by

$$\pi_t = log\ P_t - log\ P_{t-1} \qquad (13.5)$$

Here the true rate of inflation may be interpreted as the rate that would induce consumers to hold the observed level of broad money in the absence of price control. Our aim is to find out whether the true rate is significantly different from the official rate.

The standard specification of money demand equation would use the total real money balances, $(Qm + m_1)/P$. Here F-H use an analogue of a Baumol-Tobin model in which the consumer chooses to divide his cash holdings between bank deposits and currency. If there is an increase in excess demand (an increase in repressed inflation), then the "true" real interest rate or the saving deposit declines. As a result, the gap between the real return on currency and quasi-money narrows. Currency thus becomes relatively more attractive due to its high liquidity (ready ability to buy goods if goods are available).

Third, the F-H model uses the ratio of broad money balances to retail sales to measure the deviation between "true" and official inflation. Here broad money, M, is defined as the sum of currency and consumer holdings of bank deposits. The true price level is equal to the sum of the official price level and a term which reflects repressed inflation.

$$log\ P_t = log\ P + \alpha log\ (M_2/PR) \tag{13.6}$$

where P is the official price level and R is the real volume of consumer retail sales. If $\alpha = 0$, then the true and official rates of inflation are equal. If, at the other extreme, $\alpha = 1$, then a 10 percent increase in the ratio of money to retail sales will cause the true rate of inflation to be 10 percent higher than the official rate.

Fourth, the model assumes that inflationary expectations are adaptive such that the expected value of the true inflation rate for the next period depends on the predicting error made this period.

$$\pi_t^e - \pi_{t-1}^e = \beta(\pi_t - \pi_{t-1}^e) \tag{13.7}$$

where π_t^e is the expected true inflation rate for next period at this period; π_t is the true inflation rate of this period and β is an estimated constant which lies between 0 and 1.

Fifth, the model assumes that the real stock of quasi-money balances, valued at the true price level, adjusts with a log to the desired level. That is,

$$log\ qm - log\ qm_{-1} = \tau(log\ qm^d - log\ qm_{-1}) \tag{13.8}$$

where qm_{-1} is the real stock of quasi-money of the previous period and τ is a parameter to be estimated. The economic implication of the model is that the stock of currency plus household bank deposits are exogenous and represents nominal purchasing power. Consumers adjust their quasi-money balances based on their inflationary expectations and income levels.

Finally, because the real disposable income, y, for China is not available, the model constructs values of y as the sum of real retail sales of consumer goods plus savings and changes in the end-of-period currency held by households.

$$y \equiv R + \frac{[(QM - QM(-1)) + (M_H - M(H-1))]}{P} \tag{13.9}$$

where M_H denotes household currency holdings. Equation 13.4 to 13.9 constitute the F-H model.

By using the quarterly data for the period 1979-1988, the optimal values of parameters $\alpha = 0.89$ and $\beta = 0.92$ are found by grid search in the reduced form of the equations such that the log-likelihood is maximized within the range $\alpha \geq 0$ and $0 \leq \beta \geq 1$. The value for α indicates that a 1 percent change in the (M_2/PR) ratio (the measure of the monetary overhang) will lead to a 0.89 percent change in the true rate of inflation. The parameter $\beta = 0.92$ implies that the expectation of inflation appears to be revised fairly fast, which is plausible in an economy with rapid institutional changes. The estimated τ is 0.361, which indicates that the real quasi-money balances take about $(1 - \tau)/\tau = 1.7$ quarters to adjust to the difference between the demand and actual amount in the last quarter.

Feltenstein and Ha also test the following four hypotheses. First is to test if the true rate of inflation is equal to the official price index, which is equivalent to seeing if $\alpha = 0$. A likelihood ratio test rejects the hypothesis $\alpha = 0$ at a 1 percent level. Second is to test the hypothesis that the true velocity of money is constant. The likelihood ratio test cannot reject the null hypothesis that the true velocity is constant. Therefore, F-H conclude the true velocity is approximately constant; the apparent rapid decline in the velocity of money is actually the result of using the distorted official price index. Third is to test whether the monetization process played an important role in the demand for quasi-money. F-H introduce a trend variable (with first quarter of 1979 equal to 1, second quarter of 1979 equal to 2, etc.) in the demand equation (13.4). It turns out that both the t-statistic and likelihood ratio test cannot reject the hypothesis that the coefficient of the trend variable is insignificantly different from zero. Fourth, to check whether real interest rates are useful explanatory variables in the demand for quasi-money, F-H substitute the true interest rate variable (which is the difference between the nominal rate and the true inflation rate) in the place of the true inflation rate. The result is that the coefficient of the true real rate of interest has the wrong sign and its t-statistic is insignificant. This confirms that the expected true rate of inflation out performs other variables in determining the Chinese quasi-money demand.

To sum up, F-H construct a monetary model to estimate to what extent inflation is repressed in China for the period 1979-1988. According to their model, by the end of 1988 the true price index was 114 percent higher than the official index, assuming that the two were equal at the beginning of 1979. Therefore, they conclude that the annual rate of true inflation is approximately 12.4 percent higher than the official price index for the

10-year period under study. Most results in the F-H model are plausible. However, two things should be mentioned here for the reader to contemplate. First, one should consider whether saving in China is voluntary or forced. Second, one should note that a result that the monetization process is insignificant is surprising and probably due to the oversimplification of the monetization process by using a trend variable. Chapters 8 and 9 of this book have discussed the monetization process in detail and concluded differently from the F-H model. Here, readers are asked to compare the two points of view and judge which one is better to explain the reality in China.

Figure 13.1
Rising money supply and inflation

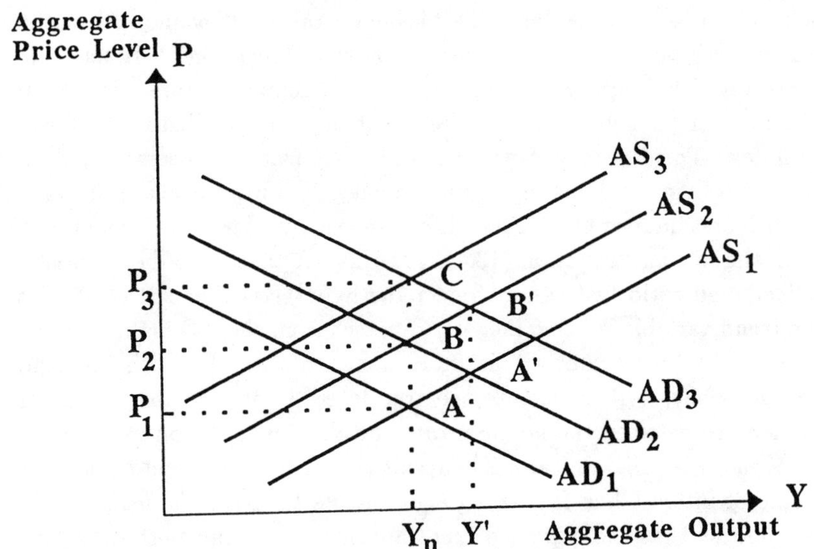

Figure 13.2
Impact of a one-shot increase in government expenditure

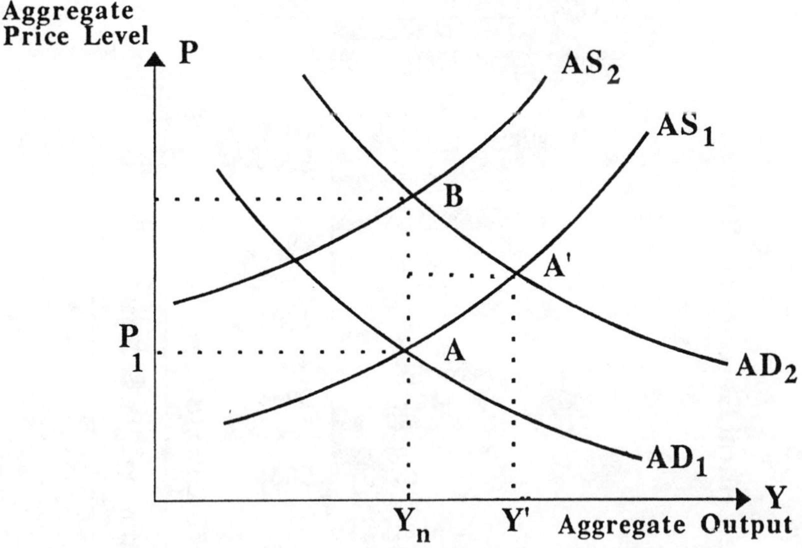

Figure 13.3
Response to a supply shock

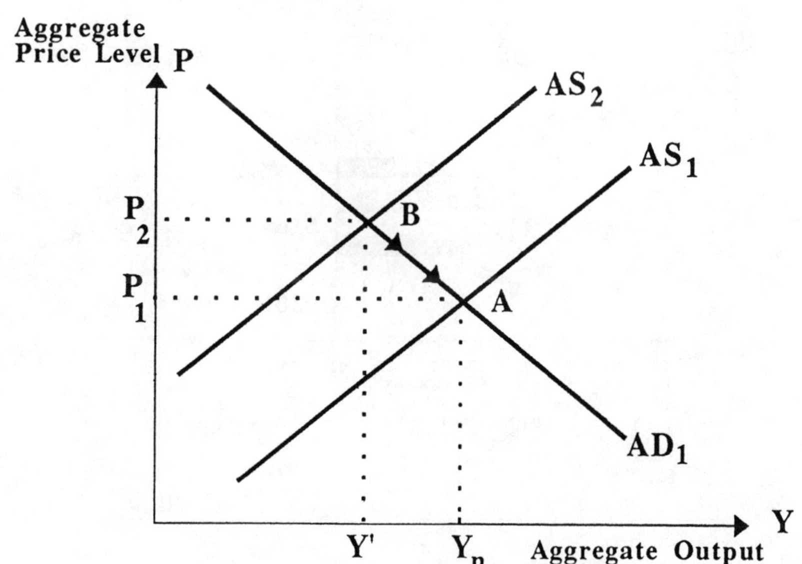

Figure 13.4 The Chinese Central Government Deficit

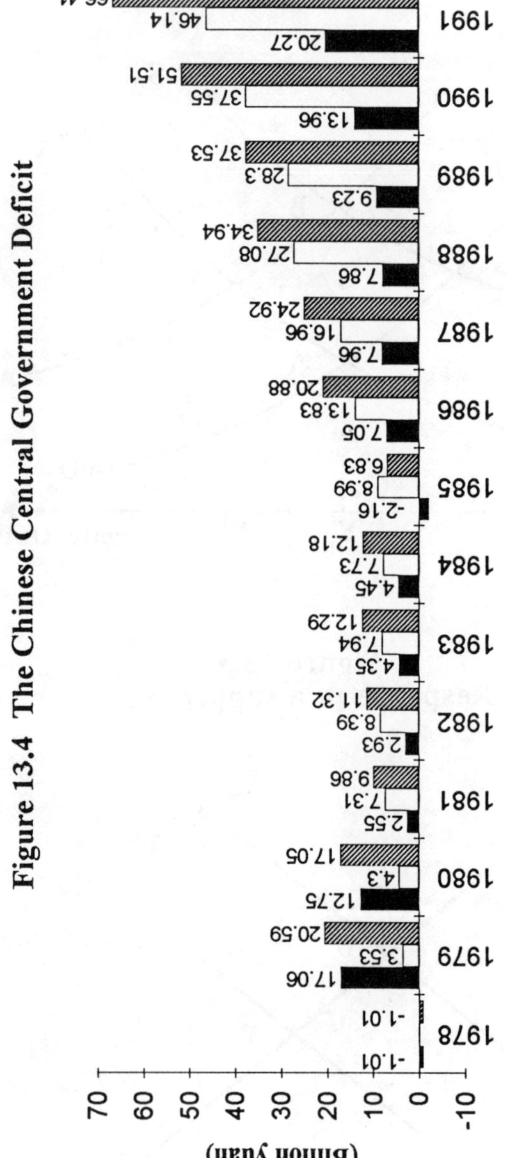

Source: Statistical Yearbook of China, 1992, page 215, 226.

14

Money and Economic Activity

As we discussed before, money played a subordinated role in the centrally-planned economy, because resources were by and large allocated by mandatory plans. Money was passive and accommodating to the physical allocation plan. There was neither a central bank nor an independent monetary policy. In this environment, clearly money was an endogenous variable. The central planners always first worked out plans for physical allocation of resources, according to which the cash and credit plans were determined.

During the economic reform, the role of money in the Chinese economy has changed. Casual observation and statistical evidence have suggested that the monetary variable in China has become increasingly active in income determination. Money looks more like an exogenous variable in China in the sense that it precedes the economic activity since the mid-1980s. This observation is not surprising. After all, China has a central bank with a money supply system based on reserve requirements and the multiplier effect. More importantly, the whole economy is moving towards a market system.

The debate between monetarists and Keynesian economists has focused on the role of money. The advantage and disadvantage between Keynesian and monetarist models have been fully debated and well documented. Most Keynesian arguments are based on structural models, which describe the transmission mechanism between money and income as follows: The money supply affects interest rates, which in turn affect investment, which in turn affects aggregate demand and output. The monetarist views are primarily based on the reduced form models, which examine the effect of money on economic activity by looking at if movements in income are tightly linked to movements in money.

The structural model approach is superior if we know the correct structure of the model. However, this is a big *if*. Even in developed countries, where the relationships among economic variables are relatively clear, there have been endless debates over the right structural models. For an economy in transition, where institutional changes have occurred rapidly in the process of establishing a market mechanism, it is very difficult (if not impossible) to construct a structural model. Perhaps, the reduced form model approach is the more feasible method with which to analyze the relationship among economic variables during the transition period.

In this chapter, we will do a preliminary study of the role of money in China after the central bank was established; the focus of the discussion is on the relationship between money and income variables.

14.1 Causality Analysis for Monetary and Income Variables

There is a great deal of concern over the endogeneity of the money supply in China (Zhou and Zhu 1987). The central bank of China does not have an independent monetary policy. The targets of money supply are not credible. The central bank obeys the central government's orders and its branches are led simultaneously by the central bank and local governments. The central bank and its local branches face tremendous pressures from the corresponding governments to supply extra money to support economic growth in their localities. The excess money supplies in 1958, 1984, and 1988 are examples of how economic conditions and the government's policies have tremendous influence on the money supply. Does this imply that the income variable determines money supply or is it the other way around? In this section, we investigate the causal relationship between the monetary and income variables in China.

It is worth pointing out that the degree of independence of the central bank is important. Alesina and Summers (1990) have shown that when central banks are ranked from the least independent to the most independent for 17 developed countries, the inflation performance is found to be the best for countries with the most independent central bank. The People's Bank of China was a government agency in the past and had no independent power to implement a monetary policy. The degree of independence has increased since PBC became the central bank in 1984. It was not a coincidence that a relatively independent central bank emerged at the same time that the money supply became increasingly like an exogenous variable in the economy.

There are two approaches to the endogeneity problem in econometric literature. The first one is the Cowles Foundation approach, which assumes that the classification of variables into "endogenous" and "exogenous" and the causal structure of the model are given *a priori* and not testable. The more recent second approach is to define the "exogeneity" in some specific ways so that it is testable (Eagle, Hendry and Richard 1983). Here we limit ourselves to a simple version of the latter approach.

We define causality in the Granger (1969) sense. The premise is that the future cannot cause the present or the past. If event A happens after event B, we know that A cannot cause B. On the other hand, if A happens before B, it does not necessarily imply that A causes B. In other words, the necessary condition of A causing B is that A occurs before B, but this is not a sufficient condition. In practice, we observe two time series A and B, and would like to know whether A precedes B, or B precedes A, or if they are contemporaneous. Granger causality means "precedence"; it is not causality as it is usually understood.

Granger (1969) suggested a test for causality. Consider two time series, m_t and y_t, denoting money and income respectively. The series m_t fails to Granger cause y_t if in a regression of y_t on lagged $y's$ and lagged $m's$, the coefficients of $m's$ are zero.

$$y_t = \sum_{i=1}^{n} \alpha_i y_{t-i} + \sum_{i=1}^{n} \beta_i m_{t-i} + \epsilon_t \tag{14.1}$$

That is, if $\beta_i = 0$ for $i = 1, 2, ...n$, then m_t fails to cause y_t. The lag length n is relatively arbitrary.

Chen (1989) examines causal relationships between the monetary and other macro-economic variables. By using the sample period 1951-1985, he finds that a causal relationship (feedback) exists from currency to nominal income, from currency to the budget deficit, and from currency to the trade deficit. One-way causality runs from currency to total inflation. We differ from Chen's study by investigating separately the causal relationship between the monetary and income variables for the periods before and after the reform. The profound institutional changes during the economic reform would raise serious doubts in those studies in which the common parameters (mechanism) are estimated by pooling pre- and post-reform data together.

14.2 Empirical Results of the Granger Test

To test Granger causality between the monetary and income variables, we have regressed the growth rate of national income, GNI, on its own lags and the lagged values of the growth rate of M2 for the annual data 1953-1978, with lag length n equaling 2 and 3. The results are striking. None of the coefficients of the lagged GM2, the growth rate of M2, is significant.

The simple correlation coefficient between the growth rate of M2 and the real growth rate of national income is only 0.26 for the period 1953-1978. The student t test ($t = 1.57$) indicates that the correlation coefficient is not significantly different from zero at the 5 percent level. This indicates that M2 did not cause income in the period 1953-1978 in the Granger sense. This result can also be seen in Figure 14.1, where the growth rate of M2 and the growth rate of real national income are plotted together. (The annual data used in Figure 14.1 are provided in Table 14.1.) No consistent pattern can be observed between the two variables before 1978. This finding supports the hypothesis that in a centrally-planned economy, money was passive and accommodating, and did not play an active role in the economy.

It would be interesting to look at the relationship between the growth rate of M2 and the income variable by using the quarterly data for the reform period. The quarterly data on national income are not available. In China the agricultural products still account for a large proportion of the income, and their production cycle is a year. Estimating the quarterly income is tedious and less rewarding, we therefore use the industrial output or the total retail sale as the economic activity variable. The quarterly data of M2, industrial output, and the total retail sales are available. Notice that some kind of seasonal adjustments should be done before the causality test. The money supply in China usually has a spike in the fourth quarter each year (before the Chinese new year, Spring Festival, cash injection). There are usually two peaks for the total industrial output, the second quarter and the fourth quarter.

Both casual observation and preliminary statistical analysis have suggested that the money supply (M0 or M2) has led the economic activity variable (industrial output or the total retail sales) by two quarters on average during the reform period (1983-1991). Although a conclusive answer depends on a formal investigation, our conjecture is that the monetary variable has preceded the income activity variable during the reform period. The precise lag length (one quarter to three quarters) varies for different measures of money and economic activity variables.

The possible explanation of this conjecture is that the economy has changed dramatically since 1979. The reform made the market share increase and firms and individuals started to respond to market conditions. The government and the banking system have tried to use economic leverage instead of administrative orders to adjust and tune the economy. The money supply became one of the most important instruments to control the general credit condition and the aggregate demand. Money has played an active role in determination of income. This conjecture is also consistent with the previous studies in this area for industrial economies. For example, Andersen and Jordan (1968) concluded in their well-known paper that the monetary variable (the change of money supply) had a significant impact on the change of GNP and hence played an active role in income determination for the United States, whereas the fiscal variables were not significant.

The above result suggests that the monetary variable was passive and accommodating in the period when the economy was centrally-planned. However, since the economic reform started in 1979, the monetary variable is getting increasingly active and is playing an important role in income determination. Further research is needed in this area to verify this conjecture.

The relationship between money and income variables is extremely important for policy makers. Monetarists, led by Milton Friedman, have presented their arguments convincingly by a comprehensive analysis, which contains timing, statistical, and historical evidence. What we have done in this chapter is no more than to raise the question regarding the relationship between the monetary and income variables. The above preliminary results should be viewed with the following two principles in mind. First, although we have shown that there is a high correlation between the change of money supply and income for the reform period, correlation does not necessarily imply causation. That movement of one variable is tightly linked to another does not necessarily mean that one variable causes the other. Second, Granger causality test has indicated that the change in money supply precedes (is ahead of) the change of economic activity (industrial output). This test only explains which variable happened first and which has followed. Based on the Granger causality test, it is premature to conclude that the change of money supply has caused the change of income because the possibility of *reverse causation* (Mishkin 1992, pp. 637-650).

Table 14.1
Growth Rate of M2 and Real National Income

Year	Growth of M2[a]	Growth of national income
1953	12.24	14.0
1954	16.45	5.8
1955	10.20	6.4
1956	19.95	14.1
1957	12.97	4.5
1958	58.42	22.0
1959	25.06	8.2
1960	4.44	-1.4
1961	7.50	-29.7
1962	-0.82	-6.5
1963	0.09	10.7
1964	-0.44	16.5
1965	14.47	17.0
1966	13.81	17.0
1967	11.20	-7.2
1968	5.91	-6.5
1969	-1.15	19.3
1970	-1.23	23.3
1971	9.80	7.0
1972	5.60	2.9
1973	15.29	8.3
1974	7.64	1.1
1975	8.61	8.3
1976	6.59	-2.7
1977	2.09	7.8
1978	4.68	12.3
1979	25.80	7.7
1980	26.39	6.4
1981	21.25	4.9
1982	15.90	8.2
1983	18.74	10.0
1984	34.84	13.6
1985	17.80	13.5
1986	28.20	7.7
1987	22.40	10.2
1988	21.19	11.3

NOTE:
a. M2 is defined as in Table 4.2.

SOURCE: *Statistical Yearbook of China*, 1989. *Almanac of China's Finance and Banking*, 1990.

Figure 14.1 Annual Growth Rate of M2 and Real National Income of China
Data Period: 1953-1988

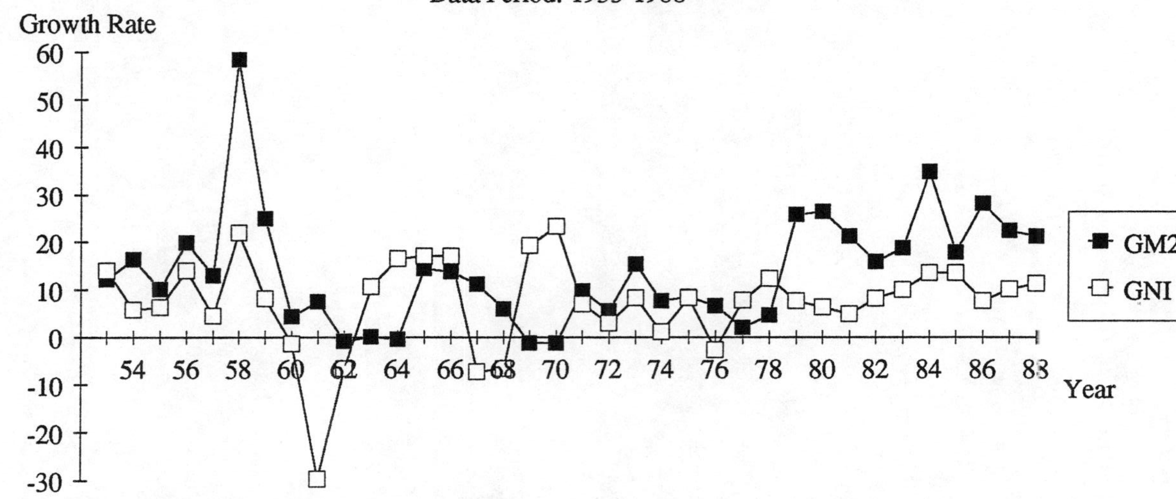

Source: Statistical Yearbook of China, 1989. Almanac of China's Finance and Banking, 1989.

PART FIVE

Financial Markets in China

15

Nonbank Financial Institutions

From the previous discussion, we see that before 1979, the financial sector was monopolized by a banking system dominated by the People's Bank. There were virtually no other financial intermediaries in existence. One of the significant developments of the economic reform during the 1980s was the emergence of nonbank financial intermediaries. The transition from a centrally-planned economy to a market-oriented economy can be characterized as a decentralization process. The emergence of nonbank financial intermediaries played an important role in this process in the sense that it broke the banking system's monopoly on financial resources. Nonbank financial institutions brought competition by channeling funds from lenders-savers to borrowers-spenders. They compete with the banking system and provide alternative ways for savers to invest and for spenders to borrow.

By the end of 1992, China had 85 financial security companies, of which about 20 were established in 1992, and 1200 trust and investment companies, of which more than 300 were newly opened in 1992. Both security and trust and investment companies are allowed to engage in stock, bond, and other securities business. In addition, there were 20 financial firms, 4 insurance companies, 9 leasing companies and more than 3000 credit cooperatives in urban areas (Lou 1993).

The total amount of bonds and stocks issued in 1992 was 120 billion yuan, of which about 10 billion were common stocks. By the end of 1992, the accumulated bonds and stocks in the financial market reached 300 billion yuan, which was 40 percent higher than in 1991. Compared with broad money, M2, which was about 2300 billion, the total amount of stocks and bonds was about equal to 13 percent of the value of broad money at the end of 1992.

During economic reform, the economy has changed to a multi-layered, diversified ownership structure. Rapid growth of the collective and private sectors and joint ventures requires a flexible and efficient financial sector. To a certain degree, the emergence of the nonbank financial institutions satisfies such a demand. In this chapter, we introduce some nonbank financial intermediaries, specifically, the People's Insurance Company, trust and investment corporations, and rural and urban credit co-ops. Other financial institutions, such as brokerage firms, will be discussed in Chapter 16 with the stock and bond markets. The discussion of this chapter will focus on the nature, the function, and the economic significance of these nonbank financial institutions.

15.1 The People's Insurance Company of China (PICC)

Founded on October 20, 1949, the People's Insurance Company of China (PICC) was the only insurance company in China until recently. Its headquarters is in Beijing.

The Nature and Responsibilities of PICC

PICC has monopolized the insurance sector in China. It deals with all kinds of insurance and reinsurance businesses, provides consulting services to other insurance companies, and has a monopoly position in the provision of international insurance. PICC has been the dominant power in domestic insurance business. Roughly speaking, provision of all required insurance, foreign exchange insurance, insurance of state-owned enterprises, and insurance of joint venture enterprises are conducted exclusively by PICC.

PICC has the following responsibilities: (1) to promulgate all kinds of regulations, procedural rules, and insurance ratings for the insurance industry; (2) to conduct domestic insurance and international insurance business; (3) to serve as an agent of foreign insurance companies and to verify, evaluate, and make payments in cases that involve foreign insurance companies; (4) to operate in real estate markets for the transactions of its tangible and intangible assets; (5) to serve as the holding company of China Insurance Company Ltd., Pacific Insurance Ltd., and other overseas subsidiaries and joint venture investments of PICC; (6) to participate in international academic and business exchanges; (7) and to conduct other business entrusted by the People's Bank of China. PICC provides more than 200 insurance services for domestic customers and more than 80 insurance services for foreign clients.

The Structure of PICC

The board of directors has the final decision making power for PICC. The board consists of 31 to 39 directors, who are appointed by the relevant departments of the government. The board of directors elects seven to nine directors as the standing directors, out of whom one president and several vice presidents are nominated. The State Council appoints the president and vice presidents upon nomination. The board of directors has an annual meeting. The president, vice presidents, and the designated standing directors are in charge of the routine business.

PICC has a supervisory board, which consists of seven to nine members appointed by the relevant departments of the government. The supervisory board elects three of its members as the standing members, out of which one chairperson is nominated. The State Council has the final say on the chairperson's appointment. The responsibilities of the supervisory board are to verify the company's annual budget, to audit all accounting procedures, and to investigate important cases. The supervisory board also has an annual meeting to discuss important matters and also to set up the work agenda for the next year.

The hierarchical structure of PICC consists of the headquarters, its first level subsidiaries, main branches, and branches, with a vertical chain of command. The headquarters is in Beijing. At the provincial, large-city, and special economic zone level, PICC has its first level subsidiaries. PICC branches are established at county level, and the main branches are formed at the regional level, which is between the provincial and county level. PICC has two special subsidiaries: The China Insurance Company and the Peace Insurance Company, both concentrating their operations in Hong Kong, Singapore, and Macao.

History of PICC

There have been three phases in the history of PICC. The first phase was during the period 1949-1958, when its aim was to "protect the state-owned assets, ensure safety of production, facilitate commodity exchanges, and promote people's welfare." In this period, PICC established about 2200 branches in China and quite a few branches abroad. It provided insurance services in enterprise properties, transportation, life, and also in accidental, agricultural, international reinsurance. PICC played a significant role during this post-war recovery period in restoring production and providing insurance for business and households, and also served as a source of income for the new government. PICC received insurance premiums totaling 1.6 billion yuan and made payment of 0.38 billion yuan for this period.

The second phase was during the period 1958 to 1979, when PICC became a department of the People's Bank, and its domestic operations were entirely suspended. The theory behind this was that insurance was a capitalist phenomenon and China was on the road to socialist/communist utopia, hence the insurance business was supposed to be consigned to the garbage bin of history. In a socialist society, all accidental losses for enterprises should be compensated from the government budget, and the government and the collective commune should take care of ordinary people's accidental losses. A big socialist family is risk free and therefore the domestic insurance operation had finished its historical mission and should be suspended. For the period 1958-1979, PICC only operated in a few port cities for international insurance, most of which were trade and shipping related. Publicly, its name was still the People's Insurance Company of China, but internally it was the foreign insurance department of the Bureau of Foreign Business under the People's Bank of China.

The third phase has run from 1980 to the present. After the Cultural Revolution, the State Council approved resumption of domestic operations of PICC. In 1980, PICC resumed its domestic operation and both domestic and international business have grown at an astonishing rate since then, reflecting demand for insurance as the economy moves toward a market-oriented system. In 1984, PICC obtained its sub-ministerial rank and established its own company leadership structure.

During the reform period, PICC has established more than 2800 branches domestically and employed more than 70,000 people. PICC had more than 13,000 authorized agencies by the end of 1980, and employed 20,000 full time agents. PICC also established branches in Hong Kong, Macao, and all over the world and has established business relationship with more than 1000 major insurance companies from 120 countries and regions.

The PICC's domestic operations have developed rapidly in both urban and rural areas and have reached industry, agriculture, commerce, service, and many other sectors, most significantly households and individuals. More and more ordinary people have understood why insurance is necessary and beneficial. They have begun to request insurance information and to carefully choose those policies that are appropriate to their situations. In this promotion process, enterprises and institutions have played important roles. A significant proportion of household insurance (most popularly household property insurance) has been purchased by employers as fringe benefits, which has a side effect that it has popularized the concept of insurance among ordinary people. The premium income of PICC increased at an astonishing rate, about 50 percent annually for the period 1985-1989.

By the end of 1989, the total value of properties insured by PICC reached 2310.9 billion yuan; 500 thousand enterprises and firms purchased enterprise property insurance, 77.92 million households obtained home property insurance, and 182.13 million people had life insurance. In 1989, the total revenue of PICC was 14.24 billion yuan, a 30 percent increase over the previous year, exceeding the target by 22.4 percent. The domestic revenue of 1989 was 12.3 billion, including insurance premiums of 8.16 billion and income from deposits of 4.14 billion.

The insurance premium revenue and compensation payments data are summarized in Table 15.1, from which we see that the rate of increase of income is fast and PICC has been fairly profitable. Notice that in Table 15.1, the revenue minus the payments is the profit of the company.

Table 15.1
Insurance Revenue and Profit of PICC
(in billion yuan)

	1986	1987	1988	1989	1990	1991
Insurance premium revenue	5.25	7.91	10.95	14.24	17.78	23.39
Compensation payments	2.14	2.71	4.26	5.96	8.11	11.78

SOURCE: *Almanac of China's Finance and Banking*, 1991, Beijing, China, page 339,and 1992, page 122.

In 1990, 560 thousand enterprises purchased enterprise property insurance; 90.89 million households obtained household property insurance, a 17 percent increase from the previous year; and 217.36 million people participated in various versions of accidental/life insurance, a 19 percent growth rate compared with the year before. The total revenue for 1990 was 17.78 billion yuan, a 23 percent increase over the previous year. The revenue from domestic operations was 15.58 billion, among which insurance premiums were 9.9 billion and deposit income was 5.68 billion. If we classify the domestic operations into property damage and life insurance, the revenue from the former was 9.6 billion (a 30.8 percent increase) and the revenue from the latter was 5.98 billion (a 30 percent increase from the last year). The foreign-related insurance revenue was 420 million US dollars in 1990, 2.4 percent higher than in 1989.

The total compensation payments outlay was 8.11 billion yuan in 1990, during which 2.78 million cases of domestic property damage were processed with a total payment of 4.23 billion yuan; 9.52 million cases of life insurance were processed with payments totaling 2.6 billion. Foreign-related payments total 250 million US dollars. The total amount of tax and profit surrendered to the government was 2 billion in 1990.

15.2 The China International Trust and Investment Corporation (CITIC)

Established in October, 1979, the China International Trust and Investment Corporation (CITIC) is a conglomerate organized by the government to conduct finance, production, trade, technology, service, and other related businesses. Its headquarters is located in Beijing. CITIC had a registered capital of more than 3 billion yuan at the end of 1989.

CITIC engages in a variety of businesses, including – but not restricted to – (1) investment in domestic and foreign projects (which can be direct, indirect, or joint venture) and research and development of new technologies; (2) entering the domestic and international financial markets (CITIC is authorized to do financial business domestically or abroad); (3) engaging in the securities business in primary and secondary markets; (4) rental and leasing business inside and outside of China; (5) foreign-related insurance (involving mainly insurance for foreign investment in China and international insurance and reinsurance); (6) domestic and international trade; (7) bidding and undertaking foreign projects and providing labor and service to foreign firms; (8) real estate and tourist services; (9) and providing trust and consulting service to domestic and foreign customers.

CITIC has actively participated in international financial markets. It has raised capital by issuing the corporation's bonds in Japan, Germany, the United Kingdom, and Hong Kong. It has initiated about 100 joint venture enterprises that involve foreign investment and about 200 joint venture enterprises among domestic partners. By doing so, it has promoted economic integration and cooperation among regions and sectors of the domestic economy as well as internationally. In particular, it emphasizes the introduction of new technology, management skills, and information into China. In order to attract foreign capital and create a profitable investment environment, CITIC has built many modern hotels, office, and apartment buildings that aim at attracting foreign investments, foreign companies, and foreign tourists. It also facilitates foreign investment by providing a wide range of consulting services to foreign firms regarding government policy, tax system, legal environment, etc. It plays a match-making role between foreign capital and potentially profitable projects in China. It has also made investment in foreign countries to produce some materials that are in short supply in China. For example, it has invested in lumber, aluminum, and paper production in the United States, Australia, and Canada.

The Board of Directors is the uppermost in the hierarchy of CITIC. The Board of Directors consists of one president, several vice presidents, standing directors, and directors. The president and vice presidents are appointed by the State Council. The famous entrepreneur, Mr. Rong Yiren, was the founder of CITIC and was the president of the corporation (1979-1993) until he became the Vice President of China.

The headquarters of CITIC consist mainly of a headquarters office, a department of planning and finance, a personnel department, a department of auditing, an information center, a department of development and management, an office of research and development, a CITIC research institute, and a CITIC publishing house. CITIC has many subsidiaries in China and offices around the world.

CITIC is a product as well as a symbol of economic reform and the open door policy. In the 1980s, it became a giant conglomerate worth more than 3 billion yuan in registered capital, with an employment of more than 25 thousand people. (It started in 1979 with only a dozen of people on its payroll.) At the beginning of 1990s, the total assets it controlled around the world exceeded 25 billion yuan. It is now a group that integrates productions, technology, finance, trade, and services.

The unique background of CITIC explains its astonishing success. First, CITIC is a government sponsored company. It has tremendous monopoly power that other companies did not have. It was the first company and at that time was the only company that was authorized to have the management power it enjoyed to conduct its business. Second, its leaders have unique backgrounds. For example, its president and founder, Mr. Rong Yiren, was the "number one" capitalist entrepreneur before the People's Republic was established. Mr. Rong has special personal relationships with many top leaders of the Chinese government including Deng Xiaoping. Mr. Rong's background, personality, and ties have definitely contributed to the success of the company. Third, the economic reform and open door policy created a suitable environment and degree of freedom for CITIC.

With this background in mind, let us now look at three cases of the CITIC projects.

Case 1. Yizheng Polyester[1]

There are two ways that CITIC utilizes foreign capital. The first is from direct investments of foreign capital. The second way is to raise foreign capital abroad and then invest in domestic projects. The investment on Yizheng Polyester is an example of the latter.

Yizheng Polyester was one of the key construction projects started in 1978. In 1980, the government could not afford to continue many unfinished projects under construction. Since the Yizheng Polyester project was already begun and some equipment had arrived, suspending the project would mean a tremendous loss to the government. At that time, polyester fiber was in shortage in China, and each year China imported a large amount of polyester and nylon fibers from abroad.

Under these circumstances, CITIC signed a joint venture agreement with the government (Ministry of Textile) in June 1981, according to which CITIC was responsible for raising funds for the project. CITIC raised about 200 million US dollars overseas through bank loans and by issuing bonds, and it also raised some funds domestically. In 1985, the first phase of the project was completed, which was a large factory base that is capable of producing 180 thousand tons of polyester fiber annually. The second phase of the project was launched in 1985 and was completed in 1990. Now Yizheng Polyester is capable of producing 480 thousand metric tons of polyester and other chemical fibers per year, about one-third of the total output of the country. It can provide 5 meters of cloth per person to 1 billion people.

CITIC was not only responsible for raising funds, but also involved in the management control, marketing, quality control, and export promotion of Yizheng Polyester.

To western readers, the above activities in which CITIC has engaged are pretty standard. But this was a first in China, and it had profound significance. It showed that the government monopoly in large project investment was gone. Furthermore, the joint venture setup implies that CITIC had penetrated into production and management, and it certainly broke monopolistic vertical relationships of large modern firms with corresponding ministries. One can argue that CITIC is still a government owned company. However, the important point here is that while both the Ministry of Textile and CITIC are government-owned, competition makes the two companies better than one monopoly.

Case 2. China East Leasing Company[2]

The China East Leasing Company (CELC) was founded in April, 1981, by CITIC, ORIX Company of Japan, and Beijing Electrical and Machinery Equipment Company (BEMCC). This is a typical joint-venture case. CELC had 3 million US dollars in registered capital (of which 50 percent is from ORIX, 20 percent from CITIC, and 30 percent from BEMEC). Its headquarters is in Beijing.

The CELC is a financial leasing company which serves as a window through which it is possible to utilize foreign capital, equipment, and technology. The CELC does not limit its operation to leasing equipment only, it combines leasing with international trade, joint venture investment, and technology transfers.

First, the CELC has opened new channels for attracting foreign investment. Generally speaking, foreign investment is associated with new technology embodied in advanced equipment. Leasing alleviates the shortage of hard currency. Firms and local government do not have to pay the whole value of the equipment up front. More than 80 percent of the leasing conducted by CELC is related to technical improvement and innovation.

Second, CELC engages in pay-in-kind trading and sourcing. Various pay-in-kind trading arrangements are very popular in the coastal areas of China. Foreign firms take advantage of low labor costs and set up different kinds of pay-in-kind trade arrangements in which the future exports of a firm will be the main source of repayments of the foreign investment. An export processing industry has been established, wherein foreign firms supply technology and raw materials and the products are processed in China and then re-exported to the world market. The CELC has facilitated the creation of many such enterprises through leasing arrangements.

Third, CELC explores opportunities of export leasing — leasing abroad equipment made in China. In 1985, the CELC leased out a Chinese ship to a foreign company.

By the end of 1990, CELC had arranged about 730 leasing projects for a total of 26 provinces and cities. The total amount of foreign capital utilized was near 800 million US dollars. Many projects introduced new technology and products to China. CELC has begun establishing branches in other cities, it has signed economic cooperation agreements with 19 provinces and cities, and it has business relationships with hundreds of foreign firms around the world.

Case 3. CITIC Industrial Bank (CITICIB)

CITIC has engaged in many quasi-banking businesses; it is natural that it needs a bank. CITIC Industrial Bank (CITICIB) is such a bank. Established in April, 1987 in Beijing, the CITICIB is directly affiliated with CITIC. Most of its transactions are in terms of hard currencies. The main services offered by the CITICIB are: (1) deposit and loan services in both hard and domestic currencies, (2) export loans, (3) brokerage services for domestic financial institutions and foreign banks, (4) underwriting domestic bonds, stocks, and other securities, (5) serving as a clearinghouse for domestic and international transactions, (6) providing foreign exchange, travelers checks, and credit card business, (7) arranging leasing business among domestic and foreign firms, and (8) providing financial consulting services.

The main clients of the CITICIB are the firms and enterprises of the CITIC group. It also provides services to other institutions and enterprises at the central and provincial level. Although the CITIC Industrial Bank is directly affiliated with CITIC, it is an autonomous entity, with independent decision making and management power, responsible for its profits and losses. The president of CITIC, Mr. Rong Yiren, was the honorary president of the board of directors. The directors are recruited from the People's Bank of China, the Agricultural Bank of China, The People's Construction Bank of China, the Bank of China, and the Industrial and Commercial Bank of China. As expected, the way to do business in China is to invite powerful persons from all important related institutions. The chief executive officer is in charge of day-to-day operation under the leadership of the board of directors.

In 1990, the CITICIB had total assets of 21.43 billion yuan and a total liabilities of 20.81 billion yuan. Total equity is 630 million yuan. Net profit was 121.55 million yuan in 1990.

As economic reform continues, more non-bank financial institutions appear. The monopoly position of CITIC has been challenged by other firms. CITIC has made significant contributions in exploring how to grow out of the central plan, how to introduce foreign capital and management into a planning system, and how to introduce competition and market mechanism into the government owned enterprises, reorganizing them into joint ventures or more independent firms.

15.3 China Venturetech Investment Corporation (CVTIC)

Initiated by the State Commission of Science and Technology, the China Venturetech Investment Corporation (CVTIC) is a limited stock company with the government controlling most of the shares. Established in December, 1985, CVTIC is an independent legal entity, supervised by the People's Bank of China. It is an international non bank financial institution with its headquarters in Beijing. At beginning, it had registered capital of 40 million yuan (about 5 million US dollars).

The objective of CVTIC is to raise venture capital through various channels for investment in new technology, especially in new companies and small-medium size enterprises. CVTIC emphasizes investments in information and communication, biotechnology, electronics, and new materials science. For investments with high risk and high research and development costs, CVTIC provides venture capital and shares the risks and profits. Most projects invested in are high-risk technologies and products. It is difficult for those companies that engage in high risk investment to obtain funds from other existing channels.

CVTIC deals with domestic currency as well as foreign exchange. The domestic currency operations include various kinds of investments, loans to medium and small size enterprises on research and development of new technology, underwriting stocks and bonds for new firms, leasing, arranging international operations, providing consulting services, and financial auditing services. The foreign currency operations include entrusted deposits for domestic and foreign customers, borrowing abroad, underwriting financial securities denominated in foreign currency, investments and loans, are leasing and consulting services.

The organizational structure of CVTIC is similar to the standard arrangement, with a board of directors and a chief executive officer (CEO). Directors are elected by the shareholders. The board of directors is in charge of amending the bylaws of the corporation, hiring the chief executive officer, and making decisions on other important matters. The responsibilities of the CEO are to implement the decision of the board, carry out day-to-day operations, appoint branch and department managers, approve investment projects, and submit financial and profit distribution reports to the board.

CVTIC is supervised by the People's Bank of China. The domestic currency account of CVTIC is in the People's Bank, the foreign exchange account is in the Bank of China. CVTIC has reserve deposits at the People's Bank as well as bad-debt reserve deposits. The domestic currency and foreign exchange operations are subject to the regulations of the overall credit plan. CVTIC reports on a regular basis to the People's Bank about its financial plans and important decisions. It also submits its financial statements to PBC.

By the end of 1990, the total assets of CVTIC reached 1.4 billion yuan; revenue in 1990 was 130 million yuan with a profit of 17 million yuan. From 1986 to 1990, the total assets increased 35 fold, revenue 65 fold, and profit 21 fold.

CVTIC has actively pursued business with foreign financial institutions. It has a subsidiary in Hong Kong called CVTIC International Ltd., which is its link to international business and corporations. CVTIC has offices or agencies in the United States, France, Australia, and Japan and other Southeast Asian countries. Beside business relationships with industrialized nations, CVTIC has several cooperative projects with Russia and the former Soviet Union countries. CVTIC has actively engaged in the securities business both domestically and abroad.

15.4 Postal Savings Deposit

Postal savings deposits started in China in 1919 by the then nationalist government. It flourished in the 1930s. After the Communist government took over, the postal savings deposit network was taken over by the People's Bank. In September of 1953, the service was suspended.

In 1986, the Ministry of Postal Service and the People's Bank signed an agreement (arranged by the State Council), according to which the postal deposit service would be restarted in China. The arrangement was that the post office network would be used to offer savings deposit service, basically passbook deposit and time deposit services. The interest rates paid on these deposits are determined by the People's Bank. In a sense, the postal offices serve as outlets of the People's Bank. Deposits attracted by the postal service are controlled and utilized by the People's Bank, which is the central bank of China. In return, the People's Bank pays a fee to the Ministry of Postal Service.

The growth of the postal savings deposits was rapid in the second half of the 1980s. Table 16.1 summarizes some information about postal deposits, from which we can see the following points. First, total postal deposits have been increasing every year. By the end of 1990, the total postal deposits were 18.034 billion yuan. From 1986 to 1990, the total postal deposits grew on average 138 percent per year. The total postal deposits accounted for about 0.25 percent of total residential savings in 1986. This percentage increased to 3.5% by the end of 1991, a 13-fold increase.

Second, the total number of branches that offer postal savings deposits increased rapidly. By the end of 1990 there were 17,305 postal office branches offering deposit services. This number was second only to the number of branches of the Industrial and Commercial Bank and the Agriculture Bank. Apparently, the postal savings deposit provides a convenient and accessible service to their customers.

Third, a set of regulations and laws regarding postal savings deposit were established during the late 1980s and the early 1990s. At the same time, professional personnel were trained for the postal deposit services. By the end of 1990, there were more than 40,000 professional staff members in the postal deposit service. One last thing worth mentioning is that the number of postal service accounts peaked in 1988. It declined drastically in 1989 and 1990, then it stabilized in the early 1990s.

Table 15.2
Postal Savings Deposits in China

	1986	1987	1988	1989	1990	1991
Total postal deposits (billion yuan)	.564	3.763	7.034	10.084	18.034	31.515
Total deposit accounts (million)	–	53.50	117.02	74.51	66.34	65.18
Total branches	2794	9477	13651	15609	17305	18738

SOURCE: *Almanac of China's Finance and Banking*, 1991, Beijing, China, page 182-185, and 1992 page 567.

15.5 Rural Credit Cooperatives

Rural credit co-ops in China are grassroots financial institutions organized and collectively owned by farmers. The history of rural credit co-ops was found in the Hebei province. The rural credit co-ops played an important role during the period 1950-1957, in which rural credit co-ops pooled rural financial resources and helped investment in agriculture.

In 1958, when the government launched the commune movement, the rural credit co-ops were merged with the operation of the government owned

Agricultural Bank. During the economic reform in the 1980s, the independent, collective nature of the rural credit co-ops was reemphasized. The government has given the rural co-ops relatively independent management power.

The rural credit co-ops are owned collectively by farmers through equity stock, which can be seen clearly from the liability and equity side of its balance sheet, which consists of equity stock, internal capital, deposits, borrowed capital, and other sources; this was the case even before the reform. In the early 1970s, more than 90 percent rural households had some equity stock in the rural credit co-ops. Because farmers' incomes were extremely low at that time, most households had just a few shares of stock and a typical share was worth only two or three yuan. The total equity stock of rural credit co-ops in China was less than 500 million yuan before reform. During reform, there has been a rapid growth of the rural co-ops. The total equity stock reached 7,936 million yuan by the end of 1990.

The bulk of deposits of the rural credit co-ops are from rural households. The deposits from rural enterprise account for a small proportion. By the end of 1990, the total deposits in the rural co-ops was 214.5 billion yuan, of which 30.334 billion was from rural enterprises and institutions. The remaining 184.16 billion (86 percent) was from rural households.

Internal capital has been basically accumulated from retained earnings. By the end of 1990, the total amount of internal capital of rural credit co-ops was 8.233 billion yuan. Borrowed capital is usually not a large item. Overall, rural credit co-ops as a whole are a fund provider. The amount rural credit co-ops lend to the banking system is often much larger than the amount borrowed from the banking system.

The rural credit co-op is an important nonbank financial institution. By the end of 1990, there were 58,200 independent rural credit co-ops with 327,230 service branches, employing more than half a million full time employees and more than a quarter million part-time employees. The total amount of deposits in the rural credit co-ops was about 18.42 percent of that of the entire banking system.

15.6 The Emerging Nonbank Financial Intermediaries

The trust and investment companies, rural and urban credit cooperatives, and security firms constitute the nonbank financial intermediaries, which have profoundly changed the financial sector in China.

First, the most significant change brought in by the nonbank financial institutions is that the monopoly position of the Chinese banking system has been broken. The nonbank financial institutions compete with the banking system both in usage of and attracting funds. Individuals and firms now have more alternatives for investing money. By the end of 1991, the total trust deposits of enterprises in nonbank financial institutions was 142.2 billion yuan (Xie 1992).

Second, nonbank financial intermediaries are in general outside of the plans of the central government and the central bank. Most trust and investment companies have been established by state banks and local governments. As a matter of fact, the purpose of establishing them was to circumvent the control of the credit and cash plan of the central bank. It is very convenient for local governments to use these financial institutions to facilitate the economic development of their localities. As a result, the effectiveness of the control of the central bank has been weakened. In the past, there were no other financial intermediaries and no alternative financial assets available to the general public except bank deposits. The entire money-flow process was fully controlled by PBC. Now nonbank financial intermediaries attract funds directly from households and enterprises. Local governments raise funds directly to finance their high priority projects. Enterprises issue bonds and stocks to the general public. A significant proportion of the money flow is outside of the cash and credit plan. The long run implication is that the reforms in the financial sector is irreversible. The old methods of control became obsolete. The central bank has to establish a set of instruments to achieve an effective control of money supply.

Third, nonbank financial institutions are more independent compared to banks, have more flexible management power, and are subject to less regulations. Generally speaking, managers in these institutions have more incentive to maximize profits. Consequently, the investments of nonbank financial institutions are usually more creative in terms of the types of investments (joint ventures, direct ownership, bond-financed, etc.), and are more efficient and profitable in terms of results.

Fourth, there are tremendous moral hazard problems in nonbank financial institutions. Many of them are affiliated or related to banks. They share staff, funds, and information with their holding banks, and make decisions jointly to maximize the joint profit under current regulations. Because banks are subject to more regulations and supervisions, there is high incentive for banks to divert their funds to their fully controlled trust and investment companies.

Fifth, there are very few regulations or laws regarding this sector. The boundary between banks and nonbank financial institutions is not clear. Most nonbank financial institutions are taking advantage of less regulations and seeking rent wherever possible. It is very urgent for China to decide what kind of nonbank financial institutions it needs. Whether China should follow the American model of separating banking and security business, or follow the Japanese way in creating a main bank system which allows banks to do virtually everything in the financial markets (Qian 1993). Some efforts have been made in this area. For instance, one important item in the austerity program in the summer of 1993 was to separate banks from their affiliated investment or security firms. However, the implementation of the policy and the result remain to be seen.

Sixth, most nonbank financial institutions were established in a hurried fashion. There is a shortage of qualified personnel. The professional quality and moral standards of those who are in the nonbank financial institutions are low by international standard. This factor constrains the further development of the nonbank financial institutions.

Notes

1. The information of the Yizheng Polyester case is from *Almanac of China's Finance and Banking*, 1989, page 303-304.

2. The information of the CELC case is from *Almanac of China's Finance and Banking*, 1991, page 348.

16

The Stock and Bond Markets

From 1981 to 1991, the total amount of financial securities issued in China was 377 billion yuan, of which about 160 billion had matured and had been redeemed. The remaining balance was 217 billion. Among the total issuance of financial securities, 130.8 billion were government bonds; 59.8 billion bonds were issued by financial institutions; 65.7 billion were bonds issued by enterprises; 7.54 billion were stocks, and the rest were bank certificates of deposit (CDs) in large denominations. Table 16.1 summaries the financial securities issued for the period 1981-1991.

Financial markets have been established and developed as the number of securities transactions have increased. There are two stock exchanges in China, one in Shanghai, one in Shenzhen. A computerized trading system, Security Trading Automated Quotation System (STAQS), was established in Beijing, which is linked to many major cities in China. By the end of 1992, China had over 85 professional security-exchange brokerage companies; over 1200 trust and investment firms, and many other financial institutions had established security exchange counters. There were more than 70 publicly traded stocks. The total volume of securities trade was 13.6 billion in 1990 and 48.8 billion in 1991, among which 2 and 6 billion were stock trade transactions in 1990 and 1991 respectively. Bonds, especially government bonds, are still the largest item of tradable securities in China.

It has been not very clear who is responsible for regulating the financial markets. The People's Bank of China and Commission of Economic System Reform (CESR) are the two official government agencies that have regulated the financial markets. Local governments have been also actively involved. China Financial Security Association (CFSA, Zhongguo Zhengjuanye Xiehui) was founded in August, 1991. CFSA is supposed to be a self-regulated, professional association, but its actual function remains to be seen.

Established in 1992, the Commission on Security Regulation and Supervision (CSRS, Zhongguo Zhengjuan Jiandu Guanli Weiyuanhui) is a regulating commission under the State Council, which is headed by Professor Liu Hongru, a famous economist and the former Vice Governor of PBC. CSRS has been coordinating and regulating the financial markets since 1992. Although there has been some confusion regarding who is in charge, one thing is for sure: the government has been and will be the dominating voice in regulating the financial markets. The debate is over which department of the government should be in charge, and how to organize a (government) commission that looks like a self-regulated and professional association.

In this chapter, we will discuss the composition of the financial assets in China, the government bond market, and the stock market respectively. Then the Shanghai Security Exchange will be described. The significance and implications of the financial markets in China will be discussed throughout the chapter.

16.1 The Composition of the Financial Assets

Table 16.2 provides the information of the financial assets in China for 1978 and 1991, from which we can see the following. First, there are several zeros in the column of 1978 whereas there are none in 1991's column, which indicates that at least five new financial instruments have been introduced during the reform. They are: financial bonds, deposits and loans of the nonbank financial institutions, government bonds, enterprise bonds, and stocks. As we discussed in Chapter 9, there has been a rapid monetization or financial deepening process in China during the reform as measured by the ratio of M2 to GNP, or by the ratio of total financial assets to GNP. In this process of financial innovation, new financial instruments become more and more important.

Second, by the end of 1991, 99.8 percent of financial assets were in the forms of loans and bonds, while only 0.2 percent were in equity stocks. If we look at the claims on non-financial institutions (item 9-13 in Table 16.2), most of them (93 percent) were loans; only 7 percent were in the form of bonds. These figures reflect that financial markets are at a very early stage of development in China. Although bond and equity financing have been introduced, the majority of financing has been obtained through loans.

Third, the liquidity of the financial assets was relatively low. The most liquid asset, cash, accounted for 6.9 percent and tradable bonds and stocks were only 3.6 percent of the total financial assets. Most financial claims were among state banks, state-related trust and investment companies, government agencies, and state-owned enterprises. This was probably the source of the soft budget constraint. It is conceivable that the proportion of tradable bond and stock securities will increase in the coming decade.

Table 16.3 illustrates the composition of household financial assets for 1978, 1985, and 1991. By the end of 1991, households on average held 19 percent of their financial assets in cash, 70 percent in deposits in banks and financial institutions, 10 percent in tradable securities, and 1 percent in others.

From Table 16.1 to 16.3, we see that bonds, especially government bonds, are the most important tradable securities for the period under discussion. Let us now turn to the government bonds market in the next section.

16.2 The Government Bond Market

The government bond is the largest item in the financial securities market both in terms of quantity issued and in terms of amount of trading transactions. Most government bonds are issued by the Ministry of Finance of the central government. The construction bonds are issued by the state-owned investment companies.

Types of Government Bonds

There are different kinds of government bonds, issued for various purposes and to different buyers. The following is a list of the government bonds outstanding in China.

1. *The Treasury Bond (Guokujuan).* The State Council decided to issue government bonds in 1981. To most older Chinese people, government bonds are not unfamiliar. Before 1949, under the Nationalist government, there were government bonds. After the People's Republic of China was established, the central government issued many kinds of bonds in the period of 1950-1959. During the Cultural Revolution, "China has neither internal debts nor external debts" was a hot propaganda slogan. The Chinese government and most Chinese people were proud of this for a long time and claimed that debt was a symptom of rotten capitalism. It took 22 years (1959-1981) for the Chinese government to realize that debt is not that bad after all.

From 1981 to the end of 1990, there were a total of 60.415 billion yuan in treasury bonds issued to the public, which includes the state- and collectively-owned enterprises, local governments, institutions and organizations, private businesses, and individuals.

The treasury bonds issued in the period 1981 to 1984 had the same scheme of maturity, which was between 5 to 10 years, determined by random drawings. Starting from the sixth year after the issuance, the Ministry of Finance pays back the principle plus interest to 20 percent of the bond holders each year until all bonds are redeemed (the last 20 percent are redeemed in the tenth year). The interest rates (simple) for the bonds issued in this period were 4 percent for institutional holders and 8 percent for individual holders.

The treasury bonds issued in the period 1985-1987 had a uniform maturity of 5 years. Interest rates for institutional and individuals holders were different. Interest rates were 5 percent for institutions and 9 percent for individuals in 1985, 6 percent and 10 percent for the period of 1986-1988. The maturity of treasury bonds issued since 1988 has been shortened to 3 years. Since 1989, the differential treatment of interest rates between institutional and individual holders was abolished and a uniform rate of 14 percent prevailed in 1989 and 1990. All interest paid was calculated by simple rates; no compound rates were used. The People's Bank of China is in charge of managing treasury bonds. It entrusts the specialized banks and other financial institutions with the handling of transactions of treasury bonds. According to regulations, free buying and selling of treasury bonds was not allowed at the beginning. However, trading transactions of treasury bonds were legalized and secondary markets were created in the second half of the 1980s.

2. *The Key Project Bond.* In order to guarantee sufficient funds to the key projects (such as energy, transportation, and raw materials), the Ministry of Finance for the first time issued 5.5 billion yuan in "key project" bonds in 1987. The maturity was 3 years and principle and interest were paid at maturity. Among the 5.5 billion, 5 billion was issued to institutions at a yield of 6 percent annual rate, and 0.5 billion was issued to individuals at a yield of 10.5 percent. This 5.5 billion in key project bonds was handled by the People's Construction Bank of China. In 1988, the People's Bank issued 3.0 billion yuan in key project bonds to individuals and institutions at an annual rate of 9.5 percent with a maturity of 2 years. Again the People's Bank authorized the specialized banks and other financial institutions to underwrite the bonds and to redeem them at maturity.

3. *The Fiscal Bond.* One way to make up a government deficit is to borrow money by issuing fiscal bonds. In 1988, the Ministry of Finance issued 6.6 billion in fiscal bonds, mainly to institutions. The People's Bank

is in charge of managing fiscal bonds. By the end of 1990, the total amount of fiscal bonds issued was 13.716 billion yuan.

4. *The Construction Bond.* To raise money for basic infrastructure construction, several specialized investment firms (e.g. investment firms of energy, transportation), together with the Ministry of Petroleum and the Ministry of Railroad issued 8 billion yuan in basic construction bonds primarily to specialized banks at an annual rate of 7.5 percent with a maturity of 5 years. The bonds are administrated by the People's Construction Bank. By the end of 1990, the total amount of the issuance of basic construction bonds was 9.5 billion yuan.

5. *The Value-Guarantee Bond.* To curb inflation and reduce excess demand in the economy, the Ministry of Finance issued 8.743 and 37.40 billion yuan in value-guarantee bonds in 1989 and 1990, respectively, to urban and rural residents, private businesses, insurance companies, and various fund foundations. The term of maturity was 3 years. The yield of the bond was equal to the floating rate of 3 year time deposit announced by the People's Bank plus the value-guarantee subsidy (which was a indexing scheme linked to inflation rate) and an additional one percentage point. In other words, the nominal yield of the bond was equal to the total yield of the 3 year value guarantee time deposit plus one percentage point. The value-guarantee bond was promoted by the specialized banks and post offices around the country. Each province had a sales target. In those regions that could not meet the sales quota, local governments had to buy the remaining bond by using local funds.

6. *The Special Government Bond.* In 1989, the Ministry of Finance issued 4.3 billion in special government bonds to profitable state-owned, collective, or private enterprises, to institutions and organizations, to pension funds, to unemployment insurance foundations, etc. The bond yielded 15 percent and the term of maturity was 5 years. The Ministry of Finance and local governments allocated the buying quota to all "appropriate" institutions. In other words, institutions were forced to buy the required amount of special government bonds. The Treasury issued 3.24 billion in special government bonds again in 1990.

Market Transactions of the Government Bonds

When government bonds appeared in 1981, any private transactions in the bonds was treated as illegal. As more and more government bonds were issued, the demand for a secondary market increased. On August 5, 1986, the Shengyang city branch of the People's Bank approved a request of the Shengyang Investment and Trust Inc.to open a business counter for transactions of financial securities. By the end of 1987, there were many brokerage companies, investment and trust firms, and credit unions providing financial securities exchange business in 41 cities around the country. The total amount of transactions exceeded 100 million yuan by the end of 1987, of which 90 percent were the buying and selling activities of institutions for their own accounts; the remaining 10 percent were trades for their customers' accounts.

The State Council approved the secondary markets for government bonds on a trial basis in April 1988. The first group of experimental secondary markets were established in Shengyang, Shanghai, Chongqing, Wuhan, Canton, Harbin, and Shenzhen. There were another 54 cities that got approval to start secondary markets in June of 1988. The People's Bank approved the establishment of 34 financial securities firms during the same year.

In 1988, total transactions in the security markets were 2.63 billion, of which 91.3 percent were trades on behalf of institutional accounts, and 8.7 percent of the transactions were for client accounts. If we classify the transactions in terms of the type of securities, then 91.1 percent were treasury bonds, 4.1 percent enterprises bonds, 2.5 percent financial bonds, 1.3 percent basic construction bonds, 0.5 percent bank CDs in large denominations, and 0.5 percent stocks. By the end of 1988, the secondary markets for treasury bonds became a nationwide network, consisting of security brokerage firms, investment and trust companies, and other financial institutions. Overall, the supply of treasury bonds was greater than the demand; prices were generally below the par value. Institutional traders were able to buy the treasury bonds at bargain prices. Consequently, the total amount bought by institutions (1.51 billion) was much larger than the total amount sold (0.77 billion). The ratio of the amount sold to bought was 0.51.

In 1989, the total amount of transactions in the securities markets was 2.301 billion yuan, declining by 13 percent from the level of 1988. The political environment of 1989, especially in the second half of the year (after the June 4th Tiananmen incident), had a negative impact on securities trade. During 1989, the central government launched a campaign of auditing securities firms and investment and trust companies. In addition they closed some "illegal" securities exchange firms. The other reason that the trade decreased in 1989 was that no new treasury bonds were allowed to be traded. Market trade of treasury bonds was restricted to those bonds issued in 1985 and 1986 only.

The development of the securities market had a significant breakthrough in 1990. In February, Shanghai and Chongqing started to allow treasury bonds issued in 1987 and 1988 to be traded in the market. In May, more than 20 provinces and cities approved the legal trading of treasury bonds issued from 1982 to 1988. In some coastal cities, treasury bonds issued in 1989 were also allowed to enter the market. Securities trading in 1990 had the following new developments.

First, trading was active. Total trading in financial securities for the first four months of 1990 was 1.83 billion yuan, an increase of 200 percent over that of 1989. Total trade on treasury bonds was 1.71 billion yuan, an increase of 220 percent over 1989. The most active treasury bond trading market was in Shanghai, where the total volume was 754 million for the first four months of 1990.

Second, prices were stable. Before the opening of the secondary market for securities, the government was concerned that excess supply of the government bonds would result in their prices plummeting. In fact, the prices of government bonds were very low in the black market before the establishment of secondary markets. (In the black market, the prices were usually 70 percent to 80 percent of the par value, in some regions, even 50 percent of the par value.) After large-scale secondary markets were opened, combining with the decreasing interest rates trend and an easing of inflationary expectations, there was a steady price increase for the government securities. By the end of April, 1990, in the Shanghai market, the price of a treasury bond issued in 1985 with 100 yuan par value was 142.13 yuan, and the effective annual yield was 12.1 percent. The price of a treasury bond issued in 1986 was 125.15 yuan; effective yield was 17 percent. The price and effective yield for treasury bonds issued in 1987 were 107.7 yuan and 18.1 percent; for bonds issued in 1988 the price was 108.4 yuan and yield was 17.1 percent. The prices of government securities were much higher than the previous prices in the black market, and effective yields were close to the return on time deposits with equivalent maturity terms. Although the amount bought by institutions was still larger than the amount sold, the ratio of sold to bought increased to 0.66, which was much higher than that in 1988. This is a perfect example for how people value the liquidity of a financial asset. The same government bonds, which can be assumed to be default-risk free, were more valuable if they were tradable in the secondary market.

Third, the nationwide information and exchange network was established. As the secondary market developed most rapidly in the coastal cities, there was excess demand for government securities in the coastal region, whereas in the interior and remote provinces, there were still excess supplies. Consequently, there was a flow of government securities from interior provinces to the coastal areas. A preliminary uniform national market started to function and the prices on government securities, especially on treasury bonds, converged in different regions. The total amount of trade in financial securities in 1990 was 11.85 billion yuan, which was more than 2 times higher than combined total transactions for the period before 1990. For the period of 1991-1993, the growth of government bonds trading was even faster. Figure 16.1 shows the composition of financial securities issued in 1991. Figure 16.2 illustrates the composition of government bonds issued in 1991.

16.3 The Stock Market in China

Since 1980, some enterprises have begun to raise capital directly by issuing bonds and stocks. The profound significance of this development lay in the fact that it ended the situation in which the banking system was the only source of capital. The stocks in the first half of the 1980s in China had few attributes of real stocks. Although they were named "stocks," they were primarily bonds. These "stocks" had the following characteristics. First, the purpose of stock issuance was fund-raising, not changing ownership of the company. Although many enterprises issued stocks, issued amounts were generally small. Most stocks were sold internally to the firms' own employees, and they were mostly "home made," meaning not printed very well. Second, most of these stocks had a predetermined fixed yield (dividend); a maturity date at which time the stock holders got their principle back, and there was little risk since both the yield and redemption were guaranteed. Some stocks even allowed their holders to redeem the principle before the maturity. Furthermore, there was little management participation or voting power through stock ownership. Third, there was differential treatment between individual and institutional stock owners. Generally speaking, yields (dividends) for individual holders were much higher than those for institutional holders, and some institutional shares had no dividend at all.

In September, 1984, Tianqiao Department Store, the first limited company owned by shareholders, was founded in Beijing. It issued a redeemable stock with a 3 year maturity. Then Shanghai Feilo Acoustics Inc. issued non-redeemable stock (much closer to a real stock) for the first time to the public.

As the economic reforms in the urban areas continued, how to define property rights of state-owned firms became a very difficult problem.

Some economists actively advocated stock ownership as a better way to define property rights and called for experimental stock issuance in the state-owned sector. As a result, a group of shareholder-owned corporations emerged. Among them were Vacuum Electronic Limited Inc. in Shanghai, Gold Cup Automobile Limited Inc. in Shengyang, and Yuzhong Investment & Trust Limited Inc. in Chongqing. Although the largest shareholder is still the government in most cases, this is an essential step forward toward a real stock market.

The stock ownership experiment in the large and medium size state-owned enterprises brought the stock market in China to a new stage. The emergence and popularity of non-redeemable stocks (common stock) moved the Chinese stock market closer to the international standard. Now there are mainly the following types of stocks.

First are the bond-like stocks. This kind of primitive stock was popular in China in the mid 1980s. Such stocks had guaranteed rates of return (dividends). Most of them had a maturity date at which time the principle would be paid back. Some of them included voting rights; others did not. There was no uniform standard for this kind of stock, they were pretty much enterprise-specific. Most stocks in China before 1990 belonged to this category.

Second are the common stocks. This kind of stock is essentially the same as the common stock in the West. They appeared in some stock issuance experiments of large and medium size state-owned enterprises. Common stockholders as a whole have voting rights and participate in the decision making process of the corporation. The dividend on common stocks is a function of the after-tax profits of the firm. The common stocks have grown very rapidly since 1990.

Third are preferred stocks, the holders of which enjoy a fixed annual dividend but have no voting power. The percentage of preferred stocks is small.

A new development in 1991 was that the type-B stock entered the market in Shanghai and then in Shenzhen. Type-B stock is specially designed for foreign investors; it has to be purchased by foreign exchange, but is denominated in Renminbi. Type-B stock holders have all the rights as the common stock holders (presumably type-A). On November 30, 1991, Shanghai Vacuum Electronics Inc., a Shanghai security firm, and several foreign security firms signed a contract to jointly underwrite the first type-B stock for Shanghai Vacuum Electronics Inc. in China. It seems that issuing type-B stock is an efficient way to attract foreign capitals. In the last two months in 1991 alone, 240 million US dollar worth type-B stocks were sold in Shanghai and Shenzhen.

Stockholders can be classified into three categories: the state, institutions, and individuals. The state shareholder is the government. *State shares* are those created in the process of reorganizing state-owned firms into corporations owned by stockholders; the original assets owned by the state were converted into government shares. *Institutional shares* are those shares bought by institutions with their own money (not government money). *Individual shares* are shares purchased by domestic residents and foreigners (including overseas Chinese). By the end of 1990, the total amount of stock issued was worth 4.5 billion yuan. Although the absolute amount was still small, there has been a trend of rapid increase.

Stock trading in China started in 1986 when the Investment and Trust Company of Shanghai Industrial and Commercial Bank provided stock trading services. The State Council promulgated regulations allowing stock trading in Shanghai and Shenzhen only. By the end of 1991, 35 stocks (18 in Shanghai, 17 in Shenzhen) were publicly traded and the total volume of stock trade was 6 billion yuan for the year.

Another new development worth mentioning is the establishment of an information network for the financial market in China by PBC. The network was designed to instantaneously report price and quantity information on financial securities, interest rates in the capital market, and fund availability information. The computer network is also capable of conducting securities trades. This computer information network became operational (for a trial period) in April, 1991; it operates Monday through Saturday. By the end of 1991, there were 81 members from more than 30 cities joined the system.

16.4 The Stock Market in Shanghai

The Shanghai Security Exchange (SHSE), the first securities exchange (the Wall Street of China) of the People's Republic of China was founded in November, 1990. The Shenzhen Security Exchange was founded in July of 1991, which has structure and operating rules similar to Shanghai, and is perhaps closer to the international standard. The establishment of these two securities exchange houses started a new era for the financial securities markets in China. Shanghai is the financial capital of China. It had relatively developed stock and bond markets before the People's Republic of China was founded. Naturally, the resurrection of the stock markets was started in Shanghai. In this section, we will briefly introduce the Shanghai Security Exchange. (This section is written based on the *Bylaws of SHSE* and *Rules and Regulations of SHSE*.)

The Organizational Structure of SHSE

The Shanghai Security Exchange was the first stock exchange of the People's Republic of China. The People's Bank approved its establishment on November 26, 1990, and its grand opening was on December 19, 1990. The SHSE is a non-profit legal entity organized generally by following the international standard for a stock exchange. It provides the physical space for securities trading, organizes and manages transactions among traders, provides securities trading information (price, volume, index, etc.), and conducts other business approved by the People's Bank. It consists of members, a board of directors, a general manager, and a supervision board.

1. *The Member.* A financial institution can apply for membership in the SHSE if it satisfies the following conditions: (1) It has the approval of the People's Bank to conduct securities trading in Shanghai; (2) it fully acknowledges the bylaws of the SHSE; (3) it has two years of securities trading experience; (4) it has qualified personnel and an organizational structure that conforms to the regulations of the People's Bank; and (5) it promises to pay the dues of the SHSE. After the application is approved by the SHSE and the Shanghai branch of the People's Bank, the financial institution becomes a member of the SHSE. By the end of March, 1991, there were 25 institutional members in the SHSE, among which 9 were financial institutions in other cities that had established branches in Shanghai.

2. *The General Manager (GM).* The GM is the legal representative of the SHSE. The GM is hired by the board of directors and has a term of 3 years. The responsibilities of the GM are to implement the decisions of the board of directors, to report to the members' assembly and to the board of directors, to organize the day-to-day business and administration, to hire department heads of the SHSE, and to represent the SHSE in dealing with other institutions.

3. *The Board of Directors.* The SHSE has a board of directors that makes day-to-day decisions. The responsibilities of the board are: (1) to implement the decisions of the members' assembly; (2) upon the nomination of the GM, to evaluate and approve or reject the applications of prospective new members; (3) to hire the GM and other top management personnel; (4) to evaluate and supervise the management plans and rules proposed by the GM; and (5) to approve the budget. The board of directors consists of 9 persons, 6 of whom are directors elected from members. (The term of the 9 directors is 3 years; 2 directors are elected each year.) There are three non-membership directors. They are nominated by the People's Bank and elected by members (their term is also 3 years). Both member

and non-member directors can be elected for consecutive terms. The board of directors is led by the President, who is a non-member director (whose term is 3 years), and a Vice President, who is a membership director (and whose term is 1 year).

4. *The Supervision Board.* The supervision board consists of four persons, among whom the chair and vice-chair are non-members. The chair and vice-chair of the supervision board are appointed by the Shanghai branch of the People's Bank. The primary responsibility of the supervision board of the SHSE is to check any possible wrong-doings, to examine the annual budget, and to supervise the business in the SHSE.

The SHSE is responsible for approval or disapproval of applications of securities to be traded in the SHSE. It organizes the trading and settlement process. Now let's look at the operating procedure in more detail.

Review Procedure for a Security to Be Traded in SHSE

So far most transactions in the SHSE have been government bonds, provincial and municipal bonds (for basic construction purposes), financial bonds, enterprise bonds, and stocks. At beginning of 1991, there were 31 securities traded in the SHSE, among which 6 were government bonds, 9 were financial bonds, 8 were enterprise bonds, and 8 were stocks.

For a security to be traded in the SHSE, the security issuer must first apply. The application includes the following documents: a report on the current status of the issuer's firm, official approval of the security (approval of *issuance* does not automatically imply that the security is allowed to be *traded*); the registration documents and the bylaws of the firm. In addition, the following documents must be included depending on the nature of the security. For an enterprise or financial bond, the actual outstanding bonds and credit rating report should be submitted. For a stock, the following documents must be included: A prospectus of shareholders, a consolidated asset-liability balance sheet of the firm for the past two years, a recommendation of a member of the SHSE, and a statement on how the firm regularly reports its operating status to the public. Government bonds and Shanghai municipal bonds are exempt from the above application procedure; whether they are allowed to trade is determined by the State Council or the city government.

The SHSE makes a decision within 15 days after the application is received. The criteria of accepting a security to be traded in the market are the following. For a stock to be traded, the company must be registered in the relevant department of the government; the actual amount of capital raised by stock issuing should be greater than or equal to 5 million yuan; the percentage of stocks issued to public should be no less than 25 percent; the registered shareholders must be no less than 500; the company must have been profitable in the past two years; the company must be recommended by at least one member of the SHSE and must promise to report regularly its operating status in an openly published newspaper or magazine. For an enterprise bond applicant, the requirements are: the enterprise must be formally registered; the term of the bond must be at least one year and the credit rating of the enterprise must be at least Grade A; and the total amount must be at least 10 million yuan. For a financial bond to be traded, its term must be at least one year and the total amount to be issued must be greater than or equal to 10 million yuan.

After the SHSE's approval, a formal notification will be sent to the applicant and the result will be announced to public. Those firms whose securities are traded in the SHSE pay an initiation fee and a monthly fee. For example, for bond trading the initiation fee is 0.3 percent of the total par value with a lower bound of 3000 yuan and the upper bond of 10,000 yuan. The monthly payment for bond transactions is generally set at 0.01 percent of the total par value with a minimum 100 and maximum 500 yuan.

The Operating Procedure of Trades

1. *Opening an Account.* Individuals or institutions who want to buy and sell stocks traded in the SHSE must entrust a member of the SHSE as their broker by opening an account. An individual client can open an account by bringing personal identification to a securities firm. The information needed is the following: name, sex, identification number, home address, occupation, phone, and client's seal and signature. To open an institutional account, the institution's representative should bring the official registration of the institution, the entrusted person who represents the institution and his/her phone number and signature, and a written statement which authorizes the securities firm to trade for the institution.

A client requests a securities company to perform a transaction on his behalf by telephone, telegraph, fax, letters, or (of course) by going to the firm and ordering a transaction personally. There are two kinds of orders in terms of price, market order (trade at market price) or limited order (trade at a specified price). In terms of time, an order can be effective for a day or for five days. An order usually includes the nature of the transactions (buy or sell), the name of the security and the amount, price and effective date of the order, and the form of the settlement process. The trade amount has to be a multiple of the basic trading unit (100 yuan for stocks, 1000 for bonds). Traders must pay a deposit to conduct a trade. For a bond purchase, a buyer must pay 20 percent of the total amount as deposit; for a selling order of bond, the seller must surrender an amount of bonds that are worth 20 percent of the total selling order to the trading firm before the order will be executed. For stocks, a buyer has to make the payment in full, and a seller has to surrender the total amount of stocks he wants to sell to the securities firm before the transaction is executed. In the jargon of the West, the margin requirement for bond trade is 20 percent, for stock 100 percent.

2. *Trading.* The SHSE is open five days a week (Monday through Friday) and closes on holidays. It is open from 9:30 to 11:00 in the morning (called the morning market) and 1:30 to 3:00 in the afternoon (called afternoon market). Early in its existence, bond trade dominated. Now stock trade is equally important, although the amount of trade in bonds is still much larger than that in stocks. The SHSE requires that all stock trades be done inside the market, and all bond transactions that exceed 2000 yuan have to be done inside the market. It prohibits direct trading between two securities traders (firms); i.e., all trading activities must be openly conducted through the market. Two traders working for a same company can not bid for the same security. A trader who gets orders from his clients to buy and sell the same security cannot conduct the trade with his own hand; the trade has to be done through the bidding process of the market.

The SHSE adapts price priority and time priority criteria for securities trading. When different traders bid for a same security, the one who bids the highest price has the right to buy it first. For selling a security, whoever asks the lowest price sells it first. If two traders offer the same price, the one who bids (or asks) first has higher priority.

There are three ways to bid in the SHSE: oral, written, and computer bid. Most bids are through the computer system. After receiving an order from a client, a typical securities firm informs its trader in the SHSE through computer. A trader enters the order into the computer system of the SHSE, where the mappings are found and trades are arranged. Then the computer sends messages to the terminals to inform the relevant parties that their transaction is done. Immediately after a trade is done, the involved buyer and seller sign the "Deal Is Done" form.

The oral-bids procedure is as follows. Having received an order from their company, traders should first fill out a "Security Exchange Record" form. Then they go to a pit to bid orally. (Usually this is a multi-party bidding game.) After the deal is made, the seller is responsible for filling out the Deal Is Done form, and then both buyer and seller sign it. A transaction can also be done through written bids. Traders can specify what they want on the "Security Exchange Record" form and then hand in Copy A of the form to a specialist, who works for the SHSE to organize trade. The trades are arranged by specialists according to the criteria of the SHSE.

3. *The Settlement Process.* There are three kinds of clearing settlement methods used in the SHSE: immediate settlement, ordinary settlement, and appointment clearing settlement. *Immediate settlement* occurs when the involved parties complete the settlement process both in terms of price and security transfer the same day in which the trade is conducted. *Ordinary settlement* occurs when the clearing process is completed within 4 days after the trade is made. *Appointment settlement* occurs when the involved parties negotiate a date (within 15 days after the transaction) to do the clearing settlement. The SHSE provides clearing settlement services from 1:30 to 2:30 when the market is open.

The settlement is conducted by the "net-balance transfer" method. After a trading period, all securities firms involved calculate their receivable and payable, and only the net balance will be transferred in the clearing process. If a securities firm does not have enough cash (checking account) or securities to meet the need of the settlement process, it has violated the securities exchange rules.

The settlement process consists of two parts, cash settlement and security settlement. After the market is closed, the SHSE compiles the "Overall Settlement Table" for the day, which is calculated from the quantities and prices of securities transactions recorded by the Deal Is Done forms. The bottom line of the Overall Settlement Table indicates the net balance receivable and payable of all firms involved. Then the table is sent to all relevant firms for verification. According to regulations, all firms have to pay the money balances that they owe to other firms and must transfer the securities it owes to other firms on time. Monetary payments are usually made through bank accounts. Securities transfers are mostly done through firms' accounts in the Security Storage Archive, which is a centrally administrated archive for all kinds of securities traded in SHSE.

A Summary of Trade in SHSE

In 1984, the issuance of common stock by Shanghai Feilo Acoustics Inc. marked the beginning of the stock market in the People's Republic of China. By the end of 1990, there were eleven enterprises in Shanghai (four industrial, four commercial, two financial and one real estate firms) that had experimented with stock ownership. The total amount of stocks of these eleven enterprises was 887.13 million yuan, of which 663.27 million (74.8 percent) was owned by the state, 157.54 million (17.8 percent) was owned by institutional shareholders, and 66.33 million (7.5 percent) was owned by individual shareholders. Presumably this distribution would guarantee a "socialist direction" of the stock market.

Trade of stock started long before the establishment of the SHSE. From 1986 to October of 1990, there were 16 stock-exchange counters together with more than 40 agencies operated to conduct exchanges of securities. During this period, demand for stocks was much higher than the supply, the result of which was that market prices were usually 3 to 4 times the par value. The establishment of the SHSE provided the physical, technical, and legal facilities to conduct formal and a large volume of securities exchange.

From the grand opening (December 19, 1990) to the end of February, 1991, the SHSE operated for a total of 49 days. During this period, the SHSE did some fine tuning of its trading rules and settlement processes. There were 31 securities traded in the market, and there were 13,850 transactions, totaling 815 million yuan, of which 350 million securities were traded in January and 403 million in February of 1991. Both months set the volume record for the market. Bond trade still accounted for most of the volume (83.41 percent), with stock value being 16.59 percent. Prices of bonds were relatively stable and appeared to be in an upward trend, primarily due to the decline in interest rates during this period. The percentage increases of bond prices were in a range from 0.64 percent to 15.21 percent. Stock prices surged initially and then stabilized. Comparing stock prices of January 18, 1991, to those of December 19, 1990, there were five stocks (out of seven) whose price had increased continuously on every trading day. The total percentage of increase was from 2 percent to 44 percent for this period. However, starting in the middle of January, stock prices stabilized. Figure 16.3 and 16.4 illustrate the average stock price index for Shanghai and Shenzhen Security Exchange respectively during 1991.

Although they are small and immature, the emergence of the securities markets is a harbinger of a very different China.

Table 16.1
Financial Securities Issued During 1981-1991
(All in billion yuan)

Financial securities	Total Issued 1981-1991	Balance at the end of 1991
I. Government Bonds	130.788	97.274
1. Treasury bond	80.315	50.366
2. Fiscal bond	20.216	20.216
3. Construction bond	3.065	0
4. Key project bond	5.500	5.000
5. Special bond	9.209	9.209
6. Value-guarantee bond	12.483	12.483
II. Bonds Issued by Financial Institutions	59.794	36.829
1. Investment bond	9.500	9.500
2. Financial bond	35.197	12.312
3. Infrastructure bond	9.461	9.461
4. Key enterprise bond	5.636	5.556
III. Enterprise Bonds	65.700	33.109
1. Local firm bond	33.941	18.633
2. Short-term bond	19.603	8.853
3. Internal bond	12.156	5.623
IV. Stock	7.542	7.505
Sub Total	263.824	174.717
V. Bank CDs in large denominations	113.144	43.025
Total	376.968	217.742

NOTE:

The total issued (second column) minus the balance at the end of 1991 (third column) is equal to the total amount redeemed during the period 1981-1991.

SOURCE: *China Financial Security Markets*, 1992, page 125-128.

Table 16.2
Composition of Financial Assets in China
Data: 1978 and 1991, in billion yuan

Financial assets	1978	1991	% of GNP[a]
1. Cash in circulation	21.2	317.8	16.2
2. Household deposits[b]	21.1	911.0	46.5
3. Enterprise and Institution deposits	90.3	706.2	36.1
4. Government deposits	18.7	50.4	2.6
5. Financial bonds	0	11.4	0.6
6. Deposits in nonbank financial institutions	0	142.1	7.3
7. Insurance reserve[c]	1.5	19.1	1.0
8. Total claims on financial institutions (sum of 1-7)	152.8	2158.0	110.2
9. Total loans of banks	185.0	1806.1	92.2
10. Total loans of urban rural credit coops	4.0	212.5	10.9
11. Total loans of trust and investment companies	0	121.1	6.2
12. Government bonds	0	116.8	6.0
13. Enterprise bonds	0	38.7	2.1
14. Total claims on non-financial institutions (sum of 9-13)	189.0	2295.2	117.2
15. Government borrowing from banks	0	107.5	6.0
16. Stocks	0	7.5	0.4
17. Total financial assets	341.8	4578.2	233.8

NOTE:
a. As a percentage of 1991 GNP (1985.5 billion yuan)
b. Including all household deposits in banks, postal offices, urban and rural credit cooperatives, etc.
c. The insurance reserves of PICC only.

SOURCE: Xie (1992) and *Almanac of China's Finance and Banking*, 1992.

Table 16.3
The Composition of Household Financial Assets
Data: 1978, 1985, 1991, in billion yuan except the last column

Financial assets	1978	1985	1991	% of 1991
Cash	17.38	81.34	259.02	19.16
Saving deposits	21.06	171.98	947.82	70.10
Among which:				
Time deposit	12.89	132.24	804.78	59.52
Renminbi	12.89	122.52	767.96	56.80
Foreign exchange	0	9.72	36.82	2.72
passbook savings	8.17	39.74	143.04	10.58
Securities	0	10.64	137.34	10.16
Among which:				
Government bonds	0	10.14	50.44	3.73
Other bonds	0	0.50	64.38	4.76
Stocks	0	0	22.52	1.67
Insurance	0	0.49	7.83	0.58
Total	38.44	264.44	1352.01	100

SOURCE: Xie (1992).

Figure 16.1 Composition of Financial Securities Issued in 1991

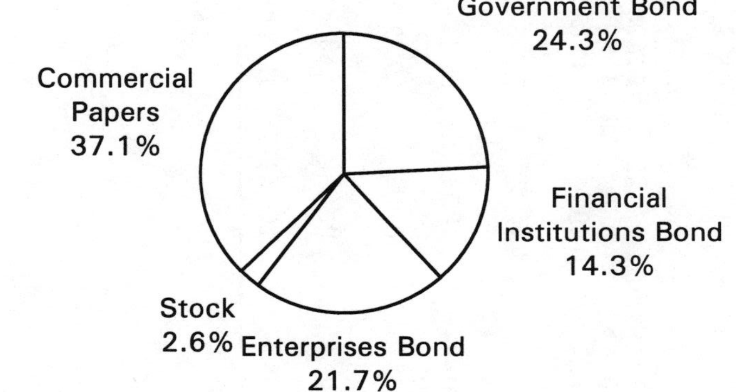

Source: China Security Markets, 1992

Figure 16.2 Composition of the Government Bonds Issued in 1991

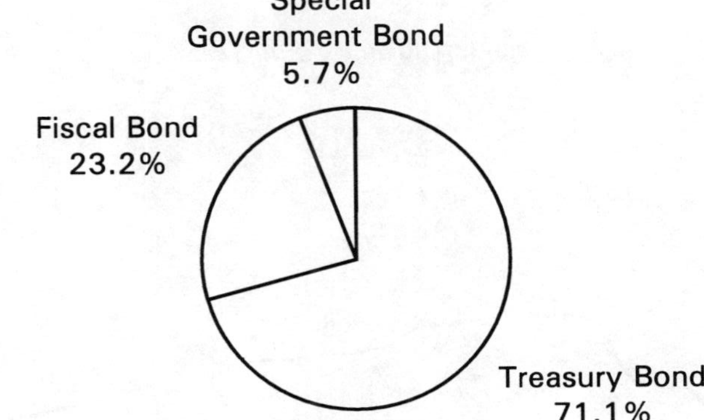

Source: China Security Markets, 1992

Figure 16.3 Average Stock Price Index of Shenzhen Stock Exchange in 1991 (Base Date: 100 = April 1, 1991)

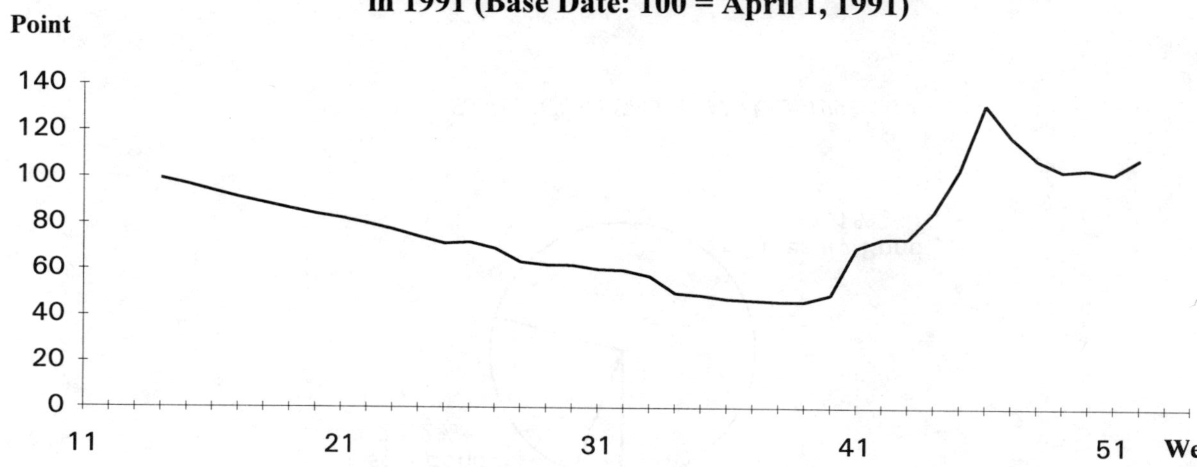

Source: China Security Markets, 1992

Figure 16.4 Average Stock Price Index of Shanghai Stock Exchange in 1991 (Base Date: 100 = December 19, 1990)

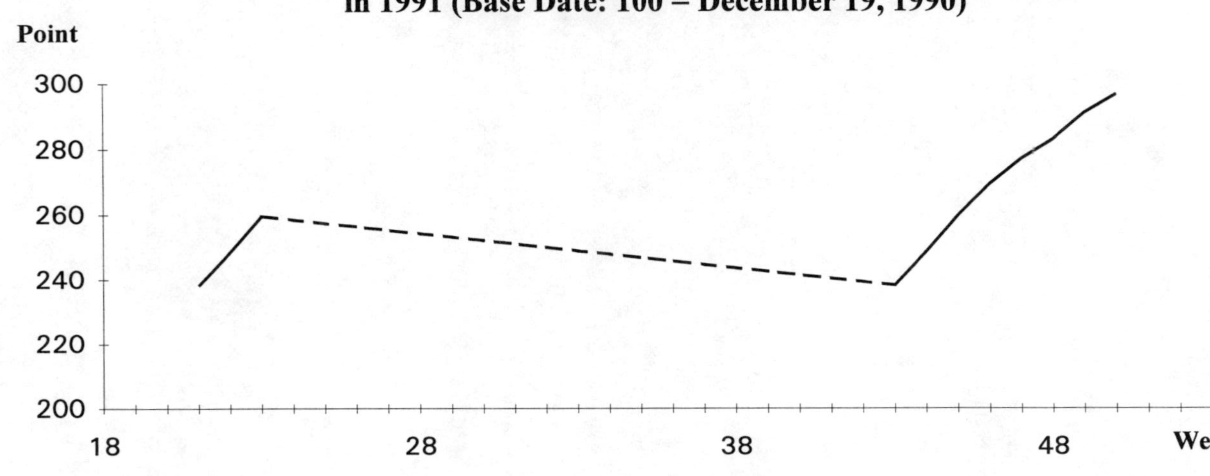

Source: China Security Markets, 1992

Epilogue

This book reviews the economic reforms of the financial sector in China for the period 1984-1993. The beginning of this period was marked by the establishment of the central bank and it ended with the austerity program in the second half of 1993.

The experience of the implementation of the 1993 austerity program indicated that the macro control mechanism in China has not been freed from the stop-go cycle. At the beginning of 1994, the Chinese government launched a new round of economic reforms in the financial sector with the following objectives.

First is to allow PBC be a real central bank. The most urgent problem in the Chinese economy is still the danger of runaway inflation. The GNP of 1993 was 3138 billion yuan, a 13.4 percent increase over the previous year, and the official inflation rate based on the general retail price level was 13 percent. The consumer price index of 35 large cities went up 19.6% (*People's Daily*, March 2, 1994). The Chinese government has been trying to strengthen the role of PBC in controlling macro economic conditions; it has been emphasized on several occasions that the primary objective of PBC is to maintain price stability by controlling the money supply, total credit, interest rates, and the reserve ratio (He 1994). However, it is still not clear how independent PBC will become in the future, reporting to the People's Congress or continuing to be under State Council.

Second is to let the specialized banks be real commercial banks. The minimum prerequisite to achieve this objective is to separate specialized banks from the state-owned enterprises and government intervention. Neither is easy to accomplish. The percentage of loss-making state-owned enterprises increased from 26.4 percent in 1992 to 30.3 percent in 1993, reconfirming an observation of Chapter 6 of this book: loss-making firms would increase during a tightening period. Most of these loss-making firms are supported by the specialized banks, which implies that delinquent debts have increased further in 1993. To a certain degree, the specialized bank is a second fiscal source of the government at various levels in addition to the government revenue collected from taxes. Therefore, it takes time and pressure (such as fiscal reform, legislative actions) to get rid of government intervention.

Third is to establish several policy banks. The State Council has tentatively approved establishing the following three policy banks: The National Development Bank, The Import & Export Credit Bank, and the Agricultural Development Bank of China. The establishment of policy banks is an important step toward making the specialized banks become commercial banks by transferring their policy function to the policy banks. However, the ultimate solution of the problems of the banking system lies in property rights reform and the separation of the banking system from the state-owned enterprises, without which the government just transfers losses from one pocket to an other.

Fourth is to move toward the convertability of Renminbi. The Chinese government ended the two-track foreign exchange system by abolishing the Foreign Exchange Certificates (FEC) beginning January 1, 1994. The unified exchange rate is controlled and regulated by PBC. During the first quarter of 1994, the exchange rate was maintained around 1 US dollar = 8.72 yuan. PBC promulgated the new foreign exchange settlement methods, which has replaced the so-called "foreign exchange retaining" method. Firms are allowed to buy foreign exchange for transactions under the current account if certain conditions are satisfied, and foreign exchange market will be established among banks.

Fifth is to develop the financial market further. A well established financial market is very crucial to the stability of the economy. A relatively large scale government bonds market is a necessary condition for a successful open market operation of the central bank. The government will promote institutions to hold government bonds in their portfolio, which can be used as collateral to borrow from the central bank. The stock market has been a focal point and will continue under strict control by the government. The Commission on Security Regulation and Supervision (CSRS) announced that the total quota for stock issuance is 5.5 billion yuan in 1994 and CSRS does not rule out the possibility that part of this quota might be postponed until 1995 if the economy is overheated.

Sixth is to establish the legal environment for the financial markets. PBC has completed the draft of the "Central Bank Acts of PRC" and the "Bank Acts of PRC." These two drafts will be discussed in the coming People's Congress and are expected to be promulgated in 1994. "Securities and Exchange Acts" has been drafted by a team led by Professor Li Yining, a famous economist at Peking University. So far, most laws and regulations in China have been drafted by government agencies. The possible conflict of interest is obvious. For instance, PBC has drafted the Central Bank Acts. The significance of the Securities and Exchange Acts is that it is the first important law drafted by "outsiders." It is also expected that the People's Congress will pass and promulgate Securities and Exchange Acts in 1994.

The experiences of Chinese economic reforms suggest that it is very difficult to change the behavior of existing state-owned enterprises. The astonishing growth of the non-state sector in the Chinese economy had unexpected results. It increased the market share of the economy and forced the state-owned enterprises to join the competition. The rapid growth of non-state financial institutions recently in China may have similar consequences for the financial sector in the future. Although it is hard to anticipate private firms in the financial sector (due to the large capital requirement and the restrictions on foreign banks), there are still many other viable alternative ownership structures to be explored, such as joint ventures, branches of foreign financial institutions, local-government-owned financial firms, collectively-owned companies, etc. The key desideratum is to break through the monopoly of the state-owned banking system and introduce competition into the financial sector. In terms of reform strategies, it is probably much easier to nurture (or at least not suppress) non-government-owned financial institutions than it is trying to change the behavior of the state-owned banks. When the market share of non-state financial institutions becomes significant, the rules of the game will be changed and the state-owned banks will be forced into a competitive market environment, and their behavior will be changed accordingly. Without competition, little real change will be brought by restructuring or reorganizing the existing state-owned banking system.

References

Akaike, H. 1969. "Statistical predictor identification," *Annals of the Institute of Statistical Mathematics*, Vol. 21, pp. 203-217.

Akaike, H. 1974. "A new look at the statistical model selection identification," *IEEE Transaction on Automatic Control*, AC-19, pp. 719-723.

Alesina, Alberto and Lawrence Summers. 1990. "Central Bank Independence and Macroeconomic Performance: Some Comparative Evidence," Harvard University, mimeo.

Amemiya, T. 1980. "Selection of Regressors," *International Economics Review*, Vol. 21, pp. 331-345.

Andersen, L. C. and J. L. Jordan. 1968. "Monetary and Fiscal Actions: A Test of Their Relative Importance in Economic Stabilization," Federal Reserve Bank of St. Louis *Review*, 50, November, pp. 11-23.

Barro, R. and D. Gordon. 1983. "A Positive Theory of Monetary Policy in a Natural Rate Model," *Journal of Political Economy*, Vol. 91, No. 4, pp. 589-610.

Bei, Duoguang. 1989. *An Analysis of Fund Circulation in China*, Sanlian Press, Shanghai, China.

Belsley, D. A., E. Kuh, and R. E. Welsch. 1980. *Regression Diagnostics: Identifying Influential Data and Sources of Collinearity*, New York: Wiley.

Box, G. E. P. and G. M. Jenkins. 1976. *Time Series Analysis: Forecasting and Control*, Revised Edition, San Francisco: Holden-Day.

Breusch, T. S. 1978. "Testing for Autocorrelation in Dynamic Linear Models," *Australian Economic Papers*, Vol. 17, pp. 334-355.

Bush, K. 1973. "Soviet Inflation," in Laulan, Y. (ed.) *Banking, Money and Credit in the USSR*, NATO, Brussels, pp. 97-106.

Byrd, W. A. 1987. "The Impact of the Two-tier Plan/Market System in Chinese Industry," *Journal of Comparative Economics*, Vol. 11, pp. 295-308.

Byrd, W. A. 1989. "Plan and Market in the Chinese Economy: A Simple General Equilibrium Model," *Journal of Comparative Economics*, Vol. 13, pp. 177-204.

Byrd, William A. 1990. "Rural Industrialization and Ownership in China," *Comparative Economic Studies*, Spring, pp. 73-107.

Chang, Gene H. 1994. "Monetary Overhang: Do Centrally Planned Economies Have Excessive Money Stocks?" Working Paper, Department of Economics, The University of Toledo.

Chang, Gene H. 1992. "On Inconsistencies between Disequilibrium Aggregates," *Journal of Comparative Economics,* Vol. 17: pp. 70-91.

Chen, Chien-Hsun. 1989. "Monetary Aggregates and Macroeconomic Performance in Mainland China," *Journal of Comparative Economics*, June, Vol. 13, No. 2, pp. 314-324.

Chen, Nai-Ruenn and Chi-ming Hou. 1986. "China's Inflation, 1979-1983: Measurement and Analysis," *Economic Development and Cultural Change* July, pp. 811-835.

Cheng, Chu-yuan. 1982. *China's Economic Development*, Boulder: Westview Press.

Cheng, Hang-Sheng. 1988. (ed.) *Monetary Policy in Pacific Basin Countries*, Kluwer Academic Publishers.

Chinese Economic System Reform Research Institute. 1985. "Reform, Challenges and Choices Faced by Us," *Jingji yanjiu (Economic Research)*, 1985.11, pp. 3-18.

Chow, Gregory C. 1960. "Tests of Equality Between Sets of Coefficients in Two Linear Regressions," *Econometrica*, Vol. 28, pp. 591-605.

Chow, Gregory C. 1987. "Money and Price Level Determination in China," *Journal of Comparative Economics*, Vol. 11, pp. 319- 333.

Dai, Genyou. 1990. *Macroeconomic Analysis of the Central Bank*, Beijing: China Finance Press.

Darlington, R. B. 1968. "Multiple Regression in Psychological Research and Practice," *Psychological Bulletin*, Vol. 69, pp. 161-182.

De Wulf, Luc and David Goldsbrough. 1986. "The Evolving Role of Monetary Policy in China," *IMF Staff Papers*, June, pp. 209-242.

Dickey, David A. and Wayne A. Fuller. 1981. "Likelihood Ratio Statistics for Autoregressive Time Series With A Unit Root," *Econometrica*, Vol. 49, pp. 1057-71.

Du, Haiyan, Chang Ronggang, Zhong Jiyin, Chen Yimin and Dai Rui. 1989. "The State-owned Enterprises' Behaviors Under the Current Inflation," *Jingji Yanjiu*, 1989.2, pp. 41-50.

Durbin, J. 1960. "Estimation of Parameters in Time-series Regression Models," *Journal of the Royal Statistical Society*, ser.B, Vol. 22, pp. 139-153.

Durbin, J. 1970. "Testing for Serial Correlation in Least Squares Regression When Some of the Regressors Are Lagged Dependent Variables," *Econometrica*, Vol. 38, 410-421.

Engle, R. F. 1982. " Autoregressive Conditional Heteroscedasticity with Estimates of the Variance of U. K. Inflation," *Econometrica*, Vol. 50, pp. 987-1007.

Engle, R. F., D. F. Hendry, and J. F. Richard. 1983. "Exogeneity," *Econometrica*, Vol. 51, March.

Fan, Gang. 1989. "Reform, Adjustment, Growth and Frictionary Inflation," *Economic Research*, January.

Feltenstein, Andrew and Jiming Ha. 1991. "Measurement of Repressed Inflation in China: The Lack of Coordination Between Monetary Policy and Price Controls," *Journal of Development Economics*, Vol. 36, pp. 279-294.

Feltenstein, Andrew and Ziba Farhadian. 1987. "Fiscal Policy, Monetary Targets, and the Price Level in a Centrally Planned Economy: An Application to the Case of China," *Journal of Money, Credit, and Banking*, Vol. 19, No. 2, pp. 137-156.

Feltenstein, Andrew, David Lebow and Sweder Van Wijnbergen. 1990. "Savings, Commodity Market Rationing, and the Real Rate of Interest in China," *Journal of Money, Credit, and Banking*, Vol. 22, No. 2, pp. 234-252.

Foster, E. 1978. "The Variability of Inflation," *Review of Economics and Statistics*, Vol. 60, pp. 346-350.

Friedman, M. 1963. "Inflation: Causes and Consequences," Council for Economic Education, Bombay: Asian Publishing House, reprinted in *Dollars and Deficits*, Prentice-Hall, 1968, p. 39.

Friedman, M. 1966. "Interest Rates and the Demand for Money," *The Journal of Law and Economics*, Vol. IX, Oct., p. 85.

Friedman, M. 1977. "Nobel Lecture: Inflation and Unemployment," *Journal of Political Economy*, Vol. 85, 451-472.

Friedman, Milton and Anna Schwartz. 1991. "Alternative Approaches to Analyzing Economic Data," *The American Economic Review*, Vol. 18, No. 1, pp. 39-49.

Fry; Maxwell J. 1988. *Money, Interest, and Banking in Economic Development*, The Johns Hopkins University Press.

Glezakos, C. and J. B. Nugent. 1984. "Price Instability and Inflation: the Latin American Case," *World Development* , Vol. 12, pp. 755-758.

Godfrey, L. G. 1978. "Testing for Higher Order Serial Correlation in Regression Equations When the Regressors Include Lagged Dependent Variables," *Econometrica*, Vol. 46, pp. 1303-1310.

Goldfeld, S. and R. Quandt. 1972. *Nonlinear Methods in Econometrics*, Amsterdam: North-Holland Publishing Company.

Goldsmith, Raymond. 1969. *Financial Structure and Development*, New Haven: Yale University Press.

Granger, C. W. J. 1969. "Investigating Casual Relations by Econometric Models and Cross-spectral Models," *Econometrica*, Vol. 37, pp. 424-438.

Grossman, G. 1966. "Gold and the Sword: Money in the Soviet Economy," in H. Rosovsky (ed.) *Industrialization in Two Systems*, New York: Wiley, pp. 204-236.

Guo, Kesha. 1989. "The Relationship between the Growth Rate of the Economy and the Money Supply," *Jingji Yanjiu*, 1989.3, pp. 64-68.

Guo, Shuqing. 1992. *Economic Transition and Macrocontrol*, Tianjin People's Press, China.

Hafer, R. W. 1992. "Inflation and Price Instability in China: A Comment," *China Economic Review*, Vol. 3, No. 2, pp. 213-218.

Hall, Robert E. 1982. *Inflation: Causes and Effects*, A National Bureau of Economic Research Project Report, The University of Chicago Press.

Harvey, A. C. 1980. "On Comparing Regression Models in Levels and First Differences," *International Economic Review*, Vol. 21, No. 3, October, pp. 707-720.

He, Guanghui. 1994. "The Reform Tasks in 1994," *China Reform*, January, pp. 6-14.

Hendry, David and Neil Ericsson. 1991. "An Econometric Analysis of U.K. Money Demand in Monetary Trends in the United States and the United Kingdom by Milton Friedman and Anna J. Schwartz," *The American Economic Review*, Vol. 18, No. 1, pp. 8-38.

Hsiao, C. 1981. "Autoregressive Modelling and Money-income Causality Detection," *Journal of Monetary Economics*, Vol. 7, pp. 85-106.

Hsiao, Katharine Huang. 1971. *Money and Monetary Policy in Communist China*, New York: Columbia University Press.

Hua, Sheng, Zhang Xuejun and Luo Xiaopeng. 1988. "The Reform in China in the Past Decade: Retrospect, Contemplation and Perspective," *Jingji Yanjiu*, 1988.9, 11 and 12.

Huang, Xiaoxiang. 1988. "Inflation and Economic Growth." *Management World*, March.

Huang, Xu. 1988. "Supply and Demand for Money and the Determination of the Price Level." *Jingji Yanjiu* (Economic Research), February, pp. 35-45.

Hui, Xiaoping. 1994. "Choosing a Proper Banking Model During the Economic Transition," *Economic Research*, January, pp. 17-23.

IESR (The Institute of Economic System Reform). 1988. *Macroeconomics of Reform*," People's Press of Sichuan.

Jefferson, Gary. 1992. "Measuring China's Gross National Product," Working Paper, Department of Economics, Brandeis University.

Jin, Lizuo. 1993. *Monetary Policy and the Design of Financial Institutions in China (1978-90)*, unpublished Ph. D. thesis, Oxford University.

Judge, G., W. Griffiths, C. Hill. H. Lutkepohl and T.C. Lee. 1985. *The Theory and Practice of Econometrics*, Second Edition, New York: Wiley.

Kaufman, G. G. and C. M. Latta. 1966. "The Demand for Money: Preliminary Evidence from Industrial Countries," *Journal of Financial and Quantitative Analysis*, September, pp. 75-89.

Koenker, Roger. 1982. "Robust Methods in Econometrics," *Econometric Reviews*, Vol. 1, No. 2, pp. 213-255.

Kornai, J. 1980. *Economics of Shortage*, Amsterdam: North-Holland Publishing Company.

Li, Yining. 1991. *Chinese Economy in Its Disequilibrium*, Beijing: Economic Daily Press.

Lin, Justin Y. 1992. "Interest Rate Liberalization and Inflation Control," Development Research Center, Beijing, China.

Liu, Hongru. 1980. *The Issues of the Socialist Money and Banking*, The Press of Financial Economics of China, Beijing.

Lou, Jiwei. 1993. "Financial System and Policy," Mimeo, the State Commission for Economic System Reform, Beijing, China.

Lucas, R. E. 1972. "Expectations and the Neutrality of Money," *Journal of Economic Theory*, Vol. 4, pp. 103-124.

Lucas, Robert E. 1976. "Econometric Policy Evaluation: A Critique," in *The Phillips Curve and Labor Markets*, edited by K. Brunner and A. Meltzer. *Journal of Monetary Economics*, Suppl. 1976, pp. 19-46.

Maddala, G. S. 1992. *Introduction to Econometrics*, Second Edition, New York: Macmillan Publishing Company.

Mallows, C. L. 1973. "Some Comments on Cp" *Technometrics*, Vol. 15, pp. 661-676.

Marx, Karl. *Capital*, edited by F. Engels and translated by Ernest Untermann, Charles Kerr & Company.

Mayer, Thomas, James Duesenberry and Robert Aliber. 1987. *Money, Banking and the Economy*, Third Edition, New York: Norton & Company, Inc.

McKinnon, Ronald I. 1973. *Money and Capital in Economic Development*, Washington, D. C.: Brookings Institution.

McKinnon, Ronald I. 1993. *The Order of Economic Liberalization*, Second Edition, The Johns Hopkins University Press.

Mishkin, F. S. 1992. *Money, Banking, and Financial Markets*, Third Edition, Harper Collins.

Muth, J. F. 1961. "Rational Expectations and the Theory of Price Movements, *Econometrica*, Vol. 29, pp. 315-335.

Naughton, B. 1987. "Macroeconomic Policy and Response in the Chinese Economy: The Impact of the Reform Process, *Journal of Comparative Economics*, Vol. 11, pp. 334-353.

Naughton, Barry. 1991. "Why Has Economic Reform Led to Inflation?" *American Economic Review*, Papers and Proceedings, May, pp. 207-211.

Nelson, Charles R. and Charles I. Plosser. 1982. "Trends and Random Walks in Macroeconomic Time Series," *Journal of Monetary Economics*, Vol. 10, pp. 139-162.

Nerlove, M. 1958. "Adaptive Expectations and Cobweb Phenomena," *Quarterly Journal of Economics*, Vol. 73, pp. 227-40.

Newbold, Paul. 1984. *Statistics for Business and Economics*, Englewood Cliffs: Prentice-Hall, Inc.

Okun, A.M. 1971. "The Mirage of Steady Inflation," *Brookings Papers on Economic Avtivity*, Vol. 2, pp. 485-498.

Pagan, A.R., A.D. Hall and P.K. Trivedi. 1983. "Assessing The Variability of Inflation," *Review of Economic Studies*, Vol. 50, pp. 585-596.

People's Bank of China. 1983. *Survey of Banking* (Jinrong Gaikuang), Beijing, China.

People's Bank of China. 1984. "Tentative Methods of Managing Credit and Loans," *China Finance*, December, pp. 19-24.

People's Bank of China. 1988. *Survey of the Distribution of the Money in Circulation*, Beijing: China Finance Press.

Perkins, Dwight H. 1988. "Reforming China's Economic System," *Journal of Economic Literature*, Vol. XXVI, pp. 601-645.

Perron, Pierre. 1990. "Testing for a Unit Root in a Time Series with a Changing Mean," *Journal of Business & Economic Statistics*, April, Vol. 8, No. 2, pp. 153-162.

Plosser, Charles I. and G. William Schwert. 1978 "Money, Income, and Sunspots: Measuring Economic Relationships and the Effects of Differencing," *Journal of Monetary Economics*, Vol. 4, pp. 637-660.

Portes, R. and A. Santorum. 1987. "Money and the Consumption Goods Market in China," *Journal of Comparative Economics*, Vol. 11, pp. 354-371.

The Price Reform Research Group of Chinese Academy of Social Sciences. 1986. "A Contemplation on the Price Reform in the Past

Seven Years," in Gao Shangquan, (ed.) *China: Development and Reform*, Chengdu, China, pp. 132-147.

Qian, Yingyi. 1988. "Urban and Rural Household Saving in China," *IMF Staff Papers*, December, pp. 592-627.

Qian, Yingyi. 1993. "Lessons and Relevance of the Japanese Main-Bank System for Financial System Reform in China," Working Paper, Department of Economics, Stanford Univerity.

Qiao, Rongzhang. 1986. "Price Subsidies in China,"*Jingji Yanjiu Cankao Ziliao (Information for Economic Research)*, Vol. 58.

Qin, Duo. 1993. "Money Demand in China: The Effect of Economic Reform," Working Paper, University of London.

Ram, R. 1985. "Level and Variability of Inflation: Time Series and Cross-Section Evidence from 117 Countries," *Economica*, Vol. 52, pp. 209-223.

Rawski, Thomas. 1991 "How Fast Has Chinese Industry Grown?" Working Paper, the World Bank.

Reynolds, Bruce. 1987. *Reform in China: Challenges & Choices*, M. E. Sharpe, Inc.

Riskin, Carl. 1987. *China's Political Economy: The Quest for Development Since 1949*, Oxford University Press.

The Rural Development Research Center. 1987. "Peasants, Markets and the New Institutions' Creation," *Economic Research* (Jinji Yanjiu), January, pp. 3-16.

Sachs, Jeffrey and Wing Thye Woo. 1994. "Structural Factors in the Economic Reforms of China, Eastern Europe and the Former Soviet Union," Working Paper, Department of Economics, Harvard University.

Schwarz, G. 1978. "Estimating the Dimension of a Model," *Annals of Statistics*, Vol. 6, pp. 461-464.

Shan, Weijian. 1992. "The Hybrid System and Continued Marketization of the Chinese Economy," *China Economic Review*, Vol. 3, No. 2, pp. 57-74.

Shi, Xiaomin and Liu Jirui. 1989. "Economists Should First Respect the History and Facts," *Jingji Yanjiu*, 1989.2, pp. 10-33.

Singh, Inderjit. 1991. "Is There Schizophrenia about Socialist Reform Theory?" *Transition*, the World Bank, Vol. 2, No. 7, pp. 1-4.

Stiglitz, Joseph. 1993. *The Role of the State in Financial Markets*, The Institute of Economics, Academia Sinica, Taiwan.

Szapary, Gyorgy. 1989. "Monetary Policy and System Reforms in China," Working Paper, International Monetary Fund, Washington, D.C.

Tang, Mingfong. 1990. (ed.) *Ten Years of Reform*, China: Beijing People's Press.

Tian, Jiyun. 1990. "The Current Situation of the Agricultural Sector and Our Tasks," *People's Daily*, October 29, 1990.

Turnovsky, Stephen. 1977. *Macroeconomic Analysis and Stabilization Policy*, New York: Cambridge University Press.

Wang, Yan. 1994. "Permanent Income and Wealth Accumulation: A Cross Sectional Study of Chinese Urban and Rural Households," forthcoming in *Economic Development and Cultural Change*.

Wang, Yijiang. 1991. "Economic Reform, Fixed Capital Investmant Expansion, and Inflation: A Behavioral Model Based on the Chinese Experience," *China Economic Review*, Vol. 2, No. 1, pp. 3-27.

Woo, Wing Thye, Wen Hai, Yibiao Jin, Gang Fan. 1993. "How Successful Has Chinese Enterprise Reform Been?" Working Paper, University of California at Davis.

Wu, Jinglian and Xiaochuan Zhou. 1988. *The Comprehensive Design of the Chinese Economic Reform*, China: China Outlook Press.

Wu, Lanjun. 1989. "On the Strange Phenomena in the Reform of the Financial Sector," *Financial Studies*, March, pp. 7-9.

Wu, Renhong and Zhengqing Zou. 1989. "The Transformation of the Excess Labor Force in Rural Areas and Inflation." *Jingji Yanjiu* (Economic Research), 1989.10, pp. 60-70.

Wu, Xiaoling and Ping Xie. 1993. "Monetary Policies in China's Economy in Transition," Working Paper, People's Bank of China.

Xia, Bin and Yuqi Sun. 1990. "The Research of the Money Supply Theory in China," *Financial Studies*, March, pp. 2-10 (Part I); May, pp. 8-14 (Part II).

Xiao, Geng. 1991. "State Enterprises in China: Dealing With Lossmakers," *Transition*, Socialist Economic Reform Unit, the World Bank, December.

Xie, Ping. 1992. "The Structure of Financial Assets in China," *Economic Research*, November, pp. 30-37.

Xu, Jian. 1989. "The Framework, Principle, Mechanism and the Effectiveness of the Macro Financial Control in China," *Financial Studies*, March, pp. 16-22.

Xu, Nuojin. 1989. "Money Multiplier: Theory and Practice," *Financial Studies*, October, pp. 14-20.

Yang, Guansan, Yang Xiaodong and Xuan Mingdong. 1987. "The Public Response to Price Reform," in *Reform in China: Challenges and Choices*, edited by Bruce Reynolds, M.E. Sharp, pp. 59-73.

Yang, Xiaokai and Yew-Kwang Ng. 1993. *Specialization and Economic Organization: A New Classical Microeconomic Framework*, Chapter 18, Amsterdam: North-Holland Publishing Company.

Yang, Zhongwei, et al. 1988. "Diagnosis of the Inflation in China," *Jingji Yanjiu (Economic Research)*, 1988.4, pp. 3-11.

Yi, Gang. 1988. "Market Efficiency and Property Right," *China: Development and Reform*, December, 1988, pp. 14-20.

Yi, Gang. 1990a. "Inflation and Price Instability: An Empirical Study of the People's Republic of China," *China Economic Review*, Vol. 1, No. 2, pp. 155-165.

Yi, Gang. 1990b. "The Price Reform and Inflation in China, 1979-88," *Comparative Economic Studies*, Winter, pp. 28-61.

Yi, Gang. 1991. "The Monetization Process in China During the Economic Reform," *China Economic Review*, Spring, 1991, pp. 75-95.

Yi, Gang. 1992a. "The Money Supply Mechanism and Monetary Policy in China," *Journal of Asian Economics*, Vol. 3, No. 2, pp. 217-238.

Yi, Gang. 1992b. "Inflation and Price Instability in China: Reply," *China Economic Review*, Vol. 3, No. 2, pp. 219-223.

Yi, Gang. 1993. "Towards Estimating the Demand for Money in China," *Economics of Planning*, Vol. 26, pp. 243-270.

Yi, G. and G. Judge. 1988. "Statistical Model Selection Criteria," *Economics Letters*, Vol. 28, pp. 47-51.

Zeng, Kanglin. 1989. "On the Outside Circulation of Money." *China Finance*, September, pp. 39-41.

Zhang, Weiying and Gang Yi. 1994. "China's Gradual Reform: A Historical Perspective," Working Paper, Nuffield College, Oxford University.

Zhang, Zhuoyuan. 1988. "A Discussion on the Theories and Practices of the Price Reform in Recent Years," *Jingjixue Wenzhai (Economics Digest)* , April.

Zhao, Ziyang. 1987. "Marching along the Socialist Road with Chinese Characteristics," *People's Daily* , October 25,1987.

Zhong, Pengrong. 1990. *On Inflation in China*, Nanchang: Jiangxi People's Press.

Zhou, Xiaochuan and Zhu Li. 1987. "China's Banking System: Current Status, Perspective on Reform," *Journal of Comparative Economics*, Vol. 11, pp. 399-409.

Zhu, Delin. 1989. "On the Forced Money Supply Mechanism in China," *Financial Studies*, September, pp. 8-12.

Almanac of China's Economy, Beijing, China, 1984-1991.

Almanac of China's Finance and Banking, 1989-1993, Beijing, China.

Almanac of China's Prices, 1988-1991, Beijing, China.

China Finance (Zhongguo Jinrong), various issues, Beijing, China.

China: Financial Sector Policies and Institutional Development, the World Bank, Washington, D.C. December, 1990.

China Security Markets, 1991, 1992, edited by Jin Jiandong, Xiao Shuoji and Xu Shuxin, Beijing: China Finance Press.

Excerpt of Statistical Yearbook, 1988-1993, State Statistics Bureau, Beijing.

The Great Ten Years, State Statistics Bureau, Beijing, 1959.

Handbook of Chinese Banking Practices, (HCBP), 1991, edited by Zhou Zhengqing, China: Jilin People's Press.

International Financial Statistics, IMF, Washington, D.C., various issues.

Monthly Bulletin of Statistics of China, 1985-1989, various issues, State Statistics Bureau, Beijing, China.

Statistical Yearbook of China, Beijing, State Statistics Bureau, 1983-1993.

World Development Report, 1978, 1979, 1991, 1992, the World Bank, Washington, DC.

Author Index

Subject Index

About the Book and Author

This book offers the first comprehensive study of the money, banking, and financial markets in China since the establishment of the central bank system in 1984. The author analyzes the impact of the profound institutional changes of the 1980s and the early 1990s and highlights the fundamental transformation of the role of money—from a passive accounting tool in the centrally planned system to an active and intrinsically important factor in determining the growth and stability of the present economy.

The theoretical and empirical analyses of the book are based on the newly established financial system and the most recent data available. The transitive nature of the financial sector during economic reform is especially emphasized. The author's central arguments are supported by in-depth analyses of every important aspect of the financial sector, including the function of the central bank and its relationship with specialized banks and other financial institutions, money supply and demand, monetization, price reforms and inflation, nonbank financial institutions, and new developments in the financial security markets. Extensive use is made of case studies and illustrative examples. A complete set of data from all empirical studies is provided to allow readers to examine the models and confirm the econometric results.

Gang Yi is associate professor of economics at Indiana University, Indianapolis.